Wilber's War (abridged) *is a condensation of the trilogy of the same name by Hale Bradt, which received the following accolades:*

SILVER MEDALIST: Foreword Reviews' IndieFAB Awards: War & Military

SILVER MEDALIST: Independent Book Publishers Association's Benjamin Franklin Awards: Biography

FINALIST: National Indie Excellence Awards: Military, Non-Fiction

"informed and informative … thoughtful and thought-provoking…inherently fascinating read … deftly crafted … very highly recommended for both community and academic library … collections." [Midwest Book Review, June 2015]

"This is a unique epic of monumental scale about an American soldier's fight in battles in various parts of Oceania during the Second World War, and intricately pieced together by his son." [Biz India Online News, Aug. 21, 2015]

"Hale Bradt relates a story that could resonate with the multitude of families who also sacrificed a father, a husband, or son [to war]." [*Foreword Reviews*, Fall 2015; Five Hearts rating]

Amazon reviews:

K: **A Must Read** (5 stars): "a fascinating story that I found nearly impossible to stop reading from the first chapter until the end."

Dee Long: **A Front Seat to World War II Action** (5 stars): "an amazing historical record of how World War II affected the life and family of one senior Army officer who spent three years overseas."

Society Nineteen: **A Rich Read and a Beautiful Gift** (5 stars): "It's a narrative with resonance far beyond its World War II focus … gorgeous design and high quality."

Luther and Joyce Lovely (5 stars): "a collector's item … a valuable addition to any education institution's library."

WILBER'S WAR

(ABRIDGED):
An American Family's Journey
through World War II

Hale Bradt

Wilber's War (abridged): An American Family's Journey through World War II
(A one-volume condensation of the Wilber's War trilogy)
Copyright © 2017 by Hale Bradt

Van Dorn Books,
P.O. Box 8836
Salem, MA 01971
www.wilberswar.com

Every effort has been made to trace and credit accurate copyright ownership of the visual material
used in this book. Errors or omissions will be corrected in subsequent editions
provided notification is made in writing to the publisher.

Book editor: Frances B. King: HistoryKeep.com
Book design: Lisa Carta Design, lisacartadesign@gmail.com
Typefaces: Minion, Chaparral Pro
Front cover image: U.S. Army
Back cover images: Bradt family
Printed by CreateSpace

ISBN 978-0-9966939-0-5
Library of Congress Control Number: 2016946699
Contents: 358 pages, 2 charts, 21 maps, 72 photos/facsimiles.
1. World War II (1939–1945). 2. History—Nonfiction. 3. Biography/Memoir—Nonfiction. 4.
Military History—Nonfiction. 5. American History—Nonfiction. 6. Wilber E. Bradt [1900–1945].

In memory of Wilber and Norma

And for Valerie and Abby

—this is their story too

CONTENTS

FIGURES

CHARTS

MAPS

ILLUSTRATIONS

Prologue

LLUSTRATIONS Continued

Front page headline on August 14, 1945, announcing the end of the war. [FACSIMILE: *THE EVENING STAR* (WASHINGTON, D.C.)]

Prologue
WASHINGTON, D.C., 1945

Joy and optimism were in the air. Germany had capitulated three months before, and on August 14, 1945, Japan had surrendered and accepted the terms of the Potsdam Agreement. People the world over celebrated wildly, while some were quietly relieved they or their loved ones would no longer be in harm's way. One American soldier in the Philippines—who would have faced the Japanese in the forthcoming invasion of the Japanese homeland—was heard to say, "So it's over. Well! I think I'll go sit under that tree."

At the time, I lived in Washington, D.C., with my mother Norma and sister Valerie. I was 14, and they were 39 and 13 respectively (Chart 1). My father Wilber, an army artillery officer, was not with us nor had we seen him for nearly three years. (Charts and Maps follow this Prologue.)

On October 1, 1942, Wilber's division—the 43rd Infantry, a New England outfit (Chart 2)—had shipped out to the Western Pacific where it had fought through three sustained phases of intense combat. Wilber had been wounded twice but had soldiered on, and was honored with several medals. At the end of the war, he was a lieutenant colonel and commander of the 172nd Infantry Regiment, the famed Green Mountain Boys of Vermont. If the war had continued, he and they would have crossed the beaches of Japan under fire on November 1, 1945. All had wondered whether they would have survived that bloodbath, and many would not have.

With the war's end, plans changed, and the 43rd Division did indeed go into Japan, near Tokyo, but as an occupation force. Six days after arriving in Japan, the division received orders to return to the United States. I was sitting in a study hall in high school when the school's newscast, read daily by a student, announced that the 43rd Infantry Division was being shipped home—an item of little direct interest to any other student in that Washington, D.C. school. But I knew it meant my father would be coming home, and I let out a little "whoop," but nothing more; I did not want to make a scene. The teacher raised her head to look at me curiously and then returned to her work.

Wilber on board the USS General Pope on the day of his return to San Francisco, October 8, 1945, after three years overseas. Wilber was the senior army officer on board. [PHOTO: BRK00012315_24A; *SAN FRANCISCO NEWS-CALL BULLETIN*, NEWSPAPER ARCHIVES, COURTESY BANCROFT LIBRARY, UNIV. OF CALIFORNIA, BERKELEY]

My sister Valerie remembers it as a bright, hopeful time; her daddy was coming home at last. Our lives would be happier, even joyous, with him back in our midst. We did not go to the West Coast to meet his ship, on which he was the senior army officer, but a news photographer did and captured him on board ship in a happy, smiling, perhaps even laughing moment.

Wilber reached our Washington, D.C., home in mid-October to a festive family-only homecoming, and he seemed to Valerie and me to be the same daddy we had known so well before. To clear up some seemingly minor issues before separating from the service, he was assigned to the hospital at nearby Fort Meade, Maryland, and would return home weekends. We were becoming accustomed to being a family of four again, when there came a day that was to be—and remains—imprinted on our hearts and minds till the end of our days. Here is my story of that day from my recollected youthful perspective.

X·O·Ø·O·X

It is a bright December Saturday morning in 1945 at our Alton Place home in northwest Washington, D.C. I am a lanky 14-year-old boy, and I'm off to a downtown violin lesson. My sister Valerie, age 13, accompanies me; she has a dance lesson, also downtown. We leave the house and wave goodbye to our parents. Our father Wilber has recently returned—just six weeks earlier—from three years of overseas duty with the army. Our mother Norma is busy with household chores. We walk the few blocks to Tenley Circle where we catch the trolley with the new streamlined cars that have finally replaced the classic turn-of-the-last-century cars.

My violin teacher, Jan Tomasov, is the concertmaster of the National Symphony Orchestra. My talent and level of accomplishment do not merit such a teacher, but Mother reaches high for her two children. I have been studying with Mr. Tomasov for the last few months. He is a conscientious and demanding teacher with a stern demeanor and is not given to easy praise. At the lesson, I am challenged by new material and incur his occasional displeasure.

After the lesson I head for home, again on the number 30 Wisconsin Avenue trolley to Tenley Circle followed by the walk down Ablemarle and 44th Streets. At our front door, I encounter my Aunt Josephine and Uncle Paul, my father's brother. They live across town on First Street, NW; I know them well but am puzzled about why they are here. They tell me I should go to our church (St. Columba's Episcopal) and see the minister because he has something to tell me. And I should do this straight away.

I was 15 in the summer of 1946, and here, I was leaving the back yard of our Alton Place home just as I had done on December 1, 1945, on my way to see the minister who would tell me my father was dead. My right pants leg is rolled up to keep it from getting caught in the chain.
[PHOTO: BRADT FAMILY]

Perplexed but obedient, I go to the back of the house and grab my bike. I walk it out of our back yard into the alley behind the house and bicycle the several blocks to St. Columba's. My apprehension grows as I pedal up that final hill to the church.

The minister, whom I know well through our youth group activities, ushers me into his study and asks me to sit down. With little preliminary, he says, "I am sorry to tell you this, but your father is dead."

An accident, he says. I am stunned. I learn little more from him about the circumstances. My father had been in apparent good health, though that day he had had a recurrence of malarial symptoms and had decided not to report to the Fort Meade Army Hospital where he was being treated for other apparently minor ailments.

Shaken and disoriented, I go out to the street and get on my bicycle for the downhill ride home. My usual skill and agility fail me as I start down the steep grade. I almost lose control, but don't. In a few minutes I am home.

The details of what transpired upon my arrival at the house have faded from my memory. In the subsequent days, we managed to get through the military funeral and burial in Arlington National Cemetery on a dreary rainy day. We were given welcome support by a young half-brother of Mother's, Stonewall Sparlin, a navy medical corpsman who was attending the navy diving school in Washington.

My violin teacher, upon reading of my father's death and realizing that it had actually occurred before my lesson, called to offer his condolences and to assure himself that I had not known of it during the lesson. When I told him I could not continue lessons, in part because of money, he generously offered lessons at no cost. I demurred, preferring not to continue under his stern critical teaching. I did not resume violin study until college, three years later. I am surprised that Mother did not object to my decision, but she was facing much larger issues.

X · O · Ø · O · X

My sister Valerie recalls that day in this account, "The Day Daddy Died."

It was a big day. The plan was for me to go downtown with my brother, a year older, for a dance lesson for me and some other appointment for him, but I would come home on the trolley by myself, from Georgetown to Tenley Circle.

I had made it almost home that day, walking from the trolley stop on Wisconsin Avenue down to Alton Place. When I passed the neighbors two doors from our house, they stopped me and insisted I come in for lunch. I did not want to because it was the first day of my first menstrual period and I was afraid to have an "accident." (Mother had taught me that it was a natural process, but I was still afraid.) They insisted I stay for lunch and even blocked my way, so I gave in and went into their dining room for lunch.

Their three daughters stared at me the whole time. I was uncomfortable, but I did not know what to say to them. Then the rector of St. Columba's Episcopal Church came to the house and I was told to meet him in the living room. He ordered me to sit down.

I did not trust him because he had stood passively by weeks earlier when the boys were tickling me on the floor in the church parish hall and I was almost hysterical. In that small living room, I sensed that something was wrong. He said, "Sit down." I said, "No." He repeated, "Sit down." I said, "No" again. He said, "Okay, your daddy is dead."

I felt a sort of dead anger. I walked out of that house and went down the sidewalk to our house, onto the porch, and into the dining room to find my

Fatal Shooting of Colonel, Pacific Hero, Probed by Army

Officer Is Found Dead in Basement Trophy Room

Washington police and Coroner A. Magruder MacDonald are awaiting completion of an Army investigation of the circumstances surrounding the gunshot death of Lt. Col. Wilber E. Bradt, 45, Pacific war hero and former college professor, who was found in a weapon-filled basement trophy room at his home yesterday morning with a gaping wound in his chest.

Walter Reed Hospital authorities, who assumed charge of the investigation immediately after a neighbor found the often-decorated officer's body in the Bradt home at 4421 Alton place N.W., are expected to conduct an autopsy today. Meanwhile Walter Reed officials have re-

LT. COL. WILBER E. BRADT.

Wilber's death announced in the Washington, D.C., Sunday Star *of December 2, 1945, page A6.* [SOURCE: *WASHINGTON (D.C.) STAR*]

mother sitting in a chair crying. There were police and military investigators throughout the small frame building. I asked her what happened. She said there was "a terrible accident." My brother arrived and he was told to go see the minister. He left on his bike for what I knew would be up the long hill to another message of death.

I walked into the kitchen and picked up a paper bag, went upstairs and stuffed my nightgown and a toothbrush into it, walked out and went to Mary Ann Frankenhauser's house. We were not friends, but I did not know where else to go. I said nothing to anyone and stayed there at least a week. I guess her mother called mine and left me alone.

I did not go to the funeral at Arlington National Cemetery. My brother went in the heavy rain with my mother, helping her to accept the folded American flag. I felt terrible about that.

Our daddy had come home after three years overseas and was now gone. I did not know why. I was left in a bleak, dry, empty space that turned into anger. I was driven to get a degree from Columbia University, which led to an extensive career in journalism. The anger finally dissipated, but never my regret for losing those years with my father.

x·o·ø·o·x

I am Hale Van Dorn Bradt, 85 years old in 2016 and the namesake of my grandfather F. Hale Bradt; we pronounce our name "brawt," not "brat." I am a retired physicist and professor, and a resident of Salem, Massachusetts, with a wife and two grown daughters.

My intense interest in my parents' story began on the evening of my 50th birthday, December 7, 1980 (Pearl Harbor day!), with a discussion I had with my middle sister, Abigail, then 37, about her uncertain paternity. I was driving her and her husband Tom back from our house in Belmont, Massachusetts, where we had had a small birthday dinner celebration, to their hotel in Cambridge. We got into a discussion about whether Abigail was really the daughter of my father, Wilber Bradt, a former university professor and a much decorated army officer who had died in 1945, or of Monte Bourjaily, a prominent journalist whom my mother Norma had married in 1947. Abby had been born during the war, and we knew both men were candidates for the paternal honor, but neither of us knew which it was. Abigail and I approach our histories from different perspectives, and our discussions could become a little warm. She "felt like a Bradt," and I felt the circumstances favored her being a Bourjaily. However, as on previous occasions, this conversation played out with no resolution.

Upon returning home, I immediately went looking for dated letters from Wilber, my father, that might clarify his whereabouts at the time of Abigail's conception. I knew he had written many letters to the family during the war and that maybe I had some of them. I rummaged in the old basement file cabinet where I always threw stuff that related to family. Indeed, I found a large manila envelope with about a dozen letters from my father to me. During the war, Mother had gathered them and sent them in that envelope to the *Atlantic Monthly*, which was holding a contest for the best letters written by a serviceman to his children. Wilber's letters did not make the cut and were returned. Decades later she found that manila envelope in one of her many file folders and sent it with its contents to me. I put it in the basement cabinet and promptly forgot about it.

So there I was, on the evening of my birthday in 1980, sitting on the cement basement floor reading my father's hand-written letters. The dates and places of their writing shed no light on Abby's paternity, but I found them to be well written, informative, beautifully descriptive, humorous, and self-consciously fatherly. They were also riveting and some brought tears to my eyes. I knew he had written home profusely from overseas and I even remembered some of the contents, but I had not appreciated the quality of his writing. I knew, then and there, that I had to find more of them. I had long been interested in the Pacific campaigns of World War II and had collected histories and books about them, but had never delved deeply into the details of my own father's involvement. The possibility of retrieving a mother lode of his correspondence that could shed light on his experiences greatly excited me. Abigail's paternity, in that context, became a secondary issue for me.

I met Abigail and Tom the next day and described for them the impact on me of Wilber's letters, along with my eagerness to seek out more of them with the aim of learning his entire wartime story. In doing so, I said, I could plausibly discover the truth about Abby's parentage. "Would you mind?" I asked. She responded, "After our conversation last night in the car, Tom and I went to the hotel's rotating sky bar and talked for at least two hours. I came to realize that I really didn't want to know the truth … but then again, I did." She then gave me her blessing, saying, "Do what you have to do."

That launched my search for people, places, and letters.

I eventually found some 700 highly literate, descriptive letters my father had written during his wartime service. To fill out the story, I interviewed family members, as well as his academic and military associates in the U.S. and elsewhere. I spent one afternoon with a Japanese former colonel who had fought directly opposite my father in the Solomon Islands, ferreted out documents and photographs from the National Archives in Washington, D.C., and elsewhere, and visited the Pacific areas where Wilber had served: New Zealand, the Solomon Islands, Luzon in the Philippines, and Japan. Much of this I did in the early 1980s when many participants in the story were still alive. More recently I have delved into letters written by my father's parents and his sister Mary that reveal their profound influences on his life. In recent years, I have found additional fresh material on the internet. Beginning in 1943, Wilber wrote important events and dates on a few pages in a loose-leaf notebook, which I was fortunate to find.

In all this, I uncovered a fresh and unique view of the Pacific war as experienced by an observant and committed U.S. Army participant, as well as a complex story of an American family during the war. And now I'm compelled to share the story with a wider audience. As my sister Valerie put it, "You must do this, Hale; it is everyone's story."

Wilber consistently dated his letters and, when permitted by censorship rules, gave his location. He wrote often of censorable events and places, but would

WEB

145th Inf Aug. 6, 1943
8. WEB in Baanga I. direct support of 169th Inf. and
172d Inf. from Aug 11 to Aug. 1943
9. WEB in Arundel I. direct support of 172d and 27th Inf.
from Sept. 13 to Sept. 22, 1943.
10. 169th FABn was in Direct Support of:
   a) 169th Inf. from July 7 to July 20, 1943
   b) 145th Inf. from July 20 to Aug. 6, 1943
   c) 148th Inf. from July 20 to July 28, 1943
   d) 169th Inf. in Baanga I. fr. Aug 11 to Aug 18, '43
   e) 172d Inf. "   " fr. Aug 16, to Aug. '43
   f) 172d Inf. in Arundel I. fr. Sept 11, 1943 to 22 Sept '43
   g) 27th Inf. "   " fr. Sept. 15, 1943 to Sept 22, '43
   h) 161st Inf. (no combat) fr. Sept 30 to Oct 15, '43
11. WB Inducted as Capt Feb 24, 1941 Bangor, Me. Regs 3
Moved Arr to Camp Blanding, Fla. 30 Mar, 1941 (12) S-3, 152 FA
Arr Camp Shelby ca 10 Feb 1943. Reg bec 152 FA.
Tr'd as Major to 169th FABn as Exec. 19 Feb 1943
Arr. Fort Ord. 0200 Sept 7, 1942.
10/1/42 Sailed fr. S.F, Cal. 1145 Mar. on USAT "Maui."
Oct '42 Arr Auckland, N.Z. OCT 22, . Disembarked OCT 24, 1943
Arr. Warkworth, N.Z. 24 Oct, 1943 at Wynyards Camp.
1942 Embarked at Auckland Nov. 23, 1943 on USS "American Legion" (NTS)
HB Sailed 24 Nov. 1942 and Arr Noumea Harbor Nov 27, 1943.
Arr on Quengi River Nov. 30, 1943 near Boulapari, N. Cal.
Left Noumea on USS "President Adams" 0530 Feb. 15, 1943
Attacked by Jap planes at "Torpedo Junction" near Malaita Feb. 17 '43
Arr Guadalcanal on Feb 18, left Guadalcanal on "Sau Fley" Feb. 22.
Arr. Pavuvu I, R. I. Feb. 23, 1944.

A page of Wilber's journal written in 1943 after the Solomon actions. He recorded highlights of those actions in the upper half and some of his earlier history in the lower half where he occasionally mistakenly wrote 1943 for 1942 or 1941. The smudged ink corrections in the lower third are erroneous corrections by Norma. The pencil marks in the left margin are mine, to restore correct dates. I overlooked the last entry (arrival in the Russell Islands), which should be 1943, not 1944. [FACSIMILE: HALE BRADT] delay mailing those letters until it was allowed, typically a month after the action described. He clearly was writing for the historical record. Sadly, few of my mother's extensive letters to Wilber survive, but her thoughts and concerns are reflected in his responses. As this book's narrator, I fill in events that Wilber could not or chose not to tell. I also help ground the reader in the local context, the wider events of the war, and the activities of our family at home in the United States. I also tell *my* story of delving beyond what my parents revealed in their letters, including my visits to the Pacific sites. Finally, I offer my take (as Wilber's and Norma's son) on the events of the story.

This volume is a condensed and reworked version of my trilogy, *Wilber's War: An American Family's Journey through World War II*, which I view as the formal publication of my dad's letters. It immerses the reader in Wilber's view of the Pacific war. In this single volume, I recount the story through short segments of Wilber's writing that carry the story forward. Of necessity, much of the rich content of his wartime experience is omitted, but much is retained and the essential story is preserved. Wilber's words constitute 40% of this volume, but they are only 10% of the words in his 700 extant letters.

Infrequent abbreviated references in brackets provide a sense of my sources, which are more fully described in the bibliography. Statements referenced to Wilber's letters, e.g. "letter 12/31/43," may be found in the *Wilber's War* trilogy, if not herein. In this volume, photographs of places and people and facsimiles of documents are interspersed throughout the text, but frequently referenced material—maps and charts—are placed together following this prologue.

The segments of Wilber's letters quoted herein are very lightly edited. For the most part, the inconsistencies of Wilber's impromptu writing, including his casual use of dashes and various date formats, were left untouched. If the recipient of the segment is not given, the reader should assume it to be his wife, Norma. Deletions within the body of an excerpt are indicated with ellipses.

MAPS & CHARTS

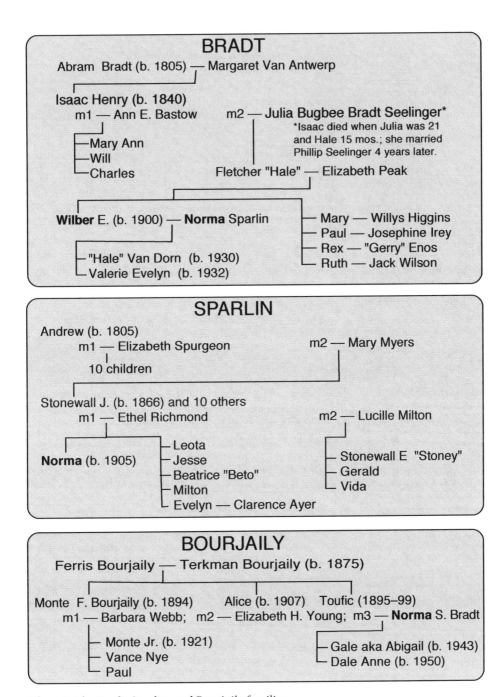

BRADT

Abram Bradt (b. 1805) — Margaret Van Antwerp

Isaac Henry (b. 1840)
m1 — Ann E. Bastow   m2 — Julia Bugbee Bradt Seelinger*

*Isaac died when Julia was 21
and Hale 15 mos.; she married
Phillip Seelinger 4 years later.

— Mary Ann
— Will
— Charles   Fletcher "Hale" — Elizabeth Peak

Wilber E. (b. 1900) — **Norma** Sparlin   — Mary — Willys Higgins
                                                     — Paul — Josephine Irey
— "Hale" Van Dorn (b. 1930)   — Rex — "Gerry" Enos
— Valerie Evelyn (b. 1932)   — Ruth — Jack Wilson

SPARLIN

Andrew (b. 1805)
    m1 — Elizabeth Spurgeon   m2 — Mary Myers
          |
    10 children

Stonewall J. (b. 1866) and 10 others
    m1 — Ethel Richmond   m2 — Lucille Milton

                    — Leota
Norma (b. 1905) — Jesse   — Stonewall E "Stoney"
                    — Beatrice "Beto"   — Gerald
                    — Milton   — Vida
                    — Evelyn — Clarence Ayer

BOURJAILY

Ferris Bourjaily — Terkman Bourjaily (b. 1875)

Monte F. Bourjaily (b. 1894)   Alice (b. 1907)   Toufic (1895–99)
    m1 — Barbara Webb; m2 — Elizabeth H. Young; m3 — **Norma** S. Bradt

    — Monte Jr. (b. 1921)   — Gale aka Abigail (b. 1943)
    — Vance Nye   — Dale Anne (b. 1950)
    — Paul

Chart 1. The Bradt, Sparlin, and Bourjaily families.

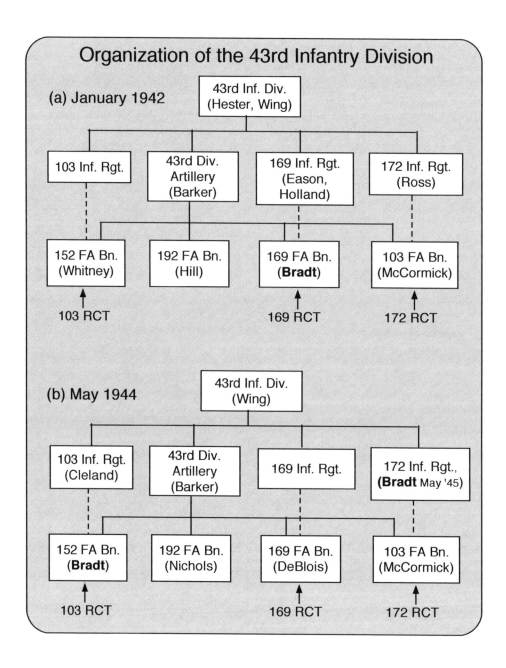

Organization of the 43rd Infantry Division

(a) January 1942

43rd Inf. Div. (Hester, Wing)

103 Inf. Rgt. | 43rd Div. Artillery (Barker) | 169 Inf. Rgt. (Eason, Holland) | 172 Inf. Rgt. (Ross)

152 FA Bn. (Whitney) | 192 FA Bn. (Hill) | 169 FA Bn. (**Bradt**) | 103 FA Bn. (McCormick)

103 RCT | 169 RCT | 172 RCT

(b) May 1944

43rd Inf. Div. (Wing)

103 Inf. Rgt. (Cleland) | 43rd Div. Artillery (Barker) | 169 Inf. Rgt. | 172 Inf. Rgt., (**Bradt** May '45)

152 FA Bn. (**Bradt**) | 192 FA Bn. (Nichols) | 169 FA Bn. (DeBlois) | 103 FA Bn. (McCormick)

103 RCT | 169 RCT | 172 RCT

Chart 2:

1. The commanding officers (C.O.) shown are those in command during the Solomon Islands and Luzon actions and who were also mentioned in Wilber's letters.

2. The division (Div.) had numerous other supporting elements.

3. The three "light" field artillery (FA) battalions (103rd, 152nd, and 169th) each consisted of three batteries of howitzers, each of which carried four 105-mm (4-inch) howitzers, for a total of twelve howitzers for each battalion. These howitzers had a maximum range of about five miles. The "medium" battalion (192nd FA) carried twelve 155-mm (6-inch) howitzers, which had a greater range.

4. The four artillery battalions were under the command of General Harold R. Barker, but could be assigned to regimental combat teams (RCT), which could operate independently of one another. The three light artillery battalions were normally assigned to the infantry regiments shown (dashed lines), but assignments could vary. The medium artillery battalion was reserved for general support where needed.

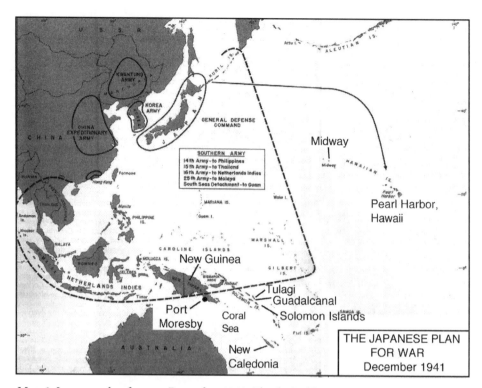

Map 1. Japanese plan for war, December 1941. The dashed line encompasses the planned Japanese sphere of influence, called the East Asia Co-Prosperity Sphere, which was attained in the months following the Pearl Harbor attack of December 7, 1941 (December 8 in Japan). The Japanese drive was halted on the ground at Guadalcanal in the Solomon Islands and at Port Moresby in New Guinea in the fall of 1942. The naval battles of the Coral Sea (May 1942) and Midway (June 1942) blocked planned Japanese attacks on Port Moresby and Midway, respectively. [UNDERLYING MAP: MORTON, *STRATEGY*, MAP 1, P. 106–7]

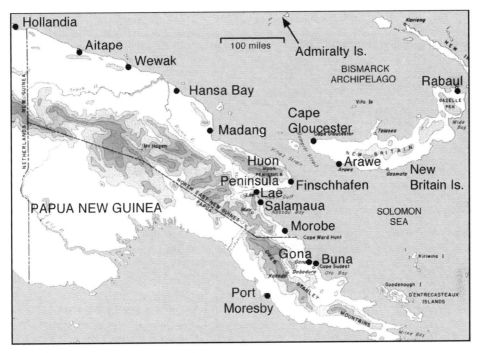

Map 2. *Eastern New Guinea. The Japanese had been driven from Guadalcanal (off map to east of Buna) and from the Gona-Buna area on New Guinea in January–February, 1943. When the 43rd Division began its attack on Munda Airfield, Solomon Islands, in July 1943, the Japanese had retreated to the Lae-Salamaua area of New Guinea. Simultaneous drives up the Solomons (under navy command) and up the New Guinea coast (under army command) were intended to isolate and eventually neutralize the major Japanese naval base at Rabaul (upper right). The advances in the two theaters were coordinated to allow the use of common naval and air resources. This strategy was given the name "Cartwheel."*

The Allies landed at Hollandia and Aitape in April 1944, bypassing the Japanese 18th Army at Hansa Bay and Wewak. The 43rd Division arrived at Aitape July 17, 1944, to help hold the line against Japanese moving westward. The Allies, by this time, held the coast southeast of Madang (center) and had rendered Rabaul ineffective as a Japanese base. [UNDERLYING MAP: MILLER, CARTWHEEL, MAP 3, P. 23]

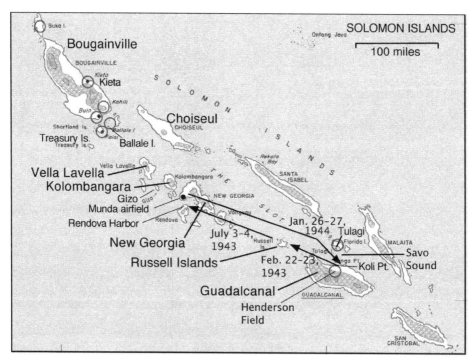

Map 3. Solomon Islands including Guadalcanal, the Russell Islands, and the New Georgia group, all of which are featured in Wilber's story. The circles indicate Japanese bases prior to the marine landings on Guadalcanal in August 1942. The major Japanese stronghold at Rabaul was on New Britain Island, 200 miles farther to the northwest (Map 2). Another Japanese airfield was built on New Georgia at Munda during the Guadalcanal fighting. The three moves of the 43rd Division during its 11 months in the Solomons are shown.

During the battles over Guadalcanal, Japanese ships would approach Guadalcanal from the northwest through "the Slot," while American ships would approach from the southeast. Both were trying to reinforce and supply their troops on Guadalcanal. Many ships were sunk in Savo Sound ("Ironbottom Sound"), which lies between Tulagi and Guadalcanal. [UNDERLYING MAP: MILLER, *GUADALCANAL*, MAP III, CROPPED]

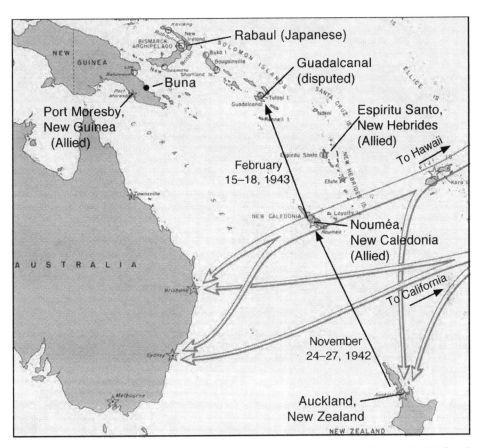

Map 4. *Southwest Pacific, July 1942, showing lines of communication (broad double lines) from Hawaii and California, the American bases (stars), and the Japanese bases (circles). The marines were doing battle on Guadalcanal when the 43rd Division arrived in New Zealand in October 1942, less the 172nd Regimental Combat Team, which had lost all its equipment in the sinking of the USS Coolidge at Espiritu Santo. In late November 1942, most of the 43rd Division moved from New Zealand to New Caledonia (lower black line with arrowhead); the balance arrived December 29. This released the Americal Division for duty on Guadalcanal. In mid-February 1943, the 43rd moved further north to the front lines in the Solomon Islands (upper black line with arrowhead). The naval battles arising from attempts to reinforce Guadalcanal by both sides were supported from the major naval bases at Rabaul (Japanese, upper left) and at Nouméa, New Caledonia (Allied, center right).* [UNDERLYING MAP: MILLER, *GUADALCANAL*, MAP II]

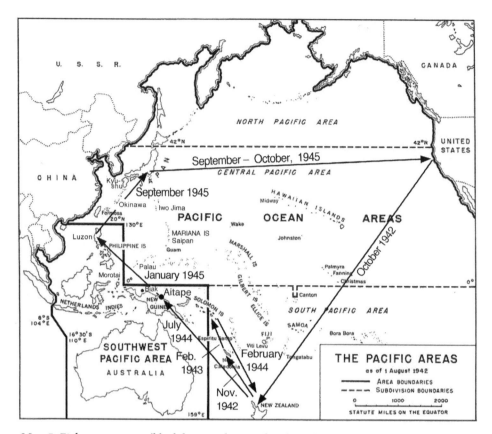

Map 5. *Eight sea voyages (black lines with arrowheads and dates) made by the 43rd Division in the Pacific Ocean during its three years overseas. Three additional (overnight) voyages were made within the Solomon Islands. Also delineated are the four military command areas of the Pacific Theater. The North, Central, and South Pacific Areas were the domain of the U.S. Navy (Admiral Chester Nimitz), and the Southwest Pacific Area, the domain of the U.S. Army (General Douglas MacArthur).*

[UNDERLYING MAP: R. JOHNSTONE, IN MILLER, *CARTWHEEL*, MAP 2, P. 3]

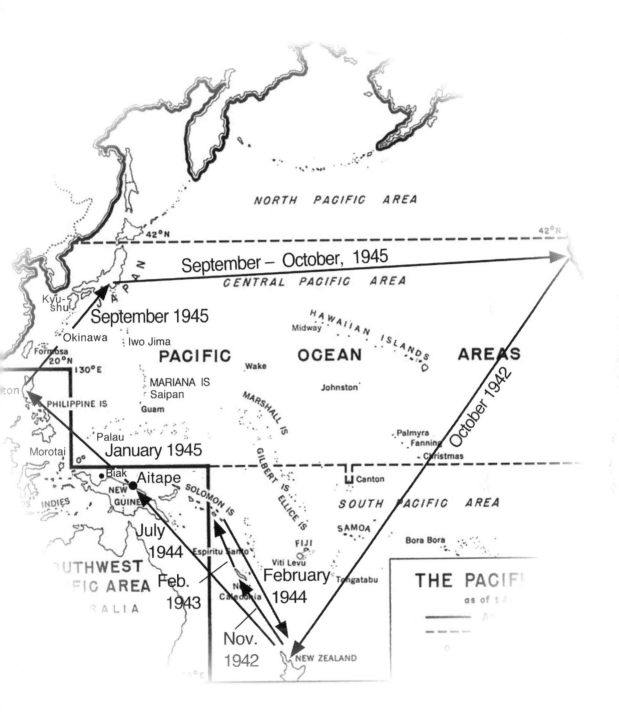

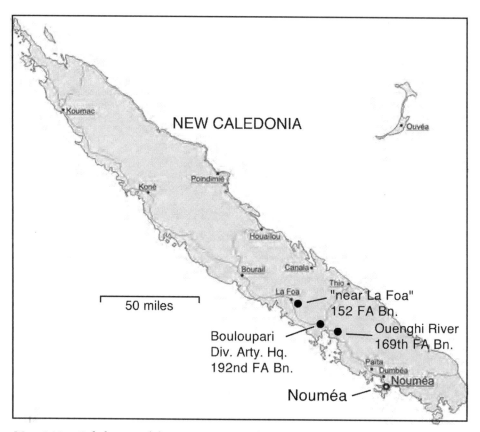

Map 6. *New Caledonia with locations mentioned in the text. The location of the 152nd FA Bn. is not known precisely.* [OUTLINE MAP: D-MAPS.COM)]

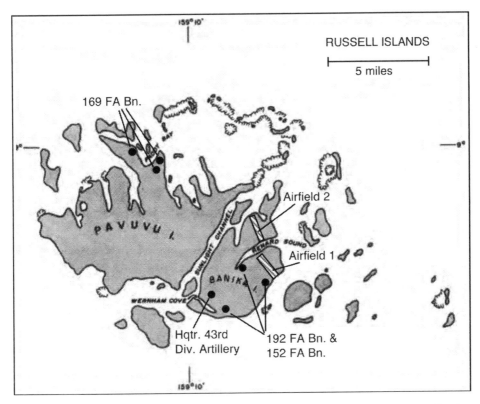

Map 7. *Russell Islands showing the locations of Wilber's battalion (169th Field Artillery) on Pavuvu Island, and on Banika Island, the division artillery headquarters, the other two field artillery battalions (152nd and 192nd), and the American airfields. Wilber's outfit, the 169th, was quite a long boat ride from the artillery headquarters and Wilber's immediate superior, General Barker.* [UNDERLYING MAP: MILLER, *GUADALCANAL*, P. 353, MAP 15; UNIT LOCATIONS: BARKER, MAP P. 30; AIRSTRIP LOCATIONS: SEABEES MAPS, WWW.SEABEES93.NET]

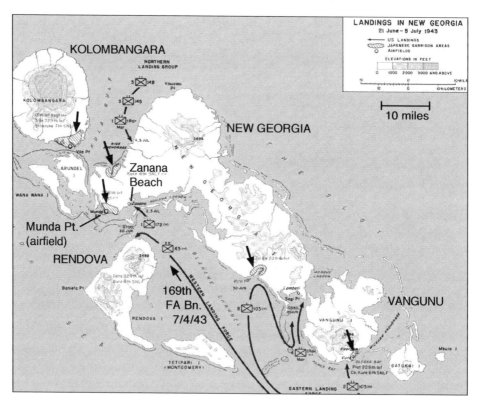

Map 8. Allied landings in the New Georgia Island Group (solid lines) June 21–July 5, 1943. The outlined hatched areas (arrows) indicate Japanese strongpoints. The long tracks show the approach of the American Western, Eastern, and Northern Landing Forces. Wilber was wounded on the north end of Rendova Island on July 4. The attack on Munda Airfield was mounted to the east of Munda at Zanana Beach. [UNDERLYING MAP: MILLER, CARTWHEEL, MAP 11, P. 69, CROPPED]

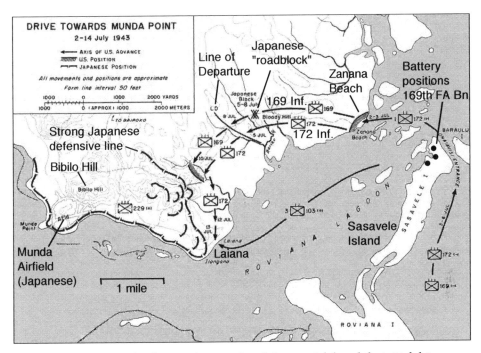

Map 9. *The American landings on Zanana Beach (upper right) and the initial drive toward Munda Airfield by the 169th and 172nd Infantry Regiments beginning July 2–3, 1943. The Line of Departure ("LD") is shown. The advance stalled at the most advanced positions shown on about July 10, after which the 172nd Infantry drove south to Laiana beach to shorten supply lines. The howitzers of Wilber's unit, the 169th Field Artillery Battalion, were emplaced on the north end of Sasavele Island (far right); from there the battalion could support the entire advance toward Munda Airfield, six miles distant at the far left.* [UNDERLYING MAP: F. TEMPLE IN MILLER, *CARTWHEEL*, MAP 9, P. 107. LOCATIONS OF 169TH FA BATTERIES: DIXWELL GOFF, WHO SURVEYED THE POSITIONS (PVT. COMM.); SEE ALSO BARKER, MAP P. 50.]

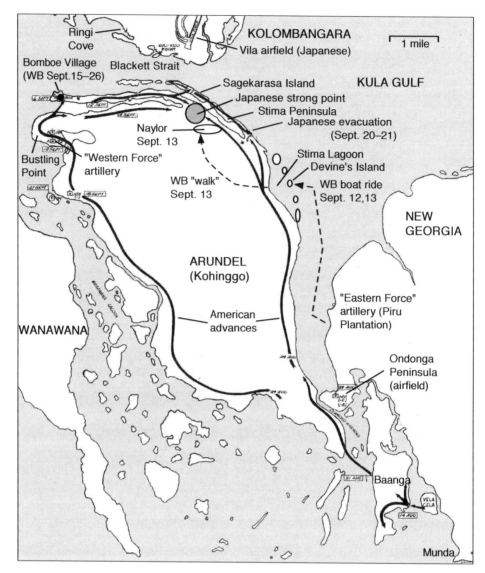

Map 10. Baanga (lower right) and Arundel Islands showing places and actions mentioned in Wilber's account. The Baanga landings on August 14, 1943, (dark arrows) were immediately above the cove where 34 men were stranded on August 12. The Japanese naval guns were emplaced on the southern tip of Baanga. The initial infantry landings on Arundel Island were at its southern end on August 29, 1943. When the infantry encountered Japanese on the north end, Wilber became involved. The position of Devine's Island is approximate. The long dark arrows show the advances of American units. The Japanese evacuated Arundel for Kolombangara on the night of September 20–21. In 1983, I circumnavigated Arundel in the clockwise direction in Arthur Basili's canoe.
[UNDERLYING MAP: BARKER, P. 96]

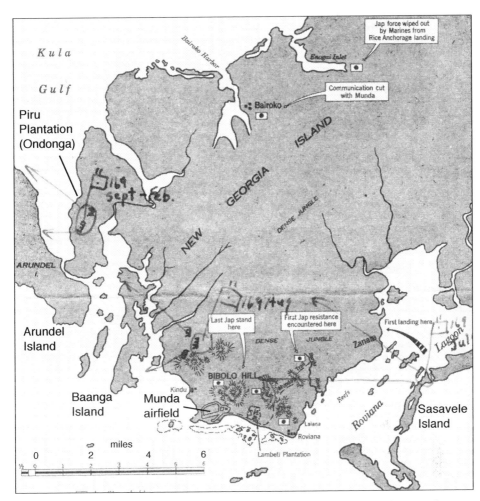

Map 11. *Munda region annotated by Wilber to show the three locations of the 169th FA Bn. during the three phases of combat in the Solomon Islands: on the north end of Sasavele Island during July 1943; north of Bibilo Hill ["Bibolo" in this map] during August; and on Piru Plantation, Ondonga, from September 1943 to February 1944. For most of the latter period, Battery A of the 169th FA was with the Provisional Battalion at Bustling Point on northwest Arundel. Wilber showed the fields of fire with long arrows.* [UNDERLYING MAP: FROM DUPUY, R. ERNEST, "BIBOLO [SIC] HILL—AND BEYOND," *INFANTRY JOURNAL,* JANUARY 1944, PP. 21–26]

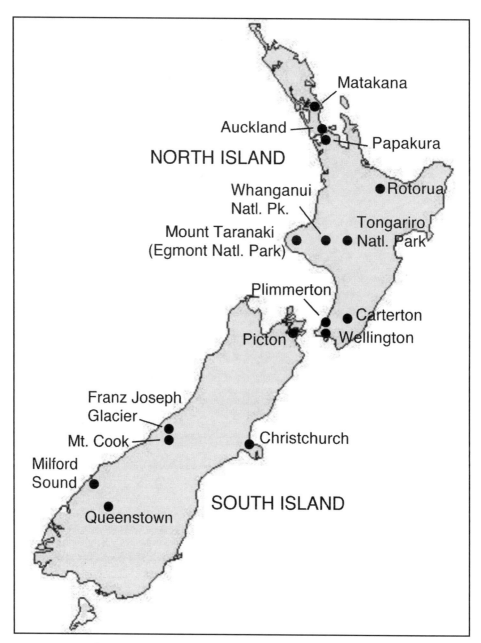

Map 12. Map of New Zealand showing the places that appear in this story. Wilber's units were stationed at Papakura and Matakana and trained near Rotorua. On leave in March 1944, he and Davis visited the three indicated national parks on North Island and also Plimmerton and Wellington. On South Island, he visited Christchurch, Mt. Cook, and Franz Joseph Glacier, and possibly also Queenstown, Milford Sound, and Picton. Olive Madsen's home was in Carterton (northeast of Wellington) when I visited her in 1984.
[MAP OUTLINE: GEOGRAPHY.ABOUT.COM/LIBRARY]

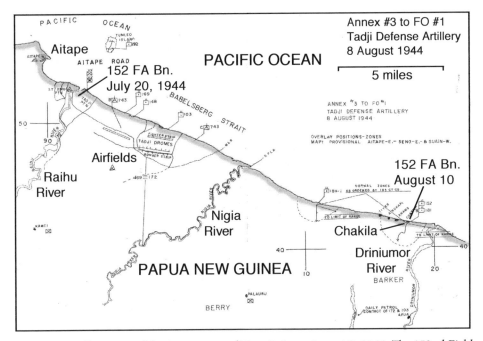

Map 13. *Artillery map of the Aitape area of New Guinea, August 8, 1944. The 152nd Field Artillery Battalion, Wilber's outfit, was initially located at the mouth of the Raihu River (to left) where it could defend the Tadji airfields and later it was at the Driniumor River to the southeast. The Japanese were mostly to the east of the Driniumor. Wilber spent a lot of time being driven between the two locations, a straight-line distance of about 18 miles. Yakamul is six miles east of the Driniumor on the coast.* [SEE MAP IV OF SMITH, *APPROACH*; UNDERLYING MAP: BARKER, P. 132]

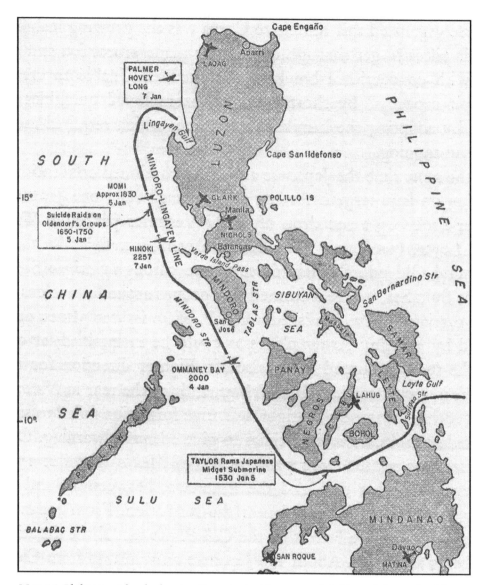

Map 14. Philippine Islands showing the principal Japanese airfields and the track of the attacking Allied convoys heading toward Lingayen Gulf in early January 1945. The U.S. Bombardment Force arrived three days before the troopships and took heavy losses from kamikaze (suicide plane) attacks, e.g. the Ommaney Bay on January 4. Wilber wrote of the sinking of a Japanese midget submarine on January 5 (lower center) and of the Japanese destroyer escort, Hinoki on January 7 (upper left of Mindoro). The full east-west width of Mindanao (lower right) is about 300 miles. The convoy could travel about 200 miles in a 24-hour day. [MAP: MORISON, V. XIII, P. 100]

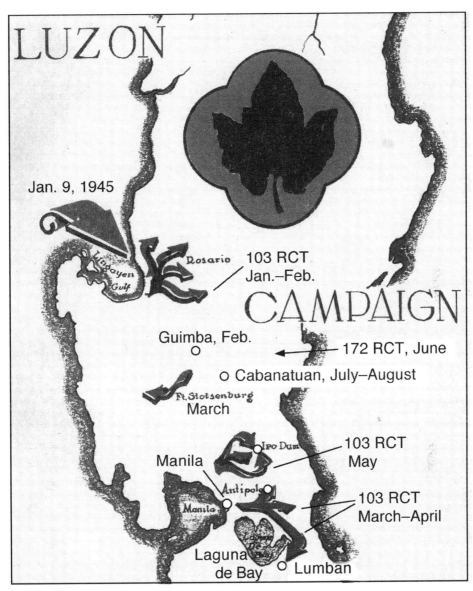

Map 15. Four actions (groups of broad arrows) of the 43rd Infantry Division on Luzon, Philippine Islands, as shown on the cover of the 43rd's report of its actions in Luzon. These actions began with the landings at Lingayen Gulf (left center) and occurred in sequence from north to south, except that the Ipo Dam action followed the Antipolo-Lumban action. The actions, locations, and action dates for the units Wilber was with are indicated. The 103rd RCT was held in reserve for the Fort Stotsenburg action. The maple leaf insignia (top center) was the emblem of the 43rd Division. [UNDERLYING MAP: *HIST, RPT. LUZON CAMPAIGN, 43RD DIV., COVER*].

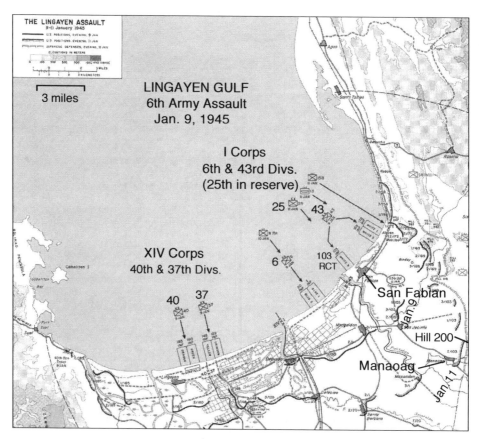

Map 16. Sixth Army assault on Luzon at Lingayen Gulf on January 9, 1945. The XIV Corps (40th and 37th Divisions) was to drive southward toward Manila. The I Corps (6th and 43rd Divisions with the 25th held in reserve) were to drive eastward to prevent Japanese forces of the Shobu Group to the north from coming south. The 103rd Regimental Combat Team, which included Wilber's 152nd Field Artillery Battalion, landed at San Fabian. The indicated landing sites extended over 18 miles. The lines of advance of the 103rd RCT for January 9 and 11 are labeled. The Japanese did not oppose the landings on the beaches but put up a strong delaying defense in the surrounding hills and mountains. Hill 200, just off the map beyond Manaoag, was the first day's objective; it was not subdued until January 17. [UNDERLYING MAP: SMITH, *TRIUMPH*, MAP I CROPPED].

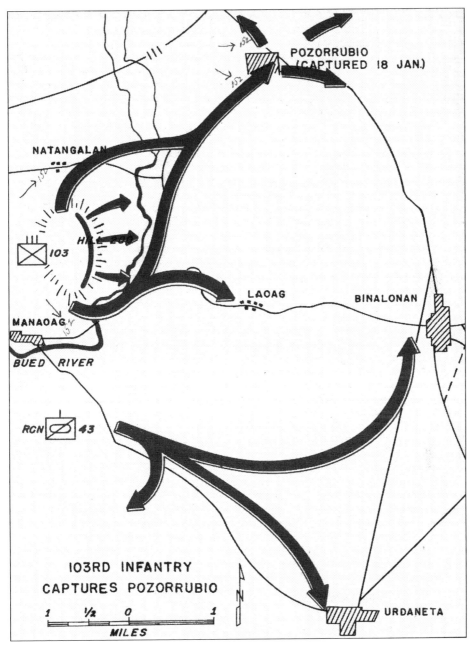

Map 17. *Capture of Pozorrubio. Hill 200 is shown at left center (label obscured); Hill 600 (not shown) is north of Pozorrubio. Hill 600 is where Wilber did the forward artillery spotting that merited him the Silver Star. Wilber's "152" notations (marked by my arrows) indicate locations occupied by his three artillery batteries for varying durations.*
[MAP: HIST. RPT. LUZON, 43RD DIV., SKETCH 7]

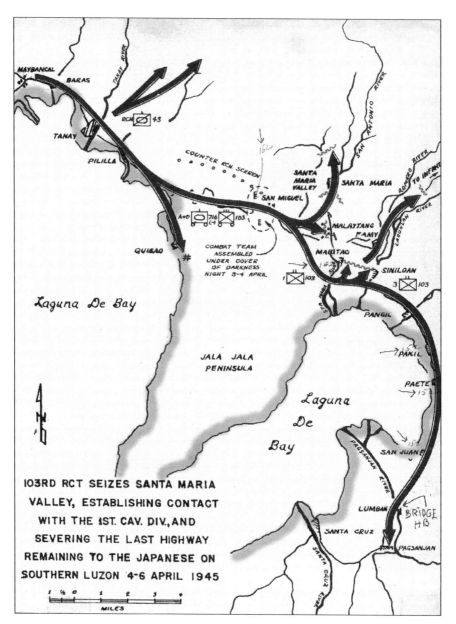

Map 18. *The drive of the 103rd RCT across the Jala Jala Peninsula and down the eastern shore of Laguna de Bay to Lumban and Pagsanjan (lower right), April 4–6, 1945. The positions of Wilber's artillery are indicated (small arrows and "152"). Wilber's actions in the capture of the bridge ("BRIDGE HB" at lower right) over the Pagsanjan River at Lumban earned him a second cluster for his Silver Star. The First Cavalry Division was driving toward Pagsanjan from the south. The large lake, Laguna de Bay, is also seen on Maps 15 and 21. The full length of the distance scale (lower left) is five miles.* [MAP: HIST. RPT. LUZON, 43RD DIV., SKETCH 15]

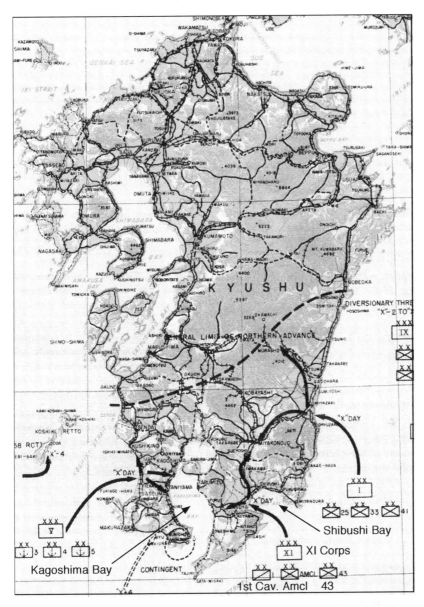

Map 19. Operation Olympic landings on Kyushu, the southernmost main island of Japan. On "X" day, scheduled for November 1, two army corps (I and XI) and one marine corps (V Corps) would land at the indicated points with the objective of securing Japanese airfields and establishing a base area to support landings in the vicinity of Tokyo on Honshu four months later. Other units would follow as needed. The 43rd Division was in the XI Corps and would land at Shibushi Bay (lower right). The 1st Cavalry Division and the Americal Division were also in XI Corps. The Americans would limit their advance in Kyushu to the area below the heavy dashed line. [MAP: REPORTS OF GENERAL MACARTHUR, V. 1, MAP 118, P. 413]

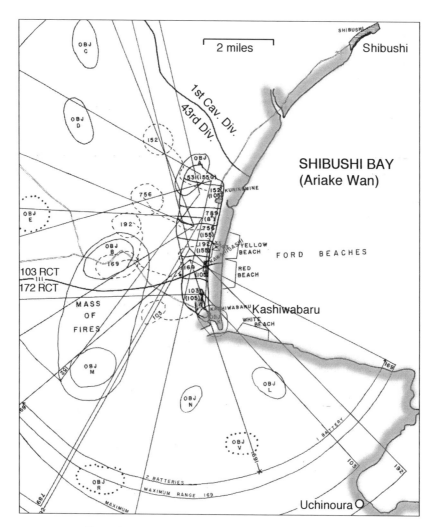

Map 20. *Artillery Plan of the Shibushi Bay landing area, dated August 5, 1945, showing positions of the 43rd Division artillery units, areas accessible to their howitzers, and objectives (firing targets). The invasion was scheduled for November 1, 1945. The 43rd Division was to land on the southern end of the long beach. The zone of the 172nd Regimental Combat Team commanded by Wilber was the entire lower part of this figure. The 103rd RCT was to be to its right (boundary line, center left), and the First Cavalry Division would be to the north on the 43rd's right. (Earlier plans had the 43rd's and 1st Cavalry's positions reversed.) The mountains in the 172nd zone (objectives L and N) reached to 2660 feet in altitude. Wilber wrote that "my regiment was given the point considered most critical to the success of the division action. That meant we couldn't take our time but would have to drive thru anything we met the costly way" [letter 9/20/45]. Uchinoura (lower right) is the town where I stayed on my 1983 visit to the nearby rocket launch facility (south of the town). The town would have been within range of the division's artillery.* [UNDERLYING MAP: BARKER, P. 231]

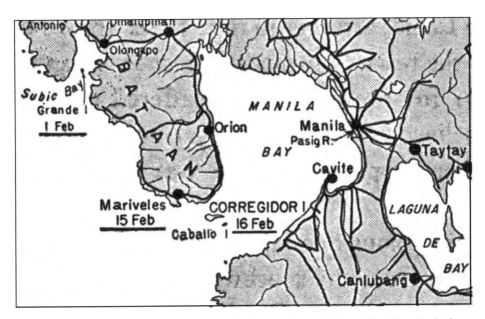

Map 21. *Manila Bay showing Bataan peninsula, Manila, and Corregidor Island, which protects the mouth of the harbor, and also Laguna de Bay (lower right). Bataan and Corregidor were the last bastions held by the Americans before they capitulated to the Japanese in April and May of 1942. The dates shown here are of Allied actions in 1945. The distance from Corregidor to Manila is 28 miles.*

[MAP: ADAPTED FROM MORISON, V. XIII, P. 190]

UNIVERSITY OF MAINE
ORONO, MAINE

24-5-37

DEPARTMENT OF CHEMISTRY
AND
CHEMICAL ENGINEERING

Dear Mother, Father + Ruth,

This is the last day of Spring vacation. During the past week I worked for the first five days then we took the children on an all day "pic-nic". About 40 miles east of here there is a low range of mountains or high hills. The highest is "chick" hill and alongside is "little chick Hill." The south slopes are clear of snow and wooded. We drove out to within a half mile of the hills and hiked in thru the woods and climbed Little chick. It was only about 1200 fts high but was steep and in some places rocky. The children had a grand time. The top gave a fine view of the surrounding county and Bangor, Orono, Oldtown, Mt. Ktaadn, 100 miles to the north and several lakes. most of the county is timbered (small second growth)

PART I

FARM TO ACADEMIA

NEBRASKA, INDIANA, WASHINGTON STATE, OHIO, MAINE
1871–1941

Formal portrait of Elizabeth, Wilber, Mary, and Hale, 1904, Portland, Indiana
[PHOTO: BRADT FAMILY]

1

"He regarded [the guard] as important even in peacetime"
MISSOURI AND INDIANA, 1871–1927

It was a cloudy day, late on a June afternoon in 2012, as I stood on a hillside in Humboldt, Nebraska, pondering two side-by-side gravestones. One was that of my great-grandfather Isaac Bradt, a Methodist provisional minister, who had died young at 32 on November 22, 1872. The other was that of Abram Bradt, Isaac's father, who had died in 1877, five years after his son. On that cold November day of 1872, Isaac's grieving young widow Julia, age 21, could have been holding her 15-month old son, Fletcher Hale Bradt, called Hale. With Julia would have been Isaac's parents, Abram and Margaret Bradt, along with Isaac's three children from a previous marriage; their mother Ann had died at 30, three years earlier.

Graves of Isaac (d. 1872), my great grandfather, left, and his father Abram (d. 1877) in Humboldt, Nebraska, with fields in the distance.. [PHOTO: JORENE HERR, 2014]

As I looked out over those Nebraska farm fields, I imagined that sad day and pondered the outcome. The 15-month-old Hale would grow up to become my grandfather, the father of my father Wilber, the soldier who had died so suddenly in our Washington, D.C., home on yet another cold day, in December 1945.

After burying her husband, Julia returned home to Michigan with her baby son Hale, where she met and married Philip Seelinger, from Versailles (pronounced ver-SALES), Indiana, a farming village in southeast Indiana. Seelinger, Julia, and Hale, now eight or nine, returned to Indiana in 1879 or early 1880.

Hale attended school in New Marion and first met his future wife, Elizabeth Peak, age six, when he was ten years old. Starting at age 17 or 18, Hale taught school for two years possibly at the New Marion School, and then entered the University of Nebraska in 1892 at age 21. He majored in chemistry and was on the football team. He graduated in 1896.

Elizabeth Peak (known in her youth as "Lizzie"), who would become Hale's wife and Wilber's mother, was born on May 1, 1875. She received an eighth grade education followed by one year of high school in North Vernon, Indiana (20 miles west of Versailles), and then became a teacher when she was still quite young. On April 3, 1899, after a four-year engagement, Hale married Elizabeth. He had obtained a job teaching science and coaching at Bloomington (Indiana) High School where he was one of only six teachers. Their first child, Wilber, the focus of this story, was born in Bloomington. The birth was difficult as Elizabeth wrote decades later,

> January 29, 1961 — The days wore along, until the next Thursday, Feb. 1st [1900]. Wilber was born at 3:20 P.M. I had never seen a newborn baby. My bed had been moved into the living room by the fire, and I saw Mother shaking and spanking and blowing her breath into the mouth of six lbs. of baby whose head was elongated; his skin was almost black. I didn't know until later that the long labor had nearly taken the child's life. I like to think Mother saved him....
>
> P.S. Our doctor bill for Wilber's birth was twenty-five dollars.

In 1903, Hale became superintendent of the Portland, Indiana, schools and moved his family there. Mary Elizabeth was born in January 1903 and a formal photo portrait of the foursome was taken a year later. Paul, the next child, was born in October 1904. The parents doted on their first born and made a list of his "cute" sayings, this one when Wilber was just short of five.

> Dec. 28, 1904 — Wilber went to visit a primary room in which there was to be a Xmas tree and other exercises. Santa Claus came in and among other things asked all the "good children" to hold up their hands. All hands went up but Wilber's. "Haven't you been good?" asked Santa. "I have been bad sometimes," replied Wilber.

In 1906, Hale obtained a position as "superintendent of Versailles." He bought an 80-acre farm three miles east of Versailles and moved the family there. It featured a large barn and a log house, their home for 13 years until 1919. The fourth and fifth of their children, Rex and Ruth, were born there in 1908 and 1916 respectively.

The log house on the Bradt farm consisted of a 22-foot-square living room, an upstairs unheated sleeping area, and a kitchen, not used in winter, tacked onto the back. And "yes, of course it had board floors; why would you think dirt?" my

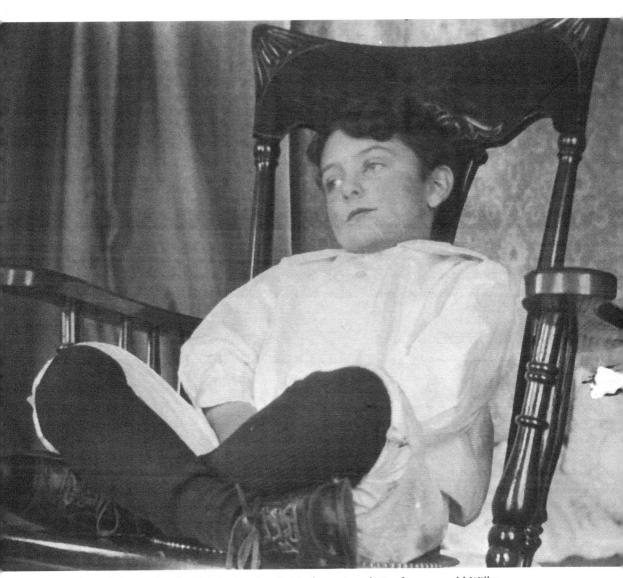

Informal photo taken by Hale in October 1904 of a contemplative four-year-old Wilber.
[PHOTO: F. HALE BRADT]

Aunt Mary was quick to clarify when I interviewed her in 1987. Toilet facilities were, of course, outdoors in the outhouse. In a 1980 letter to my niece Corinne, Aunt Mary wrote,

> 5 January 1980 — We lived in a log house then.... We all slept in the big upstairs room, with a double bed in three of the four corners of the room, and the stairway in the fourth corner. The logs could not go up to the peak of the roof, for they would roll off if they were not held fast at the corners of the house. During the winter the snow used to blow in under the boards, which closed up the space above the logs. As we slept in iron beds, Mother used to tie an umbrella to the head of the bed to keep the snow from falling on our faces.

In 1907, Hale became county superintendent of schools for Ripley County, Indiana. Five years later, from 1912 to 1914, at reduced salary, he took on teaching duties at the one-room Waterloo district school just north of the farm. His first three children were students there, and he wanted them to have a better education than the previous teacher had been providing.

The financial needs of their growing family, probably noted most often by Elizabeth, led to Hale taking positions in several school systems that were 50 to 100 miles away from home for periods during the years 1914–18. These distant positions required him to live away from his family at least during the workweek, during two of Wilber's teenage years.

When Hale was away, the responsibility for the farm duties and chores fell on Elizabeth and the children. The children later wrote that Elizabeth was the better manager of the two parents. Each child had his/her appointed duties and failure to perform required penance. According to Rex, if the wood box was not brought in, the house stayed cold. If water for cooking was forgotten, then no breakfast. Maybe he exaggerated, but if true, such things probably happened only once or twice; the Bradt kids were no fools!

But Hale's absences, during a total of three years that included his World War I service, loomed large for the children; in later years, they often mentioned it. Wilber looked up to his father and mother and sought their approval, even into his adult life. His sister Mary, in a letter to me in 1980, shed light on their parents' characters.

> Father was one of the best men I have ever known. In addition to not using profanity he worked hard all his life to keep boys from using tobacco and alcoholic drinks. He was a shy man, but always stood up to be counted for anything which he thought was right. He had a remarkable memory and could remember just what the source was for everything he had ever

read as well as the subject matter. He was a remarkable teacher and, being especially interested in scientific subjects, was always in demand....

Father had a quick temper, but he always kept it under control. Mother angered more slowly, but she boiled inside and never quite forgave anyone whom she considered her enemy.

These traits came into play in Hale's and Elizabeth's later dealings with their children. Elizabeth's long-lasting anger seemed to be rooted in an inner self-doubt that appeared in later letters. Outwardly, though, she was an assured, confident, and highly capable person.

Mary or Rex more than once told me about the time Wilber was throwing stones high up, toward the tall open-topped empty silo and claiming they were going into it. His younger brother Paul did not believe this and stepped into the silo to check, whereupon the next stone hit him on the head. He could no longer doubt Wilber's throwing ability. This was always described with great glee!

Wilber attended Versailles High School where he played basketball and had a front tooth struck and "killed"; it was always dark-colored thereafter. In his senior year, he took an examination—probably sponsored by his congressman—hoping to earn an appointment to the U.S. Naval Academy at Annapolis; this proved unsuccessful. According to Mary, he had to learn geometry on his own because the high school did not teach it. Wilber graduated from Versailles High School on April 27, 1918, in a class of 13 students. The early-in-the-year graduation date freed the students for work on their family farms during planting season.

During the Great War (World War I), Wilber's father volunteered to serve with the YMCA providing services to the troops through canteens ("huts") that sold personal supplies (stationery, shaving supplies, etc.) to the soldiers. He spent a year from May 1918 until July 1919 in Europe and participated in several battles without injury.

Hale's long absences during Wilber's teens thrust Wilber into a leadership role in the family, undoubtedly creating his close camaraderie with his mother. Hale, meanwhile, certainly did not give up his parental role. As he was preparing to leave for France, he wrote Wilber, who, at age 18, would shortly be entering Indiana University, a letter about the moral challenges Wilber would face, especially about the evils of—not sex but—smoking, a study in avoidance. By contrast years later, Wilber wrote to me, his then-13-year old son, frankly extending advice on sexual matters.

Wilber entered Indiana University (IU) as a freshman in the fall of 1918. America was at war, and Wilber became a member of the Student Army Training Corps (SATC). Early in the fall term, he contracted the flu in the great epidemic of 1918–19 that killed millions, but fortunately he recovered. He withdrew from IU in December

Portrait of Wilber Bradt in his SATC uniform with his proud mother, March 10, 1919.
[PHOTO: BRADT FAMILY]

and returned home to the Versailles farm. The war had ended on November 11. That spring, he tried again for the Naval Academy and again was rejected.

A photo taken that spring illustrates his closeness to his mother.

X·O·Ø·O·X

Upon Hale's return home in 1919, Elizabeth encouraged him to seek a teaching position again in Bloomington, Indiana, so the children could live at home while attending Indiana University. Soon, he was teaching science courses at the high school and had bought a house in Bloomington. That fall, Wilber re-entered the university as a freshman. He and each of his siblings, in turn, attended the university while living at home, and each successfully completed a bachelor's degree; the last child, Ruth, graduated in 1937.

At the university, Wilber was on the swimming team and earned his varsity letter. His soon-to-be-prominent schoolmates and close contemporaries were the wartime journalist Ernie Pyle and singer-song-writer-actor Hoagy Carmichael, both of whom Wilber knew. He had earned his bachelor's, master's, and doctoral degrees, all in chemistry, by 1926. By several accounts, he was a rather serious and dedicated student, but a graduation photo of the chemistry grads shows a cheerful Wilber.

During the Great Depression of the 1930s, Hale felt it patriotic to borrow money and hire men to do renovations, such as adding a second floor to the Bloomington house, because he had a steady salary as a teacher. However, when teachers' salaries were cut, his financial situation became precarious. Hale was always more of an optimist and spender than his wife, and this was a source of occasional conflict between them. Wilber became very wary of intra-familial bickering and revealed much of his parents' characters in a Valentine's Day (1944) letter to Norma, written from New Zealand.

> I've just read *O River Remember* [by Mary Ostenso].... The mother in the boys' family was so much like my own, I wouldn't dare send the book home, and the father was much like my father, so you see why the book moved me so.

This novel, popular in the 1940s, portrayed the mother as a strong family leader who exercised excessive, and hence damaging, control over her children, all while remaining deeply conscious of social standing and reputation. The father, by contrast, was more kindly and tolerant, but also rather laid back and impractical.

Wilber's long association with the military began during World War I, while he was at Indiana University, with his service in the Student Army Training Corps. In his sophomore year, he joined the Indiana National Guard as a sergeant, a relatively high enlisted rank. As a college student, he became eligible to be an officer and was appointed a second lieutenant the summer after his junior year. He held that rank until he finished his PhD. His unit was the 150th Field Artillery Regiment. He maintained his National Guard service, with some breaks, until World War II. His brother Paul wrote in 1961,

> He [Wilber] was always fun to be with but always serious about important things. I was with him in the guard for about six years [in the 1920s], and I assure you he regarded it as important even in peacetime.

In 1926, after seven years at IU and with a PhD in hand, Wilber found a position as an instructor in the chemistry department at the State College of Washington in Pullman, Washington. (The college was widely known as Washington State College, or WSC, and in 1959 it became Washington State University.) This position took Wilber away from home for the first time, except for those few months at IU in 1918. His destination, Pullman, was a small college town in the rolling wheat fields of southeast Washington.

Toward the end of his first year at WSC, he accepted a more lucrative position at the University of Cincinnati for the following year, again as an instructor in chemistry. The summer before leaving for Cincinnati was to be full: he was to teach a chemistry class at the college and was scheduled to serve in August as field assistant to the state geologist of Washington in the western part of the state.

He did not anticipate a major, but welcome, upheaval in his life in June of that year, 1927.

2

"It was one of the perfect days of my life"
WILBER AND NORMA, 1927–1930

On June 26, 1927, a day Wilber would never forget, a vivacious, blond 21-year-old student entered his classroom and took his breath away. She was Norma Corinne Sparlin, a music major in her senior year at WSC who needed to fulfill a science requirement. On July 4, one short week later, Wilber took Norma on a picnic. Wilber recalled this exactly 16 years later, on July 4, 1943, in a letter he wrote from a sea-going landing craft.

> I remember too that it was a July 4 in 1927 when I took Nana [Norma] out on a picnic above the Snake R. [River] canyon. We walked a path together over the river and the flowers were lovely and the air was fresh and cool. Later it rained and we sat under a blanket and talked. On the way home Norma sat on my lap and I wished we might never get home. It was one of the perfect days of my life.

Close-up of Norma taken at the picnic; Wilber was obviously enamored of her.
[PHOTO: WILBER BRADT]

They were probably sharing a seat on a crowded bus.

Who was this attractive young woman who so captivated Wilber? Norma was an accomplished pianist, organist, and writer, and was active on campus in literary and musical circles as well as in her sorority, Alpha Gamma Delta. She was not lacking for beaus and had been elected the "Sweetheart of Sigma Chi" according to her own testimony.

Norma on a picnic with Wilber, probably July 4, 1927. Sixteen years later, in a letter to Norma of July 4, 1943, Wilber remembered that picnic and, a week earlier [letter 6/26/43], recalled her black satin pleated skirt. Note the high heels (on a picnic?). [PHOTO: WILBER BRADT]

Norma was born in Barron, Wisconsin, on November 30, 1905. Her father, Stonewall Jackson Sparlin, had been born in Missouri in 1866 and named after the famous Confederate general. He left Missouri as a young man and ran a general merchandise store in Almena, Wisconsin, and later served in the elected position of county clerk. In 1887 at 21, he married Ethel Richmond who was 17 or even younger. Ethel was of early colonial English stock on both sides.

Ethel and Stonewall had six children before she left him in 1910 when Norma was four. According to Norma, contributing factors to the breakup were their strongly held differing viewpoints on the Civil War—he the Confederate and she the Yankee—as were alcohol and another woman. Ethel took their four youngest children, Beatrice (age ten), Milton (nine), Norma (four), and Evelyn (six months), to Hillyard, Washington, a suburb of Spokane. She managed to support herself and her four children with her sewing skills, along with help from an older married daughter, Leota, living in Oregon, and from growing vegetables that Milton would sell at curbside. It wasn't easy. Ethel was a marked woman; divorces were unusual and frowned upon in those days.

Norma, at age 75 and at my behest, typed an eight-page, single-spaced, self-conscious account of her life as she looked back on it. Here she describes her home life in Hillyard.

> Although money was scarce, there was a close family relationship filled with music. Singing, violin and piano practice, [and] small orchestral rehearsals kept our lives merry and bright. [Norma played the piano; Evelyn and Milton played the violin.] ... Evelyn and I were busy concertizing as early as when she was six years old and myself ten [at] ... banquets, lodge parties, weddings, showers, birthday parties.

Norma enjoyed school in Hillyard where she sang the lead in the eighth-grade musical. At age 12, she entered Hillyard High School. That summer she traveled by herself to northern Minnesota to spend the summer with her father who had established a successful logging business in the virgin forests there. This

Ethel Richmond Sparlin's four youngest children, Barron, Wisconsin, 1909: Milton (b. 1901), Beatrice (left, b. 1900), Norma (right, b. 1905), and baby Evelyn (b. 1909), probably taken at Evelyn's christening. They left for Washington State with their mother at about this time.

[PHOTO: SPARLIN FAMILY]

entailed a long train trip with one or two transfers and a night alone in the YWCA. Two years later she again traveled there for the summer. I expect that these trips, rather perilous for a 12- or 14-year-old, were not simply for a vacation or for fulfilling a father's wish to have time with his daughter. More likely they resulted from the stresses, financial and personal, in the Hillyard home.

Upon her return from the second trip, Norma entered North Central High School in Spokane because her mother had moved into Spokane. After graduation at age 16, her expert typing skills landed her a job in a law office in Deer Park, some 30 miles from Spokane. Shortly afterward, the law office owners arranged work for her as the secretary of the School of Music and Fine Arts at Washington State College in Pullman, so she could continue her education there. The dean of the school, Herbert Kimbrough, became a mentor. Of herself then, Norma wrote,

> There I wrote promotions for faculty artists, held art exhibits, arranged for plays, wrote song lyrics of the musicals, traveled with the glee club, [and] promoted everything. All this time I was intensely practicing, taking piano and organ lessons.

Norma moved on to other secretarial positions in the architecture department and in the president's office, and began giving piano lessons. She thus came to know President Ernest Holland of the college. She was a popular young woman with a circle of close friends.

A shortage of money was an ever-present concern for the Sparlins. Ethel married several times and the situation at home was probably not fully secure for the girls. By one account, sexual molestation was said to have occurred. When Norma was around age ten, she was "given away" by Ethel to another couple in another town who could better care for her, but in fact were quite neglectful. She was rescued by a man from her home parish who happened to see her unkempt and alone on a downtown street of that town. This episode was a defining experience for her; she mentioned it often in later years.

The darker aspect of Norma's home life was confirmed by Wilber in a letter he wrote to his sister Mary from the Philippines.

> February 18, 1945 — [Norma] has been a lonely and fatherless girl who early learned she had to fight her own battles herself.... She and Evelyn have fought since childhood to keep themselves free of the things they found in their own background and as a consequence look on our [the Bradt] home pretty much as their ideal.

In contrast, the strong musical and religious heritage that Ethel managed to give to her children was clearly an important and positive aspect of their lives.

On July 22, 1927, less than a month after they met, Wilber gave Norma a diamond ring and asked her to marry him before he left for the University of Cincinnati in late August. Norma was reluctant to get married so soon; she was only a few credits shy of a diploma and had, she wrote, "a super job teaching piano in a nearby high school – private pupils, all day, for two days a week, at an excellent salary."

Wilber pointed out that she could earn credits toward her degree at the University of Cincinnati and at the Cincinnati Conservatory of Music. Despite her misgivings, she acquiesced. The engagement was formally announced on August 16 at the home of Dean Kimbrough. They would be married when Wilber returned from his geological fieldwork.

On August 28, a scant two months after meeting, Wilber and Norma were married in Portland, Oregon, where her brother Milton lived. It was a small wedding with no reception; only eight guests were listed in her *Bride's Own Book*, her relatives and a friend or two. Wilber gave Norma a ring with "Comrades" inscribed on its inner surface. Norma described the ceremony and its aftermath in her *Bride's Own Book*.

Our wedding was solemnized in the dimly lighted Hinson Memorial Baptist Church in Portland Oregon at 10 p.m., Sunday evening, August 28, 1927, after which Wilber tucked me, wedding gown and all, into a taxi and took me to his hotel, the Multonomah [Portland's largest and most elegant hotel]. There were just we two at our wedding party, but red, red roses were in a bowl on the table to greet us. Wilber went out for Silver Spray [a champagne-like non-alcoholic beverage popular during prohibition] and chicken sandwiches and we celebrated hilariously with this bridal fare, eating in bed in great luxury for both of us.

Wilber knew his mother would object vehemently to the marriage because it was on such short notice and was to a woman from a broken family. Thus he did not notify his Indiana parents of the wedding until it was an accomplished fact. Wilber's socially sensitive mother did not take this lightly; she thereafter harbored a long-lived bitterness toward both Wilber and his bride that was never completely erased. Both families would soon have to confront the situation in person, as Wilber and Norma were to pass through Bloomington, Indiana, at the end of their honeymoon trip, which took them to Cincinnati.

The newlyweds arrived at the Bradt home in Bloomington, Indiana, on September 9, 1927, and received a very frosty reception as revealed in letters between Wilber's sister Mary and her mother. Norma and Wilber were so concerned about their reception that they had asked President Holland of WSC to write to the Indiana Bradts attesting to Norma's good character, which he did, but I have found no indication it altered their views.

Elizabeth's inevitable detailed report to Mary of the visit has been lost, but we have Wilber's brother Paul's take on it in a letter written after Wilber and Norma departed.

Sept. 13, 1927 — The couple [Wilber and Norma] has gone long ago. I expect you have heard mother's report. She felt very bitter against him

Norma and Wilber on their honeymoon, possibly at Lake Louise, Canada, 1927. He was wearing his red Indiana University letter sweater. [PHOTO: WILBER BRADT]

and some against her. Mother says she never wants to see them again. I believe mother would feel better if I denounced him beyond his deserts. This way she keeps expanding on his failures, etc.

Much later, Wilber reflected on this visit in a letter to Mary, "You know of the unfortunate introduction she [Norma] received to our family" [letter 2/18/45].

Wilber and Norma proceeded on to the University of Cincinnati where Wilber took up his duties as instructor of chemistry and Norma her musical studies. Norma's sister Evelyn, aged 19 at the time of their move, lived with Wilber and Norma in Cincinnati for at least part of their time there. This evidently was the best available solution to getting Evelyn some college education with acceptable and economical living arrangements.

Toward the end of the first academic year, Wilber and Norma made their next visit to his parents, a four-hour drive. Elizabeth showed little sign of the bitterness she had felt during the earlier visit but was still quite critical of the visitors, as she wrote Mary,

> May 23, 1928 — I know you want a report of our Sunday visitors.... Wilber is still wearing the suit like the sample he sent us. It has felt [been damaged with] acid and is repaired. He is much thinner. His shirt was a bright blue with collar attached and was not very becoming, but it will likely grow dimmer with age.... He seemed much more like his former self than he did last Fall.
>
> Norma looked much the same, except she has left off the rouge. Maybe only for the occasion. She was wearing a black satin dress, the upper part of which had white figures. Plain and becoming. Her slippers were black patent, trimmed with black and white. They were almost shabby from wear, but she looked nice. I think I shall like her. Her desire to be liked was very apparent and nearly pathetic. She and Wilber have "cut out" the spooning or did for that day.

Elizabeth's love of Norma ("I think I shall like her") was provisional, to say the least! At the end of the summer, Wilber and Norma visited again. They had most likely been to Washington State for the summer.

> Sept. 23, 1928 — Wilber looks very well indeed but Norma looked worn and thinner. She acted as lively as ever tho.

The summer of 1929 again took them to Washington State. On June 3, Norma was awarded her Bachelor of Arts in Music with Honors by Washington State College. A photo of her and Wilber, both in academic gowns, indicates that Wilber marched in the academic procession. These trips west allowed Wilber to nurture his contacts at WSC, to his advantage.

3

"We have a drastic cut in pay"
PULLMAN, WASHINGTON, 1930–1936

Wilber had not quite completed his three-year stint as instructor at the University of Cincinnati when he was offered an assistant professorship at Washington State College at an annual salary of $3,300, beginning in the spring term of 1930. This position was a major step up in salary and status; his initial salary as an instructor at WSC had been $2,400.

Before leaving Cincinnati, Norma and Wilber visited the Bradts in Bloomington. After they left, Elizabeth wrote Mary about the visit. She revealed a pragmatic side, a further willingness to accept Norma at some level and reduce her bitterness toward Wilber.

> Jan. 5, 1930 — Of course, we are proud he can go back where he has been [Washington State College]. Norma is thrilled to go back as a faculty man's wife. Evelyn [Norma's younger sister] is going back with them.

For the January 1930 trip to Washington State, Wilber and Norma avoided the snow-blocked passes over the Rocky Mountains and traveled southwest in their small 1928 Chevrolet roadster into which they squeezed Evelyn. Upon reaching Pullman, they moved into a small duplex and later into a little house on Side Street.

During their residence in Pullman, Norma played organ at St. James Episcopal Church, and accompanied the WSC concert band as a chaperone on a tour. Edward R. Murrow (of future radio broadcast fame), a prominent student leader, was on the tour as a WSC spokesman, and as Norma later wrote, he sought her out as a sympathetic ear for his romantic troubles.

On December 7, 1930, I was born at the Catholic hospital in nearby Colfax, Washington, and named Hale Van Dorn Bradt. Wilber gave Norma a Bulova wristwatch inscribed with "Comrades Three 12-7-30" to honor the event. (I still have the watch.)

At WSC, Wilber's academic activities and connections broadened. He not only taught and supervised research students, but also attended meetings of professional societies. He was the primary organizer of an American Association for the Advancement of Science (AAAS) meeting at Pullman and was active in Phi Beta Kappa affairs, serving as secretary of the WSC chapter. These connections led to trips east from time to time, usually by train, and he would try to fit in visits to his Indiana family.

One such trip occurred in August and September, 1931. It was a six-week excursion with wife and baby in our new, large, four-door 1930 Chrysler. The objectives were meetings in Buffalo, New York, and Providence, Rhode Island. I was a mere nine months old and slept in a hammock strung across the car just behind the front seat. In a sixth-grade essay, obviously coached by Norma, I wrote, "While we were traveling, I seemed to be most amused by looking out of the window when we were driving through cities." We stopped in Bloomington, Indiana, to see Wilber's folks and in Holton, Indiana, to see his grandmother, Julia Seelinger. On the return trip, we visited Washington, D.C., to see Wilber's siblings, Mary and Paul. Letters from Elizabeth and Mary describe these visits.

From their letters, it is clear that Wilber and Norma were traveling not only with me, but with Norma's sister Evelyn (then 22) and Marie, another young woman. Taking on two extra people (and Evelyn's violin) might have seemed a huge extra burden, but to Wilber and Norma it was quite natural to take along two young women to help with the baby. In return, they would get to see many parts of the country, and camping out would keep expenses under control.

Wilber had joined the Washington State National Guard in October 1930. The appeal of military life, a strong sense of patriotism, and the steady stipend all might have contributed to his rejoining. The Washington unit was the 161st Infantry Regiment. It held weekly drills and summer encampments. The infantry was a change from the artillery expertise Wilber had developed in the Indiana guard, requiring some make-up study and training. But he soon regained his second lieutenant rank and was promoted to first lieutenant in June 1933. Wilber was in Company E and became very close to its men and officers. After the weekly guard meetings, some of them would drop into the local Chinese restaurant, Charlie's Place, in Pullman for food and talk "of fighting the Japs" [letter 2/22/43] should it become necessary.

Our family became a foursome with the arrival of Valerie Evelyn Bradt on April 18, 1932. To commemorate it, Norma gave Wilber a Scabbard & Blade key with the inscription, "Comrades IV 4-18-32" [letter 4/2/44]. Scabbard & Blade was a military society to which Wilber belonged. This was to be their last child. Thereafter Norma suffered three or four miscarriages, and life was soon to offer further hurdles for the young family.

Valerie was born into a world sliding into the Great Depression. In the fall of 1932, industrial production and farm prices in the U.S. were at their lowest point. In response to budget pressures, faculty salaries at Washington State College were cut by ten percent. Wilber's went from $3,700 to $3,330 a year. This wasn't the only problem the family faced, as Wilber wrote his parents.

> Thursday, Jan. 12, 1933 — Norma fell on the sidewalk yesterday and broke both bones in her leg, one bone protruding through the flesh. She is in St. Ignatius Hospital in Colfax, nineteen miles from Pullman. The car is out of commission, so I can't see her often. She is suffering intensely. We are praying no infection sets in.

Valerie was an infant of nine months, and I was just two when Norma broke her leg. Wilber had his hands full. He wrote "The babies are still OK tho Hale calls for 'Mama' each morning. Rather pitiful." Norma returned home a few weeks later, but then fell and broke her leg again.

> 3-27-33 — Norma's crutch slipped on the linoleum this morning. She fell and re-fractured her leg. She is in the hospital again. Her leg had been out of the cast for three weeks and was progressing even better than we had hoped. The doctor said she could begin to put her weight on it by the middle of July and we were so encouraged.
>
> 3-28-33 — We have a drastic cut in pay and personnel of the faculty coming up next month. Hoping for the best.

Fortunately, Wilber kept his faculty position for the 1933–34 academic year, but his salary was cut an additional 15 percent, to $2,830. In April 1934, his pay was raised to $3,265 and remained there until his departure from WSC in 1936.

Two months later, Wilber's father Hale described in a letter to his daughter Mary the negative impact of the Depression on his extended family—both Mary and Rex had lost their jobs. More important, he revealed a warm concern for the well being of his grown children and their families in those trying times.

> May 16, 1933 — But, all in all, I think we have much to be thankful for and much to be hopeful for.... If this terrible crisis brings on still greater suffering and loss, I hope we can draw together and fight it out together either here or on the farm.... We will do our best to meet each problem as it comes.

Norma did recover her health, and our life in Washington State came to include outdoor activities for the whole family. There were camping trips in the rolling fields of eastern Washington State and daytime picnics.

Our family around 1935 on another outing in Washington State with an unidentified friend on the left. [PHOTO: WILBER BRADT]

In addition to family and teaching, Wilber had to keep up his academic research. His work in the electro-deposition of manganese led to a grant from the Vanadium Corporation. He was elected a fellow of the American Association for the Advancement of Science (AAAS) in 1933 and elected as executive secretary of the western division of Phi Beta Kappa in 1934. He was appointed to the PBK national committee for the revision of the PBK constitution and bylaws that same year. These associations and presentations at meetings continued to require travel to the eastern states.

In addition, he had National Guard duties. He was on summer duty in western Washington when his battalion was called up for extended "strike duty" to control crowds and strikers in Tacoma, Washington, during a bitter strike of timber and sawmill workers that shut down operations and sawmills across the Northwest. The battalion arrived in Takoma on June 23, 1935; the strike had begun officially on May 6 and extended to mid-August.

Wilber wrote his parents a dramatic and vivid account of his initial involvement. This strike duty was the precursor to the actual combat Wilber would be engaged in eight years later. His account enlivens an important event in America's history. During this period, Norma, Valerie, and I vacationed in a cabin at Pacific Beach, an ocean-side community not far from Tacoma. Here are excerpts from Wilber's account:

> July 26, 1935, Aberdeen, Wash. — It is about time that I told you something about the strike duty I have been engaged in during the last seven weeks....
>
> We found about 1000 striking men on the bridge blocking traffic to the lumber mills. They were mostly unarmed but very antagonistic toward us and determined to block the bridge, which is about 400 yards long. I was quite complimented to have the first assignment of the day – to clear the bridge. The men [in my platoon] were mostly of high school age with a few of college standing. None had ever had any experience of this type. Most men were armed with loaded rifles and a few with pistols. Bayonets were fixed on all rifles and men armed with pistols carried no other weapon. Later they received policeman's nightsticks.
>
> The main point of course was to accomplish the mission without bloodshed. I had 12 men. We placed about eight on the most crowded side of the bridge, using the others to clear the other side. I walked up the center of the street somewhat ahead of the line of soldiers, urging the strikers to move on. Those who did so kept ahead of me, and those who refused were about alongside of me, most of them on one side. These were shoved along by the soldiers. The push of a rifle at high port was usually sufficient, for anyone who insisted on his rights; the boys applied strokes with the butt, the piece against the body or of the rifle proper or barrel about the striker's head. None of them would face the soldiers.
>
> By eight A.M. the bridge was cleared, my boys had gained considerably in self-confidence, and the strikers had stopped calling the boys tin soldiers and boy scouts and had started calling them more manly but less courteous names....
>
> One man who had thrown a gas bomb back at the Major was in the street I cleared with part of Co. E. I said, "I want that man" and pointed at him. He could not have seen me point but he started on the run. I grabbed

his collar and he came back with both fists flying. He swung at me four times and each time I cracked him on the head with my night stick. The first time I eased up quite a bit and it didn't even phase him. I doubled the force of the blow next time and the last two times I was too busy to even worry about hitting him too hard. We fought all over the sidewalk, out to the middle of the street and back to the sidewalk where I threw him down against the wall of a building....

My Captain, being sick, was not able to be very aggressive in these affairs. I tried to show that I would go with my boys. As a result my status has changed considerably in the battalion. Formerly I was the college professor. Now I am the lieutenant that they want to go out on duty with....

August 1, 1935 ... I have maintained the direction by weekly mail of 4 graduate students all summer.

He had managed to monitor his graduate students in the midst of all the military activity!

Wilber had gained in leadership experience and showed that he could manage himself in tense and physically difficult circumstances. He took pride in that and wanted his parents to know. He showed little empathy toward either the strikers or the employers; he focused on maintaining order. It is amazing to me that the confrontations with troops untrained in crowd control and carrying loaded firearms did not result in accidental shootings.

X·O·Ø·O·X

In this section and occasionally later on, I step back and apprise the reader of important war-related events that were taking place elsewhere in the world. They provide us with the broader context within which Wilber and Norma were operating.

On September 18, 1931, across the Pacific in Northeast China (Manchuria), the Japanese Army set off an explosion at an isolated railroad station. This event, called the Mukden Incident, was a provocative act blamed on the Chinese. It was used as justification for the Japanese invasion and occupation of Manchuria (Northeast China), which the Japanese established as the "independent" state of Manchukuo. There was wide international outrage at these actions and the Japanese withdrew from the League of Nations. This was the beginning of tensions between the U.S. and Japan that would break out in war ten years later. The following winter, on January 28, 1932, the Japanese attacked Shanghai and took the last major Manchurian city, Harbin, on February 4. The United States issued strongly worded objections to these actions.

In January 1933, President Hindenburg of Germany appointed Adolf Hitler as Chancellor of Germany. In July, Hitler proclaimed the Nazi party to be the only legal party; all others were banned. Germany was in the depths of a depression with huge unemployment. Hitler solidified his power as fuhrer and restored Germany to relative prosperity with deficit spending on public works, industrial rejuvenation, and military arms. On March 7, 1936, he ordered three battalions of German troops into the long disputed industrial Rhineland, which had been demilitarized by the Treaty of Versailles in 1919. It was a test of French diplomatic will; the French did not respond.

4

"Our river is still behaving and is fine skating"
MAINE, 1936–1941

The fortunes of Wilber and Norma's family depended on Wilber's work. The economic climate remained grim, salaries had been lowered at Washington State College, and tenure was not certain. Wilber thus enlisted Norma in a campaign of letter writing to universities across the United States. A letter sent to the president of the University of Maine in Orono elicited a response, and letters of recommendation were sought. Most were quite positive about Wilber's research, his ability to motivate students, and his organizational abilities as demonstrated by his work on the Phi Beta Kappa committees and as organizer of the AAAS meeting at the Pullman campus.

The chemistry department at the University of Maine was at the time primarily a teaching department. The university president and dean wanted it to develop a research program. A strong head was required to change the habits of senior faculty members. A 36-year-old outsider with a credible but not outstanding research record, good teaching credentials, and demonstrated leadership skills in the National Guard may have been just what the University of Maine's Dean of Technology Paul Cloke wanted.

It was not until early in July that an offer was tendered to Wilber as full professor and head of the Department of Chemistry and Chemical Engineering. The appointment was for the nine-month academic year with a salary of $4,000. The offer occasioned queries by Wilber and Norma about conditions in Maine, particularly those pertinent to their children: schools, reduced sunlight, and tuberculosis rates. But of course, such a position could not be refused and wasn't.

Wilber purchased a new 1936 Plymouth, which I, age five, thought was absolutely terrific. That summer, the family headed east for Maine, stopping at national parks (Yellowstone and Glacier). Valerie and I danced with Native Americans at a show in a park lodge, and we saw our grandparents in Bloomington, Indiana.

We settled in Orono, Maine, in an apartment building across a small park from the Stillwater River, a tributary of the Penobscot River. It was there that I started school and a grand piano was bought for Norma. Sunday trips to Sandy Beach on Mt. Desert Island in the summer were welcome diversions. Valerie and I were not put off by the cold water and relished playing in the breakers. We would stop for fried clams on the way. Norma often told of my comment upon first viewing the Atlantic Ocean when I was five. When asked what I thought of it, I wisely responded, "It's OK, but it's not as big as the Pacific."

In January of our first winter in Maine, Wilber joined the local unit of the Maine National Guard. It provided him with exposure to the outdoors and the camaraderie of fellow soldiers who were of a different social set than his academic colleagues. It gave him breaks from his academic duties, and there was, of course, the patriotic incentive. The Maine guard unit was artillery. Wilber had thus gone from artillery in Indiana to infantry in Washington and then back to artillery. Upon leaving Washington, his guard friends there gave him a .45 caliber Colt pistol for his personal use. His notebook carefully carried its civilian serial number, C17943, which distinguished it from identical government-issued pistols.

Nine years later it was to be the instrument of his death.

That first winter, Wilber was very busy professionally but he also found time for recreation with all of us. He had many balls in the air.

> 2/3/37, Dear "folk" — Our river is still behaving and is fine skating except when the snow is on the ice.
>
> 3-15-37, Dear Father, Mother and Ruth — It is snowing here now. The natives are quite hopeful. They have predicted a terrible winter ever since I came, with no results. With the end of winter in sight they have become almost desperate. The winter here has been very mild with only occasional snow, at least three days of sunshine a week and warmer than Washington winters. Last week Norma + I went out in the woods on a south slope, built a fire and cooked steaks on sticks. What a treat!...
>
> I go to Philadelphia next month... I present two papers there before the Electrochemical Society. One paper is on manganese plating and the other is on the oxidation of lactic acid. The Vanadium Corporation of America is interested in my work on manganese and may develop the commercial aspects of it. Their lawyers are working on a patent application now.

Wilber's association with Vanadium Corporation continued into the next decade. His patent #2,398,614, "Electro-deposition of Manganese," was filed in March 1938. It was assigned to the Vanadium Corporation and was finally issued in

April 1946, four and a half months after Wilber's death. The corporation never developed it, and there never was any financial return from it for our family.

In April, Wilber wrote his parents again.

> 4-5-37 — This is the last day of spring vacation. During the past week I worked for the first five days, then we took the children on an all day "pin-pic" [picnic]. The south slopes are clear of snow and wooded. We drove out to within a half mile of the hills and hiked in thru the woods and climbed Little Chick [Mountain].... The children had a grand time....
>
> 4-14-37 — People tell us that here the month of May is a mad-house. If it is worse than April, I'll leave the state....
>
> It is only fair for [a potential student] to know that I am a slave driver when it comes to research. I won't waste time and apparatus on a man who works only for the credit. I want men who are interested enough that I have to watch them to see that they don't miss too much sleep or too many meals. Each year there are students who prefer not to work with me – for good reasons – and I am content to have it that way.

Norma entered the music scene at the University of Maine and in nearby Bangor with gusto; she stood out as a highly accomplished musician. Valerie and I were long used to hearing her play her repertoire. Beethoven's Waldstein sonata would resonate through our home as we fell off to sleep. She played with and for friends but had few opportunities for formal concertizing. She did not take on pupils other than Valerie and me.

At the end of our second winter in Orono, Norma was the piano soloist with the Bangor Symphony Orchestra in a performance of Paderewski's Polish Fantasy, Opus 19. The concert was in Bangor's city hall on May 5, 1938, and was repeated the next morning in the Memorial Gymnasium at the University of Maine in Orono. This was the high point for her on the local music scene.

Norma was a writer too. In those years, beginning in Washington State, she wrote a novel, *Grand Coulee*, named after the huge hydroelectric dam built from 1933 to 1942 in eastern Washington. The novel was never published but attempts to get it published led to many revisions over the years. Norma took seriously her roles as homemaker, mother to Valerie and me, cook for the family, and hostess to academic colleagues. I never heard her voice any frustration at not having more time for her musical and literary interests, though she may well have felt it.

In the summer of 1938, Wilber and Norma bought a house at 204 Broadway in Bangor, a Penobscot River city of about 30,000, eight miles from Orono. There we attended St. John's Episcopal Church on French Street. (Wilber's name is now inscribed in one of the stained glass windows as one of the church's war dead.)

Norma at her new grand piano in Orono Maine, about 1937.   [PHOTO: WILBER BRADT]

Valerie and I entered the Mary Snow public elementary school a half-mile down Broadway, she in first grade and I in second. It was a long walk for little kids but we did it every day through the Maine winter. Norma repaid my resistance to her piano instruction by offering me violin lessons with a local teacher, Mr. Cayting, and I eagerly took her up on this.

In our new school, I was immediately in trouble in arithmetic; everyone seemed to know the multiplication tables. They were new to me, and I was terribly confused by them. Wilber solved that efficiently. He declared that each day after school I would learn one of the "tables" prior to going out to play. The first assigned was the "sevens" because they were the hardest. I did learn them and successfully passed his verbal test. After learning several others over the next few days, I remember being happily surprised at how easy the "fives" were. I was soon back on track in arithmetic.

Wilber also attended to my mechanical education. In the kitchen one day during breakfast, I inadvertently stepped on and crushed the electric plug for the hand iron. Wilber told me I would have to fix it, handing me a screwdriver and a new plug. When I asked him how to do it, he said that I should be able to figure it out by studying the broken one without help from him. That gave me pause, but I managed to do it. I have liked working with mechanical and electrical things ever since.

It was in Maine that Wilber's weight had escalated to 240 pounds. At an even six feet, he had become quite overweight, a hurdle he would have to overcome before embarking on the military life he could now foresee.

Anticipating that his guard unit could be called to active duty, Wilber had begun in July 1940 to provide instructions to Norma should she have to run our home by herself. They were in his indestructible leather-bound seven-ring notebook and detailed the furnace and oil burner operations, electrical trouble, gas trouble, important documents, and finances. The closing paragraph was quite ominous.

> 7/4/40 — In case of catastrophe, I will look for you first in this vicinity [Maine], next in Indiana, and third in the Spokane area, and 4th in Portland, Ore. In case of bombing raids, get away from town and main highways. I'll be looking for you afterward. The safe place is usually where you are known.

Wilber was imagining the worst based on the newscasts from European countries showing refugees fleeing with their belongings on crowded roads. He and Norma had no idea how their futures would evolve.

In the fall of 1940, the New England National Guard, the 43rd Infantry Division, received notice that it would be activated in February 1941. In order to qualify for active duty, Wilber began a regimen of severe dieting: salads, no carbohydrates, and lots of exercise with handball. He successfully brought his weight down to below 200. This was an adventure in historic times that he was not about to miss. Christmas of 1940 was a somber occasion. The family was being broken up and America was on the verge of war. The future was unknown.

Upon activation, the 43rd Division would move to a Florida training camp. Norma chose neither to remain in Bangor nor to take Valerie and me to Florida. Instead she and Wilber decided that she and the children would move to New

York where she could study piano and pursue her writing. A close friend in Washington State, Gladys Anderson, had moved to New York City in 1927 to study violin at the Juilliard School of Music, as had a character, a dancer, in Norma's unpublished novel. The seeds had been planted and when the opportunity presented itself, she grabbed it. The prospect of moving to New York City must have energized her.

We rented our Broadway home in Bangor to another family on February 1, 1941, and moved into a small, depressing apartment above a grocery store a few blocks away for the few weeks until our departure for New York City at the end of the month.

Just as we moved into that little apartment, Wilber received letters from his parents with requests for financial help. This was far from the optimum time to place a new burden on Wilber and Norma, but the Indiana Bradts seemed to have missed that point altogether. There is a remarkable quartet of letters, from Hale (Sr.), Elizabeth, Norma, and Wilber, in which each provides a perspective on this request as well as on past events in their lives. Sadly, this exchange strained relations between the two families for many months, if not years.

It appears that an earlier letter from Hale requesting money did not yield a positive response. On Jan. 29, 1941, he wrote and explained again in his scrawling but comfortably legible hand that he needed $1500 for a payment to his retirement fund that would increase his retirement income from $772 to $960 per year. He claimed that it was Wilber's "share of the debt incurred in [his] education." He went on to state that a negative response would be lacking in "honesty and filial duty." This was a severe indictment. These values clearly meant a lot to Hale, and he knew they would be important to Wilber. The $1,500 was a huge sum. It was four months of Wilber's academic salary and his military salary would be significantly less.

Two days later, Elizabeth weighed in, admitting that she and Hale did not always spend money wisely. "He isn't asking that you 'help' him. He is asking you to keep your word." Again, a penalty for Wilber's noncompliance—a loss of faith—is slipped in, "Hale still has faith in you. I hope."

My parents' prompt responses on February 3 to this request would not be what Hale and Elizabeth hoped for. First was Norma's reply. She eloquently revealed the hurts she had endured upon entering the Bradt family and the effect of their other monetary requests over the past years. Her long letter gives insight into the stresses a family encounters when a member enters the military and the importance of family support. Her pent-up frustrations poured onto the paper through her skilled typist's fingers. She began with a rather cold salutation.

> Feb. 3, 1941, Dear Mr. and Mrs. Bradt — You can't imagine what your letter has done to us – indeed you have never seemed to consider our feelings and states of mind at very crucial times....

This very unfortunate demand came at the time when Wilber is most deeply troubled, when he most needs sustenance and affection and uplift. He is doing what he thinks is right for his country at great personal sacrifice, leaving a position he has dreamed of and worked for all his life. He is only condemned by you for doing so.... You should see what your letter has done to him, when he was trying so desperately to keep up his strength and courage. Your lack of faith and your importunate commercial demands seemed to crumple him....

I certainly believe Wilber when he tells me that he never promised any such thing as you mentioned.... If you would only realize it, he is a son a father and mother should be proud of in all circumstances. He has been a wonderful husband, whom I could respect in all circumstances.... I know you will be very upset by this letter and I am very sorry, but Wilber has endured so much silently, it is time you knew the way your actions have seemed to us, on this side.

Norma was undoubtedly under severe tension at this time and, indeed, had been mistreated by the Bradts. Nevertheless, there had been warm feelings and approaches on both sides in the years since their first meeting. Unfortunately, this letter—greatly shortened here— undid all that. In turn, Elizabeth, Wilber's mother, also greatly overreacted. The unnecessary pain Norma and Elizabeth caused themselves and each other saddens me to this day.

Wilber's letter was somewhat more measured and much more in control of the facts than his father's. It was dated the same day as Norma's and may have been sent in the same envelope. Though addressed to both his father and mother, he was clearly communicating with his father.

Bangor, Maine, Feb. 3, 1941 — I shall endeavor to make clear in this letter some facts, which are apparently not yet clear in your mind. You suggest in your letter that I take my pencil and do some calculations. I have done so with the following result.

During my undergraduate years, I paid you $100 a year [for room and board], and during the graduate years of my study I paid you $150 a year. According to your statements, the following year I paid you an additional $100. This figure totals $950. According to my understanding, during my undergraduate degree, in return for my services on the farm you were willing to pay for my books, clothing and tuition. This you did in part. Tuition varied from $18.00 a semester to something less than $30. We are each aware that the other items were quite reasonable. I notice that the University of Maine estimate of the cost of room and board this year is $161.00

per year. This figure of course includes profits and a retirement fund for the dormitory construction. Consequently I am convinced that your statement at the time that $100 and later $150 a year was a reasonable, non-profit estimate of my room and board cost to you.

He goes on to explain that Hale's claims of Wilber's indebtedness have varied from $3000 to $300 and that despite his good credit, there is no way the local bank will loan him—a departing military officer—such a huge sum.

I of course recognize the responsibility of a son to his parents. I regret very much that you have not appreciated my filial affection. It is my plan that beginning next June [when Hale will retire] to send you twenty dollars a month as my finances permit. This is not a promise to pay. This is a plan I hope to maintain, which will be cancelled automatically in the event of a cess[at]ion of my income. In consideration of these circumstances, and in spite of my frank and honest statements, I close by sending my real love.

The $20 per month ($300/month in today's dollars) that Wilber proposed to send his parents would have netted them $240 a year which was more than the $188 pension increase Hale was seeking, though the pension would be much more secure in the long term. Although reverberations of this conflict continued, this letter was sufficiently reasonable in tone that it left the door open for an ongoing relationship between Wilber and his father in the subsequent months and years; that with his mother was more problematical.

x · o · ø · o · x

After several months of preparation, the 43rd Infantry Division was formally inducted into federal service on February 24, 1941, for a period of one year, a period that was to be extended to over four and a half years. The next day, Wilber submitted a request for a one-year leave of absence from the university. Undoubtedly, the dean and president had advance notice that this was coming, but Wilber cautiously waited until the induction was an accomplished fact to give formal notice. His very carefully worded letter to Dean Cloke protected his options and closed on a foreboding note.

February 25, 1941 — I should like to state further that I am looking forward to an early return to this college, but if, due to international developments, my return is delayed or permanently cancelled, you should know that I appreciate very much working under your supervision. I shall look back during the next year on our association as having been the most pleas-ant and happy years of my life.

Over the next several weeks, the 152nd Field Artillery Regiment left towns across Maine, including Bangor where we lived, to travel to Camp Blanding in Starke, Florida, 45 miles southwest of Jacksonville. Convoys of military trucks and trains full of soldiers left the snowy streets of Bangor to join other elements of the 43rd Infantry Division in sunny Florida. Wilber was on the staff organizing the move, and thus did not leave until March 15.

On about March 1, 1941, Norma (age 35), Valerie (8) and I (10) left by train for New York City. Our good friends the Butlers came to see us off; Jean had been in my fourth-grade class and I was rather sweet on her. They brought flowers for Mom and Val, but not for me. I understood that flowers were not for men, but was surprised at my quietly tearful disappointment.

The two parts of Wilber's family were now off on their own separate but still entwined adventures in a rapidly changing world.

After years of skirmishes between Japanese and Chinese forces in China, full-fledged war broke out on July 7, 1937 with an exchange of gunfire near the Marco Polo bridge near Beijing. By the end of 1937, the Japanese had captured Shanghai and Nanking. Two Chinese victories in 1939 brought the fighting to a stalemate, but skirmishes and guerilla tactics continued.

In November 1937, Italy joined the Germany-Japan Anti-Comintern Pact against the Soviet Union. Hitler then felt free to move against Austria. On March 12, 1938, German troops marched into Austria, and made a triumphal entry into Vienna two days later. Britain and France protested but did nothing more. Then, in September 1938 and March 1939, the Germans occupied large portions of Czechoslovakia. This "rape of Czechoslovakia" was so blatant that finally, the spines of France and England were stiffened; it was to be their final appeasement of Hitler. If Hitler moved again, war was inevitable.

Hitler's next target was Poland, but Russian interests had to be taken into account. On August 22, the foreign ministers of Germany and Russia signed a non-aggression pact in which it was agreed that Poland could be divided between them in the event of a German-Polish war. This pact between two countries of ideologically opposed philosophies, fascism and communism, shocked the world. The ink on the pact was hardly dry when

Germany attacked Poland with airplanes and fast moving tanks (blitz-kreig) on September 1, 1939. Two days later, Britain and France declared war against Germany. Poland was fully in German and Russian hands by the end of the month.

World War II had begun.

In the following eight months, all was quiet on the German-French border despite the state of war. However, farther north, in November 1939, Russia attacked Finland and—after huge losses imposed by the well-trained Finns—succeeded in obtaining basing rights and large strips of Finish territory near the Russian city of Leningrad. Russia also moved to annex Lithuania, Latvia, and Estonia, which they eventually accomplished in June 1940.

The quiet on the western front ended dramatically on May 10, 1940, with a fast-moving German blitzkrieg attack on the Netherlands, Belgium and Luxembourg. It carried on into France, making an end run around the heavily fortified Maginot Line. By mid-June, Germany occupied the heartland of northern France, and a humiliating treaty was signed between the two countries on June 20. With the fall of France, Germany acquired Atlantic ports, which increased the effectiveness of German submarine wolf-pack tactics against Allied convoys. A total blockade of Britain by Germany was reportedly Churchill's greatest fear.

Germany's next target was England. Hitler's plans for crossing the English Channel to invade England in the favorable fall weather of 1940 were stymied because the German air force failed to win control of the skies in the Battle of Britain during August and September. Over 20,000 British civilians were killed in German bombing raids on English cities from July to December, but in the end, the British aviators, with the aid of newly developed radar, fended off the German air force.

In September and October 1940, Italy attacked Egypt and Greece from its colonial base Libya. British and Greek forces successfully counterattacked, but German forces would soon come to the aid of Italy and set back these advances. In September, Japanese troops marched into French Indochina, and a Tripartite Pact between Germany, Italy, and Japan (the "Axis") was signed. Meanwhile, the United States was actively aiding England by providing destroyers in exchange for bases on British territory.

As 1940 came to an end, Europe had become an Axis fortress, and large areas of China were occupied by Japan. American involvement in the war was becoming more and more likely. President Roosevelt proclaimed the U.S. to be the "Arsenal of Democracy," but politically he was unable to bring the country directly into the war due to strong isolationist sentiment. National Guard divisions were activated on a "temporary" basis beginning in September 1940 and conscription of individuals into the armed forces began in October. The call-ups and draft were accepted by the public as necessary steps for "keeping the peace," given the growing distaste for Adolf Hitler's actions.

Dec. 7, 1941   3:00 P.M.

Dearest Wife and My Darling children,

I am just hearing news casts of
Japan attacks on Honan and Manila.
We have expected war to come to us
for a long time. It is here and I want
you to know I love you, that
seems to be all there is in my heart.
This may and probably will mean, "all
leaves cancelled." If so I am content
until I can come back to you to stay.
The American people have given us a lot
better chance to train than the soldiers of
the last war. We are approaching a state
of being well equipped. I am not worried.
        Beloved. Do not be afraid. This time
of trial can only hurt you if you are afraid.
Bad times are ahead but we will come thru
them together. I counting on you to be my
reserves. Goodbye now. So sorry
will say Japan. He Will be sorry too. Wilber

PART II

PREPARATIONS

FLORIDA, MISSISSIPPI, NEW ZEALAND, NEW CALEDONIA
MARCH 1941–FEBRUARY 1943

Lower Manhattan seen from the S.S. Coamo leaving New York. JACK DELANO, 1941

5

"I plan to stay on this job until it is finished"
NEW YORK CITY AND FLORIDA, MARCH 1941–FEBRUARY 1942

In New York, we settled into a large one-room apartment on the ground floor of a small three-story building at 310 West 73rd Street, which Norma's college friend Gladys Anderson Gingold had found for us.

Norma commenced piano studies with the world famous Casadesus family. Her studies were mostly with Robert Casadesus's wife Gaby, with lessons in New York, at the Casadesus home in Princeton NJ, or on one occasion at their summer residence in Rhode Island. Gladys's husband, Joseph Gingold, was a first violinist in the NBC Symphony Orchestra led by Arturo Toscanini. He was also the second violinist in the eminent Primrose String Quartet. Norma quickly entered the social life of the Gingolds' musical circle, as she recounted in her memoir.

> Evenings at their [the Gingolds'] home, where the quartet rehearsed, were pure heaven. I did not ever play *with* the quartet, but at various times I accompanied individual members of that musical circle, composed of quartet wives and others, or practiced a sonata with someone. Earl Wild was the official pianist of the quartet.

As a ten-year-old, I was promptly signed up to continue my violin studies with a Mrs. Irma Zacharias, an elderly widow and friend of the Gingolds who lived in the same building. I studied with her off and on through my early 20s.

Valerie and I attended a rather depressing public school the rest of that 1941 spring term. The classes were large and unruly, the teachers harassed, and my fellow students rough and intimidating. Fortunately, we only had to endure this until the end of the academic year. New York was not yet a wartime city, but the fear of enemy sabotage was rampant; people were well aware that war was close by.

X·O·Ø·O·X

Camp Blanding, 40 miles southwest of Jacksonville, Florida, had been newly created in 1939 as a military reserve. It bordered the east and south shores of the 1.8-mile-diameter Kingsley Lake. It had (and does to this day) a varied topography of pine plantations, oak clusters, and desert-like terrain. It was rather harsh territory with extreme temperatures and biting insects; Army Rangers trained there in later years. The construction of camp buildings, streets, and facilities was still in process, and the soldiers of Wilber's division were recruited to assist the contractors [Fushak, p. 13]. The division was housed, at least in part, in a city of tents on wooden platforms. The entire U.S. Army was woefully deficient in equipment, training, and manpower due to parsimonious federal funding in earlier years, and the 43rd Division was similarly lacking.

Unfortunately, the letters written by Wilber to Norma during his stateside training have been lost. Nevertheless, letters to his parents, children, and siblings do survive and give a flavor of his and our lives in this period. Shortly after arriving at Camp Blanding, he wrote his parents,

> March 23, 1941 — I have never worked so continuously before. Tomorrow formal training begins.... I am the Regimental S-3, or Plans and Training Officer, and as such am in charge of training for the Reg[iment]. I write programs, schedules, issue training orders, correlate the work of subordinate units and pass information pertaining to training to the Battalions.... Tomorrow inspectors will be following us around all day. I'll try to look more efficient than I am.

With this letter, Wilber sent his mother a "birthday" check. She wrote on this letter that the check was for $17.78 and that on April 7 she returned it "without comment."

Six weeks later, it appeared that Wilber had received no letters from his parents other than the returned $17.78 check. He wrote his mother two days before her 66th birthday. He was walking on eggshells.

> April 29, 1941 — Happy Birthday to you. I hope it is really a happy day and the beginning of a happy year. That means that I love you and that I will be loving you a long time to come. Please don't be angry with me.... I love you and Father both and hope I have said no wrong thing here.

Wilber was 41 years old when he wrote this but was responding to his parents as a youthful offender. After several more anguished exchanges, Wilber's father Hale began accepting monthly checks of $20 or $25 from Wilber. Elizabeth held close her hurts and resentments for years, and the correspondence settled into a monthly routine of letters between Wilber and Hale.

I am sad to contemplate how much Elizabeth nurtured her grievances and took offense at statements not intended as criticisms. Nevertheless, she did not obsess about family all the time. Large parts of her letters to Mary are chatty descriptions about routine events in her life. Despite these misunderstandings, my grandparents were portrayed to Valerie and me as benevolent; I caught no inkling of this rift. Wilber, and from time to time Norma, would send Hale and Elizabeth news, via letters, of our school progress and activities.

Hale retired from Bloomington High School in June 1941 after 22 years of service; he was just turning 70. He and Elizabeth moved to the new frame, asphalt-shingled house that Hale had been building since 1939 on their Versailles farm. To supplement his income, he served as a truant officer for the Versailles school system.

These months were full of army activity for Wilber. The division was preparing for large-scale maneuvers in Louisiana in August, and this would have generated a myriad of tasks in training, supply, and transportation. The training in Florida suffered a disturbing dearth of weapons. Wilber wrote to his parents,

> July 18, 1941 — Training is slow with shortages of equipment still the normal thing. It is hard to simulate fighting simulated tanks and simulated planes with simulated weapons. Some of the men know that "there warn't nothing there." ... I am wearing a major's leaves [insignia] for the first time today.... I love you.

Wilber had just been promoted to major.

As the U.S. was mobilizing its military forces during 1941, the Axis powers made additional advances, and the one-year activations of draftees and National Guard units were extended in September by 2.5 years. Yugoslavia and Greece had been overrun in April 1941. Crete, the Greek Mediterranean island, was captured by German paratroopers and airborne troops in May. In North Africa British forces were doing battle with Germany's Africa Korps under Gen. Field Marshall Erwin Rommel in epic desert tank battles. Control of the Mediterranean was contested with fierce air and sea battles for the island of Malta, an important British military and naval fortress.

Bombing raids by British and German aircraft on their opponents' home cities continued. In March 1941, President Roosevelt signed the Lend-lease Act, which permitted China, Britain, and other allies to purchase, but delay payment for, U.S. military supplies.

On June 22, 1941, Germany invaded its ally the Soviet Union, with an overwhelming three-pronged attack. This was a shocking but well-received (by the Allies) surprise—their two enemies turning on each other. Moscow and Leningrad were soon under threat of capture. This automatically made the Soviet Union one of the Allied nations. Growing Russian resistance together with freezing weather brought the German offensive to a halt and reversed some of its gains. But the Germans did not retreat from Moscow, as Napoleon had done in 1812. Both sides dug in for the winter as they awaited the summer campaign season.

The 43rd Division participated in army maneuvers in Louisiana in August and September. These were large-scale war games involving some 400,000 men in 19 army divisions. Two armies were formed (Red and Blue) which "fought" to defend or capture key positions over 3400 square miles of the Louisiana countryside. Anti-tank defenses against German blitzkrieg tactics were tested. Two generals who later rose to great fame, Dwight Eisenhower and George Patton, were participants. Shortly after the Allies landed in North Africa, Wilber wrote on November 14, "We claim we taught Patton in maneuvers what he knows. Anyway, we taught him what FA [Field Artillery] could do to tanks in Louisiana to his sorrow."

During the Louisiana maneuvers Wilber wrote a letter to me, his ten-year old son.

> August 5, 1941 — I think every year of my life has been better than the one before. This year has been pretty bad in some ways, but I never got so many nice letters from my children or presents from them before.

Wilber stressed the positive aspects of our separation and wanted me to think likewise. This attitude contrasted to the darker, bluer moods we sometimes saw in him. Was he trying to convince himself as well as me?

During that summer of 1941, the New York branch of the family stayed in the city. Valerie and I entertained ourselves with books, music lessons, and practicing piano and violin respectively. Our apartment was near Riverside Park. On many days, I would accompany Gladys Gingold on her walks to the park with her two-year old son Georgie. I enjoyed their company.

In the fall, Norma enrolled Valerie at Blessed Sacrament School on West 70th Street. Valerie remembers that she was, quite conspicuously, the only non-Catholic in her class. Also that fall, I was accepted into the choir of Grace Church on East Tenth Street, which provided me with a salary of a couple of dollars per week and, much more valuable, free tuition at Grace Church School. The boys' school was a new scene for me; I learned to address the teachers with "Yes, Sir" and "No Sir," and studied Latin both years I was there (fifth and sixth grades).

I rapidly became expert on the Fifth Avenue #5 bus and the IRT subway as I traveled the several miles from West 73rd Street to Grace Church. I liked to stand in the front of the subway's first car looking out the front window with my hands on the brake wheel there, making believe I was driving the train as it rushed through the dark tunnels. On the way to services early Sunday mornings on the double-decker Fifth Avenue bus, I would ride in the front seat of the closed upper deck as we careened and swayed at high speed down deserted Fifth Avenue.

In November 1941, the 43rd Division participated in another session of maneuvers, this time in South Carolina. It was a large-scale war game with two armies consisting of some 300,000 troops with armor, cavalry, and aircraft. Again this was in part a test of tank and anti-tank tactics. Wilber's final assessment of his division's performance was positive. He wrote from "under a tree near Camden, S.C."

Nov. 27, 1941 — This is a short lull in the program of Gen. Drum chasing the IV Corps around the Carolinas. During the last maneuver, we were saved by the bell. It was freely admitted by the bigwigs that the stubborn fighting of the 43rd Div. saved the day for the IV Corps.

Wilber planned to be home for Christmas, but could not know then that Japanese aircraft carriers were steaming toward the U.S. Naval Base at Pearl Harbor in Hawaii. The epochal attack that brought the U.S. into the war was imminent.

The attack began on December 7, shortly before 8 a.m. in Hawaii. Wilber heard the reports on the radio and wrote to us during the raid. He was at Camp Blanding.

December 7, 1941, 3:00 P.M. [9 A.M. in Hawaii]; Dearest Wife and My Darling Children — I am just hearing newscasts of Japan [sic] attacks on Hawaii.... We have expected war to come to us for a long time. It is here and I want you to know I love you. That seems to be all there is in my heart. This may and probably will mean, "all leaves cancelled." If so, I am content until I can come back to you to stay. The American people have given us a lot better chance to train than the soldiers of the last war. We are approaching a state of being well equipped. I am not worried.

Beloved, do not be afraid. This time of trial can only hurt you if you are afraid. Bad times are ahead, but we will come through them together. I am counting on you to be my reserves. Goodbye now. "So sorry" will say Japan. He [Japan] will be sorry too.

The next day, after an inspiring address by President Roosevelt ("a date which will live in infamy"), the U.S. Congress declared war on Japan. On December 11, Germany and Italy declared war on the U.S., and the U.S. Congress responded in kind.

The United States was now a belligerent in the war.

Wilber's leave was cancelled; Norma, Valerie, and I made a hastily arranged trip to Florida to join Wilber for Christmas week. Florida still brings pleasant memories. Immediately upon arriving at our beachside cabin in Ponte Vedra, Valerie and I went out to play in the surf while our parents stayed in the cabin. The tide gradually pushed us down the beach, so that after awhile we were quite far from our cabin and quite unsure which cabin was ours. As we walked back, hoping we would recognize our cabin, our very worried folks came down the beach looking for us. Fifteen months later, Wilber recalled his afternoon lovemaking there with Norma [letter 3/27/43], undoubtedly while we were playing in the surf.

On our return to New York, I was severely chastised by the choir director for skipping out on choir obligations for the Christmas festivities at Grace Church; as a paid choir boy, I was a professional and should have known better! Needless to say, Norma's view of priorities differed radically from his. I am sure she made that very clear to him. A short while later, Wilber visited us in New York for six days.

Realizing that the war was not going to be a short one, Wilber wrote to the University of Maine, requesting that his leave be extended to July 1943. "I plan to stay on this job [the war] until it is finished." In January, 1942, Wilber was appointed as the executive officer (second in command) of one of the three artillery battalions that were an outcome of a reorganization of the division from a so-called "square" division (four infantry regiments and three artillery regiments), into a "triangular" division (three infantry regiments and four artillery battalions). His previous unit (the 152nd Field Artillery Regiment) was disbanded, and he was assigned to be the executive officer (2nd in command) of the newly named 169th Field Artillery Battalion (often written as 169th FA Bn.). It was the former 2nd Battalion of the disbanded 103rd Field Artillery Regiment, a Rhode Island outfit with a long history dating back to 1801. Wilber would later become its commander and lead it in battle.

Prior to the Pearl Harbor attack, diplomatic relations between Japan and the U.S. had been deteriorating due to Japanese expansion into China, French Indochina, and Vietnam. Retaliatory embargos, especially on oil, put in place by the U.S. and its allies, greatly increased tensions. The Japanese, to protect their economic interests in these materials-rich regions, decided to go to war to create an expansive sphere of influence called the

"Greater East Asia Co-Prosperity Sphere" in East Asia and the Western Pacific (Map 1). The attack on Pearl Harbor initiated it.

In the days following the attack on Pearl Harbor, Japanese forces swept into the Philippines, captured Hong Kong and overtook the American Pacific outpost islands of Guam, and Wake. They also moved into resource-rich Southeast Asia, capturing the fortified British naval base at Singapore on Feb. 15. The loss loss of Singapore with 130,000 troops was "Britain's greatest military disaster" according to one historian [Basil Collier; see Keegan, p. 261].

American resistance on Luzon Island in the Philippines was centered on the Bataan peninsula until its surrender on April 9, after a courageous and extended defense. This was followed by the tragic and cruel Bataan Death March, during which many American and Filipino prisoners died. The Manila Harbor island of Corregidor held on until May 6. General MacArthur had left there for Australia the previous month. He would be a leader of Allied forces in the Pacific for the rest of the war.

Borneo was attacked by the Japanese on January 1, as were Sumatra, Java, and the Dutch East Indies in February and March. Farther to the east, on March 8 and 10, Japanese landings were made on the northeast coast of eastern New Guinea (at Lae and Salamaua, Map 2) in a first move toward isolating Australia. The Japanese were aided in these advances by the long-standing resentment of British, Dutch, and French colonial rule in these areas.

The first months of 1942 were deeply discouraging for the Allies. The good news, though, was that the U.S. was finally in the war. The long-term outlook was in favor of the Allies if England and Russia could hold on until America's huge industrial and human resources could be brought to bear.

6

"My PhD didn't cut any ice here"
MISSISSIPPI, FEBRUARY–AUGUST, 1942

In the early months of 1942, fear and hysteria regarding German and Japanese agents or spies was rampant in New York City and in the country as a whole. During January and February, German submarines were sinking ship after ship off the East Coast, and President Roosevelt ordered the internment of Japanese Americans on the West Coast in February. Norma took these worries to heart and her concerns are reflected in Wilber's letters.

The 43rd Infantry Division was ordered to Camp Shelby in Mississippi on February 8, 1942, and was in place there by February 19. Wilber was put temporarily in command of the 169th Field Artillery Battalion in the absence of its commander, Lt. Col. Chester Files. Shortly after, Wilber wrote his father, with a note of fatalism.

> [About February 25, 1942] — I'm content to do any job that's pushed my way so shan't worry.... This takes me out of the "staff only" group and puts me in the "fighting" troops again.... Norma is studying hard on the piano.... I have urged this plan mainly because I have had a pretty definite and persistent feeling that I won't be back.
>
> [Wilber's marginal note:] I was invited to accept a commission as Major in the Chemical Warfare Service the other day by the head of Offensive Warfare Research at Wash D.C. I refused, admitting [to myself] I'd probably regret it in some swamp later.

At about this time, Wilber was ordered to the Field Artillery School at Fort Sill, Oklahoma, for an eight-week course beginning March 3. He became a student again. The school was a bit of a challenge for this former professor, as he wrote his father,

> March 25, 1942 — Our classes are very interesting, and the material most valuable. We attend class continuously for 8 hours a day for six days a week and study all other possible hours.... Exams are graded U or

S [Unsatisfactory or Satisfactory] So far I am specializing in the latter, but some officers I consider my betters haven't had such good luck.

April 25, 1942 — My "School Days" are almost over and I am content.... You would have been interested in the way we had to work. My Phi Beta Kappa key and my PhD didn't cut any ice here, and weren't mentioned by me either.

I was pretty discouraged for a while but finally hit the scholastic level at which I thought I belonged by getting a little more sleep....

I did achieve some publicity the other day by getting a public commendation from the most hard-boiled umpire on my ability to conduct fire. He had given me an assignment he thought I couldn't do and set another umpire on me to see [that] I got no information from anyone else. It just worked out that I got a target hit on about the 8th round.... I hope my luck holds when we play for keeps.

With schooling over, Wilber visited us in New York, but only for four days around May 10 when he described having a "special date" with Valerie for a lunch and show, while "Hale and I spent our time visiting the overturned Normandie." (The French ocean liner had been taken over by the U.S. and renamed the USS Lafayette. During its conversion to a troopship, it had burned and capsized onto its side at its Hudson River dock the previous February.) Wilber had hoped to visit his parents, but did not; neither he nor they knew this would be their last chance to see each other.

On May 20, Wilber was back with the 43rd Division where he was temporarily assigned as Plans and Training Officer under General Barker, the divisional artillery commander. He wrote his father that he enjoyed

visualizing your crops and work on the farm. If I would let myself, I could be pretty homesick about it sometimes. That is undoubtedly the just desserts of the wanderer.

Wilber refers to himself as a "wanderer," perhaps from the Old English poem wherein a solitary exile meditates "on his past glories as a warrior ... his present hardships, and the values of forbearance and faith." [see Wikipedia: "The Wanderer"]

x · o · ø · o · x

Norma, Valerie, and I spent the summer of 1942 in Hattiesburg, Mississippi, with Wilber. There, we were exposed to the cultural environment of the Deep South at a time when segregation was still in full bloom and Civil War veterans were still around. We traveled there and back on the Southerner, a streamliner train, a luxurious adventure. Valerie and I attended a day camp for part of the summer where we learned that "Yankee" was not a complimentary term. We were "foreigners," even among those with the same skin color. But we both had second-hand bicycles in Mississippi, and we loved the mobility and freedom they gave us.

The unfairness of segregation did penetrate my 11-year-old mind one day on a city bus ride from our day camp across town to our home. Valerie and I hopped on an empty bus headed for home, paid our fare, and were required to sit in the very front seats because the bus would fill up to standing-room-only with blacks.

At the end of June, Wilber wrote that the expansion of the army still dominated their training; men would be trained for certain positions and then they would be transferred to another unit to train others. By the end of July, Wilber was "back in the Bn. acting in my assigned capacity as executive officer." The entire battalion made a nighttime 25-mile march along Mississippi roads, after which Wilber remarked, "I think I can outwalk the Japs if necessary." On one occasion, about August 20, Wilber brought me to a field exercise, where I saw the 105-mm howitzers fire. I also saw two shooting stars while lying on my cot under the stars. It was a hectic time for Wilber and for the entire division, which was to be shipped overseas at the end of September. Wilber wrote his father,

> Aug. 23, 1942 — It was a pretty rushed time for me. Eight of us are running a battalion, which is supposed to have 28 officers. We were out on an exercise the night before and ended it by firing some ammunition [shells] over the heads of several generals who had, in my opinion, an exaggerated trust in the eight of us.

The spring of 1942 brought some long-awaited encouragement to the Pacific theater. In April, the American aircraft carrier, USS Hornet, sailed toward Japan and launched 16 B-25 bombers, which then bombed several Japanese cities. It was a largely symbolic raid led by Col. James Doolittle. In early May, a Japanese attempt to capture Port Moresby, the port on the south coast of New Guinea (Map 2), would have been a direct threat to Australia. It was foiled in the naval battle of the Coral Sea, which was more or less a draw. In early June, the Japanese attempted the capture of Midway Island, a scant 1000 miles northwest of Oahu, Hawaii. In a battle of carrier aircraft, the Japanese suffered devastating losses; all four of their attacking carriers were lost along with their planes and many experienced pilots. The Japanese and American carrier forces in the Pacific were now more or less evenly matched.

The Japanese then decided to strike at Port Moresby overland; this involved landings at Buna and Gona on the northeast coast of New Guinea and a march over the Owen Stanley mountain range on the Kokoda Trail to Port Moresby on the south coast. In the mountains, the trail was only a footpath; vehicles could not traverse it. From July to November the battle between the Australians and Japanese raged up and down those mountains. Finally, the Japanese, exhausted, withdrew to their bases on the north coast.

The news from Russia was less encouraging. The Germans, in their summer of 1942 offensive, did not renew their drive toward Moscow, but rather drove deeply southward into the Caucasus oil fields. They were approaching the major city of Stalingrad on the River Volga by mid-July 1942. This presaged an extended battle for the city that began with German air attacks on August 23 and lasted through January 1943.

The Japanese continued their advance into the Solomon Islands, east of southeast New Guinea (Map 3), against little or no resistance. They occupied the island of Tulagi in May 1942 and began construction of a large airfield on Guadalcanal in early July. This was a direct threat to the shipping lanes to Australia, and the navy argued strongly that the U.S. Marines should quickly capture the field before it was completed and fortified, which they did on August 7, 1942, against negligible opposition. Their toehold, though, was in great jeopardy as both sides attempted to reinforce their troops on the island. The marines were very hard-pressed at times but were able to hold onto the airfield, which was named Henderson Field after the first marine aviator lost in the Battle of Midway. The island was not completely secured until February 1943. The critical situation on Guadalcanal in the late summer of 1942 determined the immediate future of the 43rd Division.

7

"Morale is booming and so are the howitzers"
CALIFORNIA AND GREENWICH VILLAGE, SEPTEMBER 1942

Shortly after the marine landings on Guadalcanal, in early August 1942, the commanders in the area argued vociferously for more forces in the Pacific. Without them, Guadalcanal could be lost, and Japanese planes there could strike as far south as New Caledonia and could support Japanese landings in the New Hebrides, jeopardizing shipping lanes to Australia (Map 4). Despite the Europe-first strategy, the situation in Guadalcanal was deemed to be so desperate that arrangements were made to ship one more army division to the Pacific—the 43rd [Morton, p. 328].

The division was sent to California in early September 1942 for shipment to the South Pacific. Norma, Valerie, and I were still in Hattiesburg when Wilber left on September 3. We would not see him again for three long years.

About this time, we begin to see Wilber's letters to Norma. On a postcard to her, he announced his arrival at Fort Ord, California, near Monterey, 100 miles south of San Francisco. He remembered their 1930 trip in the Chevrolet roadster.

> Sept. 8, 1942, to Norma — Arrived OK. Pleasant trip. Remembered our drive over the same route every hour. Have ocean view from my tent and ants in my bedroll. Wonders of Calif. I love you.

On the day he wrote this, Norma, in one of her rare surviving letters, wrote Wilber's father of Wilber's departure.

> Sept. 8, 1942 — I want you to know he was in wonderful condition physically, spiritually, and mentally when he left. Everyone who knows him agrees there is no finer man or officer to be found anywhere. Everything he does, says, or thinks, is a credit to you. He is always fair and just – he is never mean or selfish – and is "absolutely tireless on behalf of his Battalion" (the Colonel). The men under him say he knows how to make them do their best work without rancor, and I do believe this Arty. Bn. is the best trained

in the whole U.S. Wilber has used his inventive genius on them and their training, and he is so noble and strong and good. With such a leader (Executive) they cannot help but be excellent.

Norma's eloquence most surely was reassuring to Wilber's father about his son's development as a person and soldier.

At Fort Ord, the division had an abundance of live ammunition and was training intensively.

Sept. 11, 1942 — We are firing steadily and training is going ahead by leaps + bounds. We are on the ocean. I can see it now thru my windows. Notice the fact that we have a window....

Sept. [12?], 1942 — The morale is booming and so are the howitzers. We fired over 230 rounds yesterday and 180 today.

x · o · ø · o · x

Upon our arrival back in New York, we moved into a fifth-floor apartment on West 4th Street, and I began my second year at Grace Church School, only a half-mile away. Valerie attended nearby public school PS 41 on West 11th Street. Our apartment was in Little Italy in Greenwich Village. Communication among the relatives who lived in different apartments would be carried out via loud yelling from window to window across the central courtyard.

From Wilber's letters, it's clear that Norma was his long-distance morale booster and lover as well as his helper and aide who could send him items he needed and also sign his legal documents. With his departure imminent, the passion in his letters to Norma intensified.

September 17, 1942 — It has been great to be with you [in Hattiesburg] and to feel your presence near. And such lovely nights in your arms. No one could love a man so marvelously, so sweetly, so passionately or so thoroughly. It is sweet to remember you didn't begrudge me any part of you the last night. I know you would have done anything I asked then without regret. I would never want to do anything to affront or offend you, my little white skinned slave. It is so wonderful to remember my hands on your hips and to feel the clinging folds of you caress me. It is so precious to recall my lips on your lovely breasts, to hold your soft body in my arms. I am in love with you Nana. The joy of your presence in my home can carry me thru this war and back home and it will, I know.

But the army remained on his mind.

Sept. 18, 1942 — Nothing on my mind except the three men AWOL [Absent Without Leave], the two drunks, the two who tried to fight the MPs [military police], the three who argued with the MPs, and the one who stole a cuspidor from the hotel; except the team of inspectors (officers) from the Port of Embarkation who are inspecting individual equipment, and the P. of E. inspectors who are inspecting instruments and guns, and the P. of E. inspection of chemical warfare equipment, all of which inspections are now in progress.... Just back after a shot in the arm for tetanus....

Sept. 22, 1942 — Our howitzers are gone now [to be loaded aboard ship] so the firing has been interrupted. Today we receive 60 trucks (2-1/2 ton) full of clothing and men's equipment. All that is worn has to be replaced.

He wrote that Norma was flooding him with letters, "imagine 16 letters already." At the end of the day, Wilber was in a sentimental mood. In this next letter, he recalled their intimate encounters and shared his fantasies.

Sept. 22, 1942, Little Flower of Mine [Norma] — Another day is passed and I am in my PJs that you bought on my cot in my room alone with my thoughts of you....

You have built a wonderful thing for me with your dear fingers, sweet helpfulness and beautiful guidance. My life is divided into two parts: one empty and B.N. (Before Nana) and the other W.N. (With Nana). The B.N. was barren and cold and comfortless. The W.N. has been the ringing of bells in the country in May; the light of the moon on the Ohio River; the waves on an ocean beach; the caress of a girl beside a Palouse road; everything a man could wish and more. The perfume of your hair, the music of your words, "Wilber I love you. Wilber I want to be the mother of your babies." Darling Mine you are my beloved mate. No soldier ever went to war with more reason....

I was all thrilled again too. I can see that sweet V now. Lovely knees up and apart to make it and such sweet joy inside. My eyes peep in deep and Nana I love you – I'm glad I've peeked and kissed and played and loved in that V. You have been grand to let me love you all the ways I know. It seems so amazing to me that I am permitted to possess you, that you don't mind, that you will come to my arms to be loved. I never get used to your cuddling close and reminding me of your joys by caressing and fondling me until I am all-aflame.

Few men, I think, would have revealed their thoughts so frankly. This letter made abundantly clear that they both knew the meaning of "V," and it was clearly not the

"V for Victory" rallying cry of the Allies! (This letter was a bit too explicit for my comfort. Were these really my parents?!)

Wilber then goes on to tell of a promotion possibility; the battalion commander's job had become vacant. Wilber, as second in command, was a candidate; he did keep track of the promotion possibilities. The battalion commander position was normally held by a lieutenant colonel. The major who filled it could expect a promotion.

During the last week before embarkation, Wilber wrote a series of "goodbye" letters. Each carried overtones of his uncertain future and the possibility that he might not survive the voyage or the events beyond it. He wrote several to Norma in which romance was interspersed with descriptions of the events going on around him. His first letter was to me.

> Sept. 23, 1942, 10:30 P.M. — We have been loading freight onto boxcars all day and the men are pretty tired....
>
> Son, I am proud to have a boy like you to go to war for.... I know you will do all you can to keep "the home fires burning" until I come back. I'm sorry to be away from you now but I would be sorrier and so would you if I were trying to keep from fighting for my country.... Someday you will go away from your home and then you will really know that I pray everyday that you will never be afraid and that you will be waiting for the good days we will have together some day. – I love you – My Boy

Then, to Norma,

> Sept. 24, 1942, 11:00 P.M. — Beloved Mate, Another glimpse into your life and thoughts came today. I was glad you slept a couple of nights instead of writing. Dearest ... I just love you every possible way. You are such a sweet girl to be my wife, the memories of you are so wonderful, and the comradeship of you is so strong that I am wholly yours. Last night I dreamed of you.... I would take you to this Pacific Island with me and make you sleep all day and be rested and flaming with love all night....
>
> Major [Reuben H.] King will be C.O. [commanding officer] of the 169th [Field Artillery] and is a good officer. He and DeBlois and I were at [Fort] Sill together.

Wilber showed no outward disappointment at not being chosen to lead the battalion.

Wilber, in the above letter, cautioned Norma to not "drink too much and think someone else is me." Though light-hearted, it hinted at a typical concern of departing troops. Was there reason for his concern at this time? He knew that earlier in the year, Norma had met in New York a certain Monte Bourjaily, who had been editor of the *Bangor Daily News* when we had lived in Bangor (though Norma had known him only through correspondence about items she submitted for publication). Monte became close to us in New York City and we to his family—his mother Terkman and his three grown sons. Wilber had met and liked him, and once, much later, expressed gratitude that Monte was standing by to care for the family should he, Wilber, not return.

The next evening, it was Valerie's turn to hear from Wilber. Her school, P.S. 41, was new for her, and he wanted to hear how it was going. He searched rather awkwardly for topics in her world.

> Sept 25, 1942 — Dear "Tumble Bug" [Valerie], I have been wondering how you are getting along in school. Do you walk very far? What is the schoolroom like? Do you have some new friends?... How about the bicycles? Did they get there? How did you get them from the station to the apartment [in NYC]? Pedaled down Broadway I suppose.... I was remembering our date today. We went to the place where they skate in winter [Rockefeller Center in NYC].

Then, again to Norma,

> 12:05 A.M. Sunday, Sept. 27, Bedfellow of Mine [Norma] — Two of the most wonderful letters came today from you. It is so helpful to have a little of you in my day. These were so complete too. The day's news of the children; your day including one sore thumb (I'm so sorry. I could fix it, too.); some encouragement (maybe flattery but I love it) for me; a lot of love both spiritual and physical. They do go together for us you know.... Next time I catch you I'll start at your cute little toes and cover every inch of your soft body with kisses and caresses. I'll open up the springs of your love and drink until you are drained dry and are all hot and tense with passion.

Norma was apparently reciprocating Wilber's remote lovemaking in her letters.

Later that day, a simple task brought home the reality of the division's imminent departure.

> 10:15 P.M.— I have made out "Safe arrival cards" for you, Father and Doug [acting head of the Chem. Dept. at U. of Maine]. These cards are held at this Post until our unit reports by wire that we have arrived safely less whoever fell off the boat.

The vessels that were to carry the 43rd Division to New Zealand had been loaded with the division's military cargo and were ready to take on the troops. On the evening of September 30, the men of the 169th Field Artillery marched to the train at Fort Ord for the 100-mile rail trip to San Francisco. They began boarding the USAT Maui at 2 a.m., and the ship left dockside at 11:45 a.m., October 1 [169th FA Bn. Journal].

The final five letters written by Wilber before his departure were emotionally charged and, except for the first to Norma, uncharacteristically brief. I suspect that he had been driven to the Maui, arriving well ahead of his troops and wrote them onboard the ship as he awaited their arrival. Phrases in the first to Norma strongly indicate he was overlooking the moonlit waters of San Francisco Bay. If this scenario is correct, they were written a day later than the date he wrote in the headings. He recalled many intimate moments with Norma late on this, his last night in the United States.

> Sept. 29 [30?], 1942, 11:00 P.M., My Dear Beautiful Love — It is late again but I do so enjoy writing to you. Your thrilling and so sweet letter of the 25th came today with one from Valerie. Hers was so dear I almost cried. I do love my two girls so much. That little Sparlin touch reaches right to my heart.
>
> Today has been quite busy with phone calls, court-martials, inspections, and the more efficient confusion, which only the army can devise. However I must say for the army that it feeds one well. Mail is now being censored as it leaves the division.... Then I also remember us drifting on the St. Joseph River in the evening and rowing at Twin Lakes.... There is a pretty moon tonight – just a few days past full. It reminded me of the moon on the Ohio R. and the Island Queens [riverboats]. The thing I like most about you is your sweet willingness to be loved. I do love you and do want you.... Anyway for letter number one this is longer than I had expected. Goodnight pink flesh and white body. You are a woman among women for me.... I do love you.

What wonderful sentiments and memories! Even later that evening, Wilber wrote Valerie, me, and his parents.

> Sept. 29 [30?], 1942, 11:55 P.M., Dear Daughter — Your letter was very neat. I enjoyed reading it very much.... Be my special girl friend while I'm gone and write to me when you can. I love you. Take care of Hale and Nana for me.... Please be the Army Nurse in my family while I'm gone and take care of all the hurts for me. — Goodbye my Little WAAC. Wilber

Valerie was his "little WAAC," dubbed by him as a junior member of the Women's Army Auxiliary Corps.

Sept. 30, 1942 [Oct.1, early A.M.?] — Hello Big Son — This is just a note to tell you that it is a good day here. Tomorrow is the first of October. If I were home we'd plan a camping trip for next weekend. How about Mt. Katahdin?

I want you to be my Liaison Officer in the family. A Ln. O. helps keep contact between two commanding officers, Norma and Wilber... I love you Hale, Wilber

Sept 30, 1942 [Oct.1, early A.M.?], Dear Father and Mother — I'm in a bit of a rush just now, so can only enclose the twenty I would normally try to get to you for Nov. 1.

It is beautiful here and I have enjoyed California very much. Please take care of yourselves until I finish this job. I'd like very much to know you aren't worrying.

Wilber managed to get yet another letter off to Norma before the final mail collection. He called it #2 but dated it the day before Letter #1 above, which carried the date Sept. 29, 11 p.m. (He was indeed confused about dates.) It is a final goodbye letter to the whole family.

Sept. 28, '42 [Oct. 1, early A.M.?]. Hello Beloved [Norma] — Letter No. 2 will be very short. I just want to say again that I love you more than anything else in the world. I'll come back to you just as soon as possible....

Your last letter was wonderful and thrilling. It was the one with Hale's letter and the very wide V. I was so thrilled. It's wonderful to see you and talk with you. I can use that wonderful wifey letter many times during the next weeks when I can receive none. I'll keep it in my money belt.... Don't be downcast or worried. I'll be armed and protected by your love and prayers, and I'm really counting on those prayers a lot. Love Love Love to each and every one of you, Wilber.

The USAT Maui sailed from San Francisco Bay on October 1, 1942, for a destination (New Zealand) that was unknown then to his family and probably to most of his men. After 19 months of training, he was embarking on an epic adventure (Map 5). It would be three years and one week before he would again set foot on his homeland.

8

"I will come back to my own, my beloved Nana"
USAT MAUI, NEW ZEALAND, OCTOBER–NOVEMBER, 1942

At this point, as Wilber began his three-week voyage to the Southern Hemisphere, I digress to reveal how I came to possess his letters to Norma and others.

I had been well aware since the war that Wilber had written home several times a week throughout his almost five years of military service. Did my mother (Norma) still have any of those letters? On the few occasions when I asked her, she said or implied that she no longer did. She had told my sister Abigail that she had burned them long ago, an easily believable story given the painful memories associated with them. But in 1981 when I asked again, she indicated she might have some. Upon my next visit, she produced a tattered shoebox full of them, and she willingly gave them to me. She had carried them secretly from home to home during those 35 years after Wilber's death. Later she sent me others she found in her cedar chest.

A paucity of letters from Wilber to my sister Valerie suggested there might be an envelope of letters to her similar to the set to me that I had originally found in my basement. After my many requests that she search her home thoroughly, her son found the envelope among the plethora of documents—she and her husband were journalists—in their home. Letters from Wilber to his parents ended up in the Luray, Virginia, home of Wilber's late brother, Paul. At Paul's wife's funeral in 1975, Abigail and I became aware of them, but by 1980 I had forgotten about them; fortunately Abby had not. Paul's son Alan graciously gave them to me. Other small collections came my way: Wilber's successor as department head at the University of Maine provided me a file of his correspondence with Wilber, and Wilber's brother Rex provided another small sample of Wilber's letters, including a very revealing one he wrote a week before he died. Wilber's sister Mary, in 1987,

57

gave me a collection of hundreds of letters between her and her mother, as well correspondence between her parents when Wilber was in his teens.

I have asked myself—and discussed with counselors—the ethics of sharing the Wilber-Norma intimacies publicly. The very religious Norma, and probably Wilber as well, were both from an earlier generation and would surely have objected. However, from afar and with some emotional detachment, they might well have been able to see the historical value of doing so—of presenting their lives richly and fully. Norma was a performer and a writer who fervently sought recognition through her music and writings. In fact she was a key player in a much larger drama, and in my opinion would have come to relish that role—one that typifies the challenges faced by war wives even now. For Wilber's part, he was a student of the classics and was clearly writing for history. He was well equipped to record his own odyssey.

For me, their story, told through their letters, honors both of them.

X · O · Ø · O · X

We now return to Wilber on the U.S. Army Transport (USAT) Maui. Wilber wrote a letter every day or two for a total of 17 on the 21-day voyage. I've selected and presented here portions of just a few of them. Some of them were sent as "V-Mail" (V for Victory). These one-page letters (on an 8.5 by 11-inch form) were photographed and delivered in reduced format, which could be difficult to read. Wilber found the paid airmail to be generally faster than V-mail and, thankfully for us, used it for almost all of his subsequent letters.

USS (later USAT) Maui in port, 1919. The Maui transported troops in World War I and again in World War II. This ship carried Wilber from San Francisco to New Zealand in October 1942. [WIKIPEDIA COMMONS, U.S. NAVAL HISTORICAL CENTER, NEW HAMPSHIRE, 102945; PUBLIC DOMAIN]

Sailing as a passenger on a long voyage presented Wilber with a sudden oasis of leisure. He was communing with Norma and documenting his odyssey.

Oct. 3, 1942 [USAT Maui], Dearest Norma — It is the night of Oct. 3. I am in the dining room of a former Matson Line ship....

The first night out was wonderful. Strong cross wind and waves over the side of the ship with spray blowing, and out ahead our covering protection with the convoy just dimly visible. René & I stood on the fore port of the "B" deck and wished our wives were with us.... Our boat drill is giving us good results and if needed should be OK. Willie [Wilber] is the "For'd" [Forward] Emergency Officer and stands on the upper deck receiving reports from half his Bn. and all of a sister Bn. as they clear the holds. When the last man is out he reports that to the Capt. of the ship....

Oct. 5, 1942 [V-mail], Beloved Wife and children — The crew and our (my own) .50 caliber machine gunners had target practice today and the sea was noisy with our fire. We definitely are not sneaking across this ocean but move and act as if it belonged to us.

Three days later, he reached out to me.

Oct. 8, 1942 [V-mail] — Today a big turtle like you saw in the aquarium was swimming in the sea. We soon passed him. I don't believe he was going as far as we are for he has an unambitious look on his face.

Wilber resumed his long-distance romancing of Norma in a letter that, even today, chokes me up.

Oct. 8, 1942 [V-mail] — I have just finished a letter to Hale and still want to tell you a bit about my love for you....

I remembered a night in a church in Portland Ore. where a lovely young bride named Norma heard the pastor say "Kiss the girl, Lad." Such a good beginning. All the later nights that Nana was kissed and hugged and mussed and tumbled are as precious to me.... Darling never fear but that the joy of your body will keep me from any other woman. You are my V girl and with the end of this war I will reclaim you and hope you will not have forgotten your wiles.

I send you my caresses. I hold you in my arms. My dark body presses against your white blonde skin. My lips are on your breasts. I am your lover. Please do not worry about my returning unchanged. I will come back to my own, my beloved Nana.

And he gave Valerie a view of his world that she would appreciate.

Oct. 12, 1942 [V-mail] — We crossed the equator the other day and today we were all initiated by the Navy boys who had crossed before. I have a diploma, which says I am now a "shellback." King Neptune came on board [with] Mrs. Neptune to initiate us. Mrs. Neptune was definitely a mermaid. She wore a grass skirt made of rope and very rosy apples for breasts. She sprayed the hose on most all of us and kept everyone laughing except those [persons] Neptune was paddling or giving drinks of sea water to. He also specialized in daubing grease and mashed beets on people. Everyone had a fine time and got very wet.

The letter above was written on Columbus Day, though Wilber failed to comment on it. He certainly could have drawn parallels between their respective voyages, each with its highly uncertain destination. Almost two weeks into the trip, he wrote Norma,

Oct. 13, 1942 [V mail] — It is a pain in the neck to be here and not let you know everything is OK. I know how you will worry and imagine things are bad and forget that God holds all of us in his hand. Good Old Hand! – The holds of this ship [where the men are bunked] are a lot cleaner than ever before. That is one of my jobs. The inspectors have had to increase their standards and create a new rating. Today all he could say was "Tops! Absolutely Tops!" Of such things are armies made.

Casualties in wartime from unsanitary conditions could (and did) exceed combat losses. A sanitary force was an effective force, and inspection after inspection made that possible.

Oct. 17, 1942 — You should be receiving my safe arrival card in a few days, I hope. If you don't receive this letter just keep one eye on the Hudson River, and if the fee in the Panama Canal isn't too high, I'll swim all the way home. If it's too much I'll land at Frisco and finish by train.

Wilber earned a varsity letter on the swimming team at Indiana U. His bravado regarding swimming "all the way home" struck a resonant note with me at age 11.

Five days later, the three-week voyage was nearly over. Excitement and anticipation rose.

Oct. 22, 1942 — We are pulling into the harbor [Auckland] now. The city is on low hills and we have sailed for hours along the shore. The hills come down to the shore and houses are scattered thru them. Little islands are sometimes rough and craggy, sometimes are pasture lands. It is cool and springtime and the fields are green.

As the 43rd Division approached Auckland, the U.S. Marines on Guadalcanal were desperately defending Henderson Field (airfield). Twice, the Japanese attacked the marine perimeter in force and reached to within a mile of the airfield. Japanese air raids, naval bombardments, and artillery shelling severely limited Allied use of the airfield.

The naval battles in and around Guadalcanal were historic. Both sides were attempting to land troops and to prevent the opponent from doing so. The Battle of Savo Island (August 9) was a major Allied defeat, and the Battle of the Eastern Solomons (August 24) indecisive. While the 43rd Division was mid-ocean, on October 11 and 12, the naval Battle of Cape Esperance was the first serious setback for the Japanese even though both sides suffered comparable losses [Morison, v. V].

On October 18, Admiral William F. "Bull" Halsey, Jr. was appointed as commander of the South Pacific Area; he relieved Admiral Robert Ghormley. Halsey would now command all land, sea, and air forces in the area and that included Guadalcanal. His appointment injected a welcome aggressive spirit into the area during an otherwise depressing time.

Subsequent sea battles on October 26 and 27 (the Battle of the Santa Cruz Islands) and on November 12 through 15 (the Battle of Guadalcanal) led to capital ship losses on both sides. On balance, though, the losses were more damaging to the Japanese effort. The battle for Guadalcanal was far from over, and one more major American naval defeat lay ahead. The situation was still touch-and-go. The 43rd Division was there to help tilt it in the right direction. It was only the fourth army division in the southwest Pacific.

The USAT Maui arrived in Auckland, New Zealand, on October 22, and the soldiers debarked on October 24. Wilber's unit, transported by truck, arrived at Wyngard's Camp, 50 miles north of Auckland later that same day, October 24 [Barker, p. 22; 169th FA Bn. Journal].

On October 26, the SS President Coolidge, a converted luxury liner of the American President Lines, arrived at Espiritu Santo in the New Hebrides (now Vanuatu) with the 43rd's 172nd Regimental Combat Team. One entrance to the harbor at Espiritu Santo had been mined by the Americans, and because orders to the ship's captain were incomplete, the ship entered the mined entrance. It hit two mines, after which the captain drove the ship up onto the beach. All but two people were able to evacuate the ship before it slid back into deep water, where it now resides as one of the premier scuba diving sites in the world. One of those lost was a 43rd Division field artillery officer, Capt. Elwood J. Euart, who could not exit the ship in time even as he helped others escape. He was the first overseas casualty of the division. The 172nd Infantry, which included Wilber's sister outfit, the 103rd Field Artillery (Lt. Col. William B. McCormick, C.O.), had lost all its supplies, from toothbrushes to howitzers, and did not join the 43rd Division until the Munda campaign, eight months later.

During Wilber's one-month stay in wartime New Zealand, it was still a peaceful island southeast of Australia, far from the raging combat on Guadalcanal, but a lot closer to it than California. Many of the New Zealand soldiers ("Kiwis") were off fighting for the British in Africa. The arrival of another army division of American troops provided some hope that the Japanese advance would not extend into Australia. New Zealand was a new scene for Wilber.

Nov. 1, 1942 — It's about time for me to report to my family again. It is a beautiful spring morning here with flowers in the grass, honeysuckle

Soldiers escaping from the SS President Coolidge before it slid into deep water after mistakenly striking two Allied mines in the harbor of Espiritu Santo in the New Hebrides on October 26, 1942. [PHOTO: PROBABLY U.S. NAVY]

blooming in the thickets and birds singing in all the trees. In addition the sheep are thick on all the green hills.

On November 10, Wilber sent home a package of Christmas presents, a piece of polished gum of the kauri tree for me and another for his father, a bar pin of native greenstone and sterling for Valerie, and special gift for Norma, a stone called "Black" from Lightning Ridge, Australia. It reminded him "of the flecks deep in your eyes when the sun is shining."

> Nov. 14, 1942 — I now wear a knife (stiletto type) just in case. The scabbard straps on my left arm below the elbow inside my sleeve.... [I wear the] knife up my sleeve and a pistol in an inside shoulder holster. I told the staff that my idea of "Defense in depth" was to use my driver's rifle while the Japs were 200–500 yds away, shift to my Tommie gun when they get to 100 yds, drop it for the pistol at 25 yards and use the knife from then on. "How big your teeth are Grandma."

Ten days after this letter, Wilber was on board the USS American Legion in Auckland, preparing to sail for New Caledonia. The 43rd Division was ready to begin its first assignment in the war against the Japanese, the defense of New Caledonia. Japanese landings there would threaten the shipping routes between America and Australia. The threat was minimal, but everyone remembered Pearl Harbor and Singapore!

The Allied invasion of North Africa (Operation Torch) on the Atlantic and western Mediterranean coasts (in French Morocco and Algeria) began on November 8, 1942, and good progress was made against initially negligible resistance. Rommel's battle-weary troops were far to the east, and the local French Nazi collaborators ("Vichy French") did not contest the Allied landings. This first flush of victory was not to last long because large numbers of German troops and aircraft were pouring into Tunisia.

On November 19 and 20, the Russians attacked the flanks of the German lines at Stalingrad and, by November 23, had encircled the German Sixth Army. It would be almost three months before the trapped troops surrendered to the Soviets.

The American marines with elements of the American army "Americal" Division were beginning to expand their control beyond the Henderson Field area on Guadalcanal, and another American airfield there was under construction. The Japanese were suffering from a lack of supplies. With the arrival of the 43rd Division in New Caledonia, the Americal Division could be totally committed to Guadalcanal.

On November 30, the naval battle of Tassafaronga, off Guadalcanal, was a disaster for the American fleet; one cruiser was lost and several others badly damaged.

9

"The mountains are coming closer"
OUENGHI RIVER, NEW CALEDONIA, NOVEMBER–FEBRUARY, 1943

The convoy carrying a large contingent of the 43rd Division sailed from Auck-
land on November 24 for the three-day voyage to Nouméa, New Caledonia.
Wilber was on the venerable USS American Legion, built in 1919. It carried
Wilber's battalion, less Battery B. Shipping resources, in great demand, were not
available to transfer this and other elements of the 43rd Division until the end of
December.

In this letter to Norma, Wilber clearly evoked the ambiance of being on a ship
at sea in the evening in risky submarine waters.

> Nov. 26, 1942 [V-mail] — This letter is being written at 10:30 P.M. and
> in the dining room. Outside I hear the hum of the motors, the dull rumble
> of the ship's propellers and feel the roll of the ship. The wind is blowing
> outside. The full moon is covered, thank goodness, by clouds and rain. Our
> escort is busily covering us against submarines.

The ships were less visible and hence less vulnerable to submarine or air attack
when not illuminated by moonlight.

The convoy arrived at Nouméa, New Caledonia, on November 27 (Map 6).
This was the home harbor for the U.S. fighting ships that were participating in the
Guadalcanal battles. Many were there, including the cruisers that would be lost or
damaged several nights later in the Battle of Tassafaronga. The aroma of war was
pervasive, but Wilber was not allowed to relate details.

> Nov. 28, 1982 [V-mail] — This voyage is over. We are in a lovely tropic
> harbor. It is nearly completely surrounded by coral reefs and is dotted by
> islands.... Ashore are hills and mountains with a little town of red roofs. I
> can see one church and what is probably a smelter. An occasional road leads
> vaguely into the interior.

I cannot tell you what is in the harbor in addition to our convoy but it is the most thrilling sight I have ever seen....

I'm still on the ship according to the SOP [Standard Operating Procedure] of hurry up and wait. We are now at the second phase. I don't mind for I'm in undershirt and shorts on my berth with a big electric fan doing its stuff on me. It's too hot to make love and besides you're not here so I'm just writing to you.

Did I tell you that one of our officers is being recommended posthumously for a decoration. You didn't know Capt. ___ [Euart, lost on the SS Coolidge] but he was one of our very best officers and died as he lived.

Euart's loss was the first death close to Wilber in his war experience. He tended to drop such news nonchalantly, at the end of a letter.

This same day, Wilber's unit moved to defensive positions on the Ouenghi River (Map 6). He offered his parents and us descriptions of his new home.

Nov. 28, 1942 — I am sitting on my bedroll inside a mosquito net and the net is justified. Around me are trees typical only of this island so the name must be omitted. Across a stream is a coffee and banana plantation, and a mountain range is beyond my front yard. Behind me but not visible is a very nice river of clean water, and a mile away is the ocean. Cocoanuts are ripe now and to be had for a song or a little effort. All in all it's hard to believe this is [that I am in] a tropic setting. It is quiet and beautiful and lovely in every way. The rainy season is due but has not yet arrived. Deer are plentiful and one of our Captains recently ate a steak from a sea-cow [possibly a manatee]. He said it was really good.

Dec 3, 1942 [V-mail] — Today my Christmas came. Santa came right thru the tent roof.... And such wonderful presents. They weren't damaged at all.

Dec. 6, 1942 [V mail] — The rain has stopped and the sky is all full of white fleecy clouds. Some of them are so low they are only halfway up the mountains. They wander around between the mountains like they were too tired to climb up in the sky where they belong.

Dec. 10, 1942 — Yesterday I went down to the town [probably nearby Bouloupari]. It was interesting to see all the people in different dress. Some blacks, some browns, some yellow, and some white. The native black takes off his hat as we pass. Some are labor soldiers and wear fragments of uniforms. They salute with a maximum of pride. We get some salutes from very surprising individuals.

Dec. 12, 1942 — This is a bird's paradise. I have never seen more anywhere. They wake me every morning.

Wilber's ability to get his unit into top shape is illustrated in this humorous description of an inspection by the divisional artillery commander (Barker) and his executive officer (Files).

Today we were inspected by "Harold" [General Barker] and "Chester" [Colonel Files]. It was very comprehensive but not as thorough as the one I do nearly daily on sanitation so they couldn't find anything to criticize. "Chester" tried, but he didn't have much hope because he asked me how things would be. I answered we were coming along but very slowly. He asked what things were slow. I said "Well, you will be able to see during the inspection what I mean." He said "I probably won't see half as much as you [do] that's wrong." He didn't.

Wilber could not write of the placement and registration of the howitzers and the establishment of the division's defensive plan. Possible air attacks and saboteurs mandated complete blackouts (no lights showing) [169th FA Bn. Journal].

X · O · Ø · O · X

Who is this General Barker mentioned so often by Wilber? Barker, a Rhode Islander, was the commander of the divisional artillery. He may also have been the only such officer to publish a history of a divisional artillery in World War II (*History of the 43rd Division Artillery*). It is a technical book with maps, orders, lists of personnel, and a good narrative. It has been invaluable for me in placing Wilber's letters in context. Barker was a dedicated and fearless commander and exacting in what he expected of his officers and men—often expressed with temper and profanity.

X · O · Ø · O · X

In this poetic letter to Norma, Wilber vividly portrays a riverside concert scene.

Dec. 16, 1942 — Last night we had the band down for a concert for the men. They played on my river bank and half the men were on one side of the river and the other half on the other side. About five minutes after the concert started, out of the bushes came five natives. They were fascinated by the music and waded nearly across the river until they were just opposite the band. Two were perfect physical specimens. They are brown to black. The other three could probably outwork any man in our outfit. All wore cloths wrapped around their hair. These are blue or white or red patterned cloth. They were barefooted and wore short trousers

67

or the equivalent. One wore what looked like some of your honeymoon type step-ins. They looked quite comfortable and probably would have hypnotized the feminine friends. One wore a loose flowing waist length kimono type shirt of large blue flowers on a white background. Another wore almost skin-tight shorts of a red and white pattern. Before the concert was over about 20 had collected. As it got dark they faded into the shadows until only a white (relatively only) garment or the glint of the car lights in their eyes showed. You would have been thrilled. They were all gone as soon as the music stopped.

The next day, his letter was more family oriented and playful.

Dec. 17, 1942, Darling Nana & Children — If you were here ... I could take you all swimming too. Which would you prefer the ocean or the river? You can have your choice, but in the ocean a barracuda or shark would probably take an arm or leg off you....

So we will stay home and Valerie will say "Oh dear. I wish I had something to do." So I'll say "OK. You bake a cake for me." And while you are baking a cake, Hale & I will get some cocoanuts for the top. We will make marks in the icing by letting my little brown lizard run around the top. He makes tracks....

This will be the first Christmas I ever spent swatting mosquitos. I love each of you. Let us all try to make the Bradt family a better family in 1943. I'm going to try as hard as I can to be a good Dad and Husband.

It seemed to me that he was being as good a "Dad and Husband" as was possible given his situation. He also had to maintain the morale and combat readiness of his troops in their static assignment on the Ouenghi River.

As Christmas approached, fighting continued to rage in Eastern New Guinea as the Allies advanced on Buna. American troops were on the offensive in Guadalcanal hoping to eject the Japanese entirely from the island, but were encountering strong Japanese resistance. In North Africa also, Americans and British were on the offensive in Tunisia, but the Americans had yet to face a forthcoming German counter offensive. In Russia, the German Army had not been able to break through to its encircled Sixth Army at Stalingrad. The war was progressing in favorable directions for the Allies, but slowly and not without cost.

The Bradt family spent Christmas in New York City. There was to be no repeat of the 1941 Christmas visit to Florida. I was thus able to responsibly fulfill my Christmas duties with Grace Church Choir.

On New Caledonia, the river flowed on while the men of the 43rd Division defended, trained, and waited their turn to enter combat. The monotony of rain-filled days affected morale.

> Dec. 18, 1942, Lover Mine — Again it is afternoon, just after the rain, and I am beside my river thinking of you.... Capt. Farrell has been out working on morale problems. We are taking pretty active steps in that direction. If we are here quite a while, the rain may get monotonous.

On this Sunday, December 20, the battalion underwent a simulated enemy attack by land and air, which led to moves to alternate positions. Firing exercises were frequent. They were training hard. Wilber's monthly letter to his parents included a bit about 11-year-old Valerie.

> Dec. 24, 1942 — [Hale] has made Valerie a sewing kit, which says on it 'VEB Sewing Kit'. Valerie has proudly taken it to her school and is now making herself a skirt. She woke Norma the other morning to say at 6:30 she was getting up to study. At 6:40 she woke Norma and asked for her pillow. At 6:50 she woke her again to ask about the "services" of Pennsylvania (meaning surfaces on the map). At 7:00 she woke Norma again to say it was time to get up.

On this same day, Christmas Eve, Monte's mother, Terkman, wrote Norma displaying genuine warmth between the Bourjaily and Bradt families; both had sent members off to war. The next day, Wilber described *his* Christmas Eve.

> Christmas Day, 1942 — This is Daddy sending from his river on Christmas afternoon.... Everyone drank coffee at 1:00 A.M. around a big bonfire and told everyone else the masses [religious services] were fine which was true, that the music was fine which was not true, that the moon was wonderful which was true, that the folks at home were probably having a white Christmas which was not true because your Christmas hadn't started yet. So ended Christmas Eve with everyone pretty happy and everyone having a prayer in his heart for his people back home.

As Wilber entered 1943, after almost two years of active duty, he still had not seen combat and was still on the Ouenghi River. He and his battalion commander, Lt. Colonel King, used the arrival of their Battery B and their sister battalion, the 192nd FA, on the USS Tryon as an excuse to visit the capital city of Nouméa.

Jan 1, 1943 — Day before yesterday [actually Dec. 29], King & I went to the town [Nouméa] intending to stay overnight on a ship in which some of our troops had a temporary lease [USS Tryon]....

The next A.M. we went back to the docks to watch the [43rd-Division] troops come in. There we ran into an old friend of King's who ... invited us out to his ship for lunch.... You would have been thrilled by the ride past all the ships [in the harbor]. Some of the ship's officers told us the names and where they had been recently. What stories you could write if they could be told. The dinner [on board the ship we visited] was excellent.... After dinner we went thru the ship.... The Navy makes good hosts.

A principal theme of Wilber's letters was his affection for his colleagues in his former (early 1930s) Washington State National Guard unit, the 161st Infantry Regiment. He had learned that they were in his part of the world, which pleased him greatly. He was also getting a reputation for his hiking.

Incidentally I know where Warner [Hudleson] and Donald [Downen] are now. Both are Captains.... Yesterday was an off duty day and I went with three of our officers for a climb.... This climbing for long hours is something not many of our officers have done and I am getting a bit of a reputation out of it as well as some good exposure [in the division].

Wilber had a passion for strenuous hikes. Hiking was a quasi-solitary sport as were his other athletic interests, like swimming and handball. He was averse to, and felt incompetent at, team sports. He knew he could excel at hiking, and he did not mind the attention it got him. And then there was Malcolm!

Jan. 5 — Did I tell you about our pet deer? She [He] is named Malcolm! At first all the boys were saying "Come here Malcy, Come here Sweetheart, Come have a cracker Malcolm." However, since Christmas Malcolm has discovered there are a lot of better things than crackers especially in tents. He likes figs, dates, Hershey bars, Juicy Fruit Gum, fruitcake, cookies, hard candy, mints, sweaty shirts, cashew nuts, peanuts, and sugar.

On January 5, a young soldier, Cpl. Saul Shocket, was returning to his post with the 192nd Field Artillery Battalion when he was accidentally shot and killed by a fellow soldier on sentry duty. Perhaps the sentry was overly nervous because the unit had arrived at Bouloupari only six days earlier; watching for infiltrators was taken very seriously, or perhaps Cpl. Shocket forgot the day's password.

Wilber described to Norma a distasteful aspect of the local coffee industry.

Fri. Jan. 15, 1943, Adorable Nana — Do you know the coffee grows in a small pod with two beans facing each other.... The pod is popped into the mouth of a native woman and cracked between her teeth. She spits the beans on one side and the cracked pod on the other. The beans lie on the ground until they are dry then are collected and sold. And now Dearest, you may have another cup.

And on a following Sunday,

Jan 24, 1943 — It is afternoon of a warm day here and I have just finished dinner. The breeze is good and keeps the mosquitos from being too active. Again I'm very thankful for these spikes [for shoes]. I travel over the hills with the "greatest of ease" now. Thank you very much, Beloved Wife.

X·O·Ø·O·X

I will now introduce Monte Bourjaily, who had befriended Norma and her family. He was an accomplished journalist who had experienced the giddy heights of wealth, fame, and associations with famous people, and the depths of discouragement brought on by overwhelming debts and two divorces. He was born in 1894 in Lebanon, and emigrated at the age of six to the U.S. with his young mother, Terkman. The financial needs of the family prompted young Monte, who had entered Syracuse University in 1913, to leave college a year later for full-time work on the local newspaper.

During World War I, Monte completed ground-school flight training, and was commissioned a second lieutenant on August 18, 1918. He then went on to flight training but was assigned to administrative duties before completing it, and was shipped overseas to France where he held staff positions in the U.S. Army Air Service.

After the war he continued in the newspaper business, rising to editorships and eventually becoming the editor and general manager of United Features Syndicate in New York City in 1928. There he was instrumental in starting up such well-known features and projects as Eleanor Roosevelt's column "My Day" and *Tip Top Comics*. It was he who realized the potential of these and other projects, promoted them, and made them successful.

Monte left United Features in 1936 a rich man and then proceeded to lose money to unsuccessful publishing and theatrical ventures. He returned to journalism in June 1940 as editor of the *Bangor Daily News*, the major paper in Bangor, Maine. By May of 1942, he was back in New York and down on his luck. For a time, he was actually working on the docks, helping with the daily hiring.

Monte had married a writer, Barbara Webb, in 1920 and they had three sons. The marriage failed in 1934, and in that same year, he married a 24-year old

Monte F. Bourjaily as a young Air-Service lieutenant in World War I and as general manager of United Features (newspaper) Syndicate in the mid-1930s.
[PHOTOS: BOURJAILY FAMILY]

"beautiful [stage] actress" and Mt. Holyoke graduate, Elizabeth Horner Young (aka Jalna Young, her stage name) from Pittsburg, Pennsylvania. That too failed, in 1941, while Monte was editor of the Bangor paper.

Monty's novelist son Vance wrote a moving piece about his father during Monte's low period in New York, which was when Monte and Norma first met. It appeared in *Esquire* and was called "My Father's Life." Here is a brief excerpt.

> The extent of Dad's over-qualification for the jobs available in the late Depression was ridiculous.... Dad went to work on the docks in his mid forties. The game was still comic books, in a weird way, and he earned forty-four dollars a week at it.
>
> Dad is dressing for the job. He is putting blotting paper inside his British wing tips to protect his socks in the places where the soles are worn through. The shoes were made for him in London during a honeymoon tour with the beautiful second wife and look good still, and he is still cheerful; he was always a shoeshine guy.... [*Esquire*, March 1984, p. 98, permission of the Vance Bourjaily estate]

Monte had enjoyed the high life of the rich and famous. He was a hard worker, driven to succeed. He loved fancy homes, had an engaging personality along with a mercurial temper, and was known to one of his sons as quite a ladies' man, which could have been a factor in his divorces. He was not tall but stood straight and proud. He felt he had fallen short in the upbringing of his sons, and those sons remained most loyal to their mother; one changed his surname to hers. Nevertheless they all stayed in touch with him and displayed a strong affection for him and for their grandmother Terkman. All three of Monte's sons served in World War II, two of them overseas.

Wilber had met Monte on his leave home in May 1942 and while in New Caledonia wrote warmly about him, "I feel so cared for by all of your love and prayers and those of your friends. I am remembering Monte and Gladys and Joe [Gingold] too" [letter 11/19/42]. He knew that Monte liked Norma and, much later [letter 1/30/44], wrote, "It is a peculiar situation, but in a way I'm glad he is standing by in case I am liquidated."

It was in late January 1943, that Norma became pregnant by Monte. Decades later, in 1982, Norma told me that Monte had been disconsolate because his son Vance had just gone overseas, and in his depression he had more or less forced himself on her, and that this was a one-time event. Vance had embarked overseas to the Middle East the previous November (1942), and this might have been the start of their liaison. Norma herself could well have been equally disconsolate as Wilber had shipped overseas in October and was now half a world away.

Norma was a very religious woman. She attended Grace Church regularly, where I sang in the choir. Discovering her pregnancy, possibly in early February 1943—and in the face of Wilber's consistently romantic letters—must surely have thrown her into despair. As a naive 12-year old, I had no inkling of this. Norma soldiered on through the rest of the spring, managing her children's lives as well as supporting Wilber with her letters and goods he requested. She was planning, with Monte but no others—not even her closest sister Evelyn—how to cope with a pregnancy she would not terminate. In the social climate of the 1940s, few would have been sympathetic to her plight.

Knowing nothing of this, Wilber focused his efforts on the 43rd Division's approaching move to the front lines. Wilber and Norma were each moving toward their respective fronts with outward assurance and inward misgivings.

On Guadalcanal, the campaign was winding down; the last organized resistance ended with the final Japanese evacuation on February 7 and 8. The Japanese drive toward the U.S.-Australia line of communications had been stopped, and the Japanese were now on the defensive. But a significant price had been paid: 5,845 casualties (killed and wounded) of about 60,000 army and marine corps troops committed. The Japanese lost (killed, wounded, and disease) a full two-thirds of its 36,000 troops in the conflict [Miller, *Guadalcanal*, p. 350].

In New Guinea, the Japanese in the Buna-Gona area on the northeast coast of New Guinea had finally been defeated by January 22, 1943, with huge cumulative losses on both sides. The Japanese remained in defensive positions northwest of Buna at Salamaua (Map 2) [Miller, *Papua*, p. 371–2].

In Russia, at Stalingrad, the final resistance of the entrapped German Sixth Army would end on February 2, 1943, with the surrender of 90,000 unwounded and 20,000 wounded men. Only about 5,000 of these men survived Russian captivity.

The next American objective beyond Guadalcanal was to occupy the Russell Islands 35 miles northwest of Guadalcanal. An American airfield there would materially shorten the distance to a Japanese airfield (Munda) that had been built further northwest on New Georgia Island (Map 3). On January 29, Admiral Halsey received permission to proceed with the occupation of the Russells. A week later, on February 7,

Halsey ordered the 43rd Division to Guadalcanal for transfer to the invasion craft that would take them to the Russells. Intense preparations for this move were underway, but Wilber could not refer to them, at least not directly, in this missive to Valerie.

> [Jan. 29, 1943] — It is the next evening now and I can see the three mountains across my river. I wish I could tell you their names.... My river forks and goes around each side of the center one. There are clouds hanging around their tops right now and the air is soft as it is before a rain. It probably is raining on the other side of the mountains now. These mountains are different from others because they can move. At least a lot of people say, "The mountains are coming closer," when they are pretty disgusted with not being home.

Then, to Norma,

> Feb 5, 1943, Hello Dearest — I'd love to have that nice white and clean face of yours in my two hands now. I'd look + look and look at each sweet feature and kiss all the shadows away. I'd hold it against my cheek and drink of the tenderness and love I know you have for me.

What "shadows" did Wilber refer to? Norma most likely expressed some despondency that reflected her now deeply conflicted life. Still, her letters to Wilber continued to flow.

Wilber's next letter spanned the several days prior to boarding ship.

> Feb 7–11, 1943 — I've been umpiring an[other] exercise and my job is just finished. Numerous people are probably relieved for I've had a grand time asking questions and making suggestions on survey and marching and occupation of [artillery] positions etc.... This may be the last letter for a week or so for our schedule is getting into the longer period exercises when there is less chance to mail letters.

On February 11 and 12, the three firing batteries of Wilber's unit—each with four howitzers and about 120 men—moved to Nouméa and loaded onto three different attack transport ships. Wilber boarded the USS President Adams and wrote again before leaving Nouméa, capturing beautifully the spirit of a violin recital Norma had written about, as well as the essence of Nouméa harbor on a moonlit night.

> Feb. 14, 43 — Joe's [Gingold's violin] recital must have been wonderful. I can reconstruct the whole thing. Joe, the stage, lights, people enchanted, you and so proud and worried for fear everything wouldn't be quite perfect, and above and thru everything the silver thread tying all your souls together.

Today, no yesterday [because it is now after midnight], I had an experience you would have loved. I was on one of our luxury liners and had to go ashore at night. The boat's orders were to "Take the Major ashore + obey his orders afterward." I'm not trying to be mysterious. There wasn't any mystery, but [during the boat ride] the moon was in and out of the clouds so it was bright then dark several times. The waves were not big but there was a definite swell.... Some ships were dark, some not, some quiet some busy, the air was soft, the hills lovely when the moon was out. Nearby on shore a smelter was doing its stuff in its usual noxious manner; in another cove the leper colony was dark and quiet, while a blinker station busily cut the night into dots and dashes from a [geologically] young mountain in the distance.

x·o·ø·o·x

The convoy bound for "Cactus" (the code name for Guadalcanal) departed Nouméa, New Caledonia, at 5:30 a.m. on February 15, 1943.

Meanwhile, it was 2:30 p.m. on February 14, in New York City, and Norma was attending the wedding of Monte's son, Monte Jr., to an attractive brunette, Marietta ("Billy") Dake, at St. Thomas Church on Fifth Avenue. It was surely an anguished time for the religious Norma as she contemplated her own marriage vows against her complex relationships to the Bourjailys.

In North Africa, American forces had moved eastward into the mountainous terrain of Tunisia. There, in mid-February, disaster struck. German forces drove through and routed American forces at Kasserine Pass. It was not until February 25 that the Americans, with the aid of British and French troops, were able to regain the pass. Command practices that led to the rout were rapidly revised and several senior commanders were relieved. This setback and the subsequent adjustments went far toward maturing the U.S. Army forces in Europe. Gradually, the Allies regained the initiative, but not without additional setbacks. The Americans from the west and southwest, and the British from the east and southeast, began the drive that would force the Italians and Germans into northern Tunisia with their backs to the Mediterranean Sea.

In Russia, on January 12, the Russians initiated a westward drive toward Kharkov. By February 20, they had created a large salient into the

German lines that included Kharkov and Kursk. The Germans mounted a counterattack on February 20, driving to the Donetz River by March 18, and trapping and destroying a Soviet tank army. Both armies, quite depleted, lay low during the muddy spring season, awaiting the battles sure to come in the summer.

July 23, 1943

Dear Son,

I thought you might like to get a letter written on a battlefield during a battle. Just now things have quieted down right here. However there are some Jap snipers in the trees around me. The men shoot one out every so often. Some fall, some are tied up so they stay. I have a very satisfactory slit trench with foliaged logs dirt over it. I am in it now.

I told you I was wounded by a bomb on the Fourth of July but that it didn't amount to much. On the tenth I was scratched in the side by a Jap bullet. Again it was nothing & it is all healed now. I have the bullet for a souvenir. It came in thru my jacket, hit me in the side and dropped in my pocket.

July 24. General Griswold was in the next fox hole to mine the other day. I was

PART III

JUNGLE COMBAT

SOLOMON ISLANDS
FEBRUARY 1943—JANUARY 1944

Howitzer (155-mm) of 192nd Field Artillery Battalion under camouflage netting at Bustling Point, Arundel Island, September 24, 1943. [PHOTO: U.S. ARMY SIGNAL CORPS, SC 182104]

10

"You can't tame a machine gun by looking it squarely in the eye"

USS PRESIDENT ADAMS, GUADALCANAL, FEBRUARY 1943

The 43rd Division was moving to the front lines! The move from New Caledonia to the Russell Islands in the Solomon Islands was carried out in two stages. Large ships carried the division to Guadalcanal, a four-day voyage. After four days on Guadalcanal, they would embark on smaller craft for the overnight trip to the nearby Russell Islands (Map 3).

The voyage to Guadalcanal was Wilber's third since leaving California. His ship, the USS President Adams (APA-19) carried armament that was light by warship standards, but not trivial: one five-inch cannon, four three-inch guns, and eight 20-mm rapid-fire guns. It traveled with other similar ships and escorts grouped in a convoy for mutual protection. These ships, chock-full of American troops, were tempting targets for Japanese submarines and aircraft.

The convoy passed through the Coral Sea, location of the famed Battle of the Coral Sea of the previous May (1942). Wilber wrote to Norma and his father shortly after the ship's early-morning departure from Nouméa.

> Feb. 15, 1943, Hello Sweet and Lovely — I wish I were able to have you with me tonight. You would have loved today. A little work and a few inspections in the morning, then just watching the mountains slide by on the horizon. The water is blue and calm with white foam all alongside.... The officers (Navy) on this ship are treating us royally. We were cargo on our last voyage but now we are privileged passengers. I eat at the #2 table with the Lt. Commanders and enjoy them a great deal.
>
> Feb. 16, 1943, Darling — It's a Lovely Morning and I wish I had you by my side. We'd take my canvas chair, which I carried on board, and set you by the rail on the bridge (on top of all the decks) and I'd stand beside you with

one hand on your shoulder. We'd talk and dream and watch the sky and the foam and the flying fish and the horizon for other ships....

Feb. 16, 1943, Dear Father — Today is again my second day at sea.... I was afraid we would go to the European front and this is my war over here. It's not one of maneuver and strategy. It's one where the enemy is either killed or you are killed. There is a definiteness about that that is very satisfying. These men aren't over here to play. They know it's either-or and they act accordingly. I may regret the finality of such a scrap sometime but until that time comes, here is where I want to be.

Wilber's words to his father about his own death were disturbingly cool and detached. But his views were largely theoretical because he had not yet been exposed to actual combat.

Feb 17, 1943 — We have just changed course, which will probably occasion 20 soldiers to ask 20 sailors whether this is the "zig" or the "zag." Someday a sailor is going to lose control of himself and kill a soldier just for that reason.

To frustrate submarine attacks, ships in a convoy would all change course every 10 to 30 minutes by preplanned but unpredictable amounts, making a zig-zag track that averaged to the desired course.

Last night was quiet but just now a warning came over the speaker system to gun crews to be especially on lookout for enemy "flying boats." The transports are shifting their positions probably for best anti-aircraft protection. [This] convoy has made seven of these trips, and, altho ships have been torpedoed on two occasions, no ship has ever failed to get there and back.

That evening the Japanese launched a torpedo plane attack on the convoy. Several days later, as he was waiting on a beach for the ship that would take him to the Russell Islands, Wilber wrote Valerie and me about it.

February 22, 1943 — The attack on our convoy on the way up here was one of the prettiest sights I have seen. There were Jap flares in the air to help their planes find us. The moon was calmly watching the whole fight, and its light danced on the waves just like in Maine. The planes would come scooting in toward us from the dark, and then the tracer bullets would start reaching out from the ships. When they hit the plane, a little fire would start to spread and maybe the plane would begin to go crooked. One big gun hit one plane right square in the middle before the pilot dropped his torpedoes at [toward] the ship. The shell burst in the plane and so did his torpedo. There was a great flash and thunderous report and that plane was completely gone.

All this time the ships were zig-zagging calmly just as if they were on a drill...; our escort ships were running around us dropping depth charges that went whamo so it sounded as if a thousand tons of pig iron had fallen on a hundred big steel boilers. At the same time all their antiaircraft guns were busy. All this lasted only about 20 minutes and the thing was all quiet and people began to count how many planes had been shot down by each ship.... Your Pop went down behind a steel gun shield a couple of times when things seemed to be coming his way. You know you can't tame a machine gun by looking it squarely in the eye.

The ship reached Guadalcanal on February 18. There was no harbor; dock facilities were built out from the beaches.

The 43rd Division had arrived at Guadalcanal on February 16 and 18, shortly after the cessation of organized resistance on February 9, though there were still isolated Japanese on the island; Wilber wrote of sniper fire. Although the 43rd Division was not involved in the organized fighting, its members were awarded a battle star on the Asiatic-Pacific campaign ribbon for the Guadalcanal battle because they were there prior to the official end-of-action date. The attack on their convoy the night of February 17 certainly justified it. Here is Wilber's view, for Norma, of the world-famous Guadalcanal and of a particularly vivid dream he had.

Feb. 19, 1943, Beloved — It is just getting dark and this letter will be short. We are bivouacked now in a cocoanut grove. On one side is the jungle and on the other is an open area of very tall grass. It is quite hot and sultry. The grass is full of crickets and the trees full of birds. I saw two pure white parrots that apparently were talking Japanese. There are monkeys here too who talk the same language. The mosquitos are definitely Anti-U.S. The jungle is lovely with green vines and shrubs and many colored flowers. – Too dark now [to continue writing]. Am OK + love you. Wish I could send Valerie the 6-inch butterfly that I saw.

Feb. 20, 1943, 9:30 A.M. — This A.M. I got up and bathed and it was necessary not because of the tropics but because I had had a particularly vivid dream of my wife.... You really should have been here for you missed a very enthusiastic session. Some day, My Darling, I won't dream of you. I'll hold you in my two hands and then I'll really make love to you.

Wilber's fantasies were right out in the open. There was no doubt that he and Norma had a rich sex life; he was focused on her and no one else, not even in his fantasies. But by this date, roughly a month after conception, Norma would likely have lost all hope that she was not pregnant. Wilber's long-distance romancing was surely wrenching to her.

x·o·ø·o·x

After just four days in Guadalcanal, the division moved to the Russell Islands, 35 miles northwest of Guadalcanal and the most forward position of U.S. troops in the South Pacific Area. It had not been clear whether the Japanese still occupied the Russell Islands, but recent reconnaissance had shown it to be unoccupied. Nevertheless, it was still possible that the Japanese would react strongly to the arrival of the Americans.

Wilber wrote while awaiting his ship on the beach at Koli Point, Guadalcanal.

> Feb 22, 1943, I'm in love with Norma — Have you ever received a love letter from a guy on a pile of 105[-mm] howitzer ammunition? Yes. Today you have one. The lover is at his ease on some Smoke. Not Smoke in his eyes but smoke under + all around him.

The smoke shells he was lying on were 105-mm shells, which released smoke on impact for use in adjusting aim. The shells would have been in hard cylindrical metal cans about five inches in diameter and perhaps 30 inches long. (Wilber's reference was to the popular Jerome Kern song, "Smoke Gets in Your Eyes.")

> Your dear letters came yesterday and had to be packed for this job, but I certainly recall some of the high spots. Imagine my lovely wife having an orgasm on account of me. Dearest you grow more precious to me each day. You were [a] darling to tell me. Isn't it odd that on the same day I got your letter I had mailed one describing an identical experience? Tis true "stone walls do not a prison make." ... In the meantime my arm is around your waist and my lips in your hair.

Norma was writing of having an orgasm too "on account of [Wilber]"! Was it real or simply a literary creation to match Wilber's passionate writing? It could well have been either.

Wilber goes on to tell about his reunion with his former Washington State colleagues of Company E, 161st Infantry. The visit was not without risk.

> All the old Co E. crowd was asking about you. They certainly all talked about Norma and what was she doing now and things they remembered. You seemed almost present. All sent their greetings, even a Lt. Patterson who remembered you playing [piano]. Lt Col. Morris of Spokane Paper

84

asked particularly to be remembered and Hud + Don [Downen] seemed definitely to feel you were part of the firm of We, Us + Co. Cris grinned from ear to ear and says "Housa Mrs?" The boys tell me that out of the Co E. we knew, over thirty men are now officers. Hud has the same mustache + is only a little more bald.

We recalled the nights [after National Guard drill] we sat in Charlie's place [the Chinese restaurant in Pullman, Washington] + talked of fighting the Japs in 1932 and how glad we were to be here now together.... And they all wanted me to stay for supper, but I had to get back for supper and before dark as there are still parties of Japs in the Jungle. We have a date [to meet again] for each island and each continent until the one in Pullman. Will you come to that one?

(Many years later in May 1981, Donald Downen wrote me the following assessment of Wilber, "I thought of him as always considerate of others, happy, jolly chuckle [sic], never autocratic or overbearing. Never hurried or flustered. Always seemed to have time for the occasion.")

While still on the Guadalcanal beach, Wilber got a letter off to Valerie and me.

Feb. 22, 1943 — My boat is in sight now so I must stop. Children I like to write to you about the things I see but would rather have you and Nana along so we could see them together (except the Japs). Don't worry about the famous Jap snipers. All our friends say they never hit a moving target, and one took three shots at me yesterday and missed badly. If they don't hit me I don't mind being shot at.

Wilber boarded the destroyer USS Saufley DD-465 on February 22 and would arrive at Pavuvu Island in the Russell Islands with his unit on February 23.

11

"Oh! There go 5000 rings"

PAVUVU ISLAND, RUSSELL ISLANDS, FEBRUARY–JULY, 1943

The landings were made at Pavuvu and Banika Islands in the Russells on February 21 and 23 and the Japanese made no attempt to drive the Americans from them. The landings were a learning experience. Months later, Wilber compared them to another unopposed landing, this one in Italy.

> January 15, 1944 — [it] was a little like our landing on the Russells – nobody home! Probably it was just as well as there were some definitely amateur aspects to that landing. For example Rainey's pilot confessed during the night that he had never been in "these parts" before. I don't know why he should ever [have] been there, but Rainey was certainly disappointed in his pilot, especially after he spent the night on a reef.

The 169th Field Artillery Battalion spent four months on Pavuvu guarding the front and training for future combat (Map 7). It was bivouacked in a palm tree grove planted by Lever Brothers, the international soap manufacturer. The battalion's mission was to protect the Russells and in particular an American airfield that was to be constructed on the adjacent Banika Island. Japanese bombers and fighters from Munda Airfield did occasionally attack the 43rd Division encampments and later the Banika airfield.

> Feb 27, 1943 — Darling I'm back again. It's 2:30 P.M. and the past two days have been hectic and hot. We have been rushing all things artillery and furnishing transportation to other troops at the same time. Everything is quiet and peaceful.... The Japs very thoughtlessly did not leave things in the best of conditions.... The current crop [of coconuts] is falling now and helmets are definitely in style....

I went into the jungle a couple of miles yesterday to get acquainted with it. So far it has been a long ways from being "impenetrable."... There are enormous trees with great gnarled roots, others with roots that make walls out from the tree trunk, so there are small rooms around the tree. Some are as white as birch, some stand on ten or twenty legs....

Mar. 10, 1943 —Did I tell you that we call the Jap planes that come over Washing Machine Charlie or Maytag Charlie because their motors are not synchronized and they make a rhythmic beat, RRRRRRrr RRRRRrrr RRRRRrr.

Norma was clearly writing Wilber assiduously and sending him things he needed.

Mar. 13, 1943 — I spent an hour this morning putting spikes in another pair of shoes. In the jungle they go [bad] pretty fast (shoes), and one pair is good for just one more long climb, then I'll take out the spikes + save them. In the jungle I wear them near the toe and instep ... and when I step, those in the toe dig in and no slipping back occurs. When I'm jumping from root to root or limb to limb of trees I step in the instep and stick like a cat.

Mar 27, 1943 — Our neighbors [Japanese] on the next island come over [in airplanes] frequently (nearly every night) and we all get up + stay by our slit trenches until the All Clear comes along. We aren't quite in his favorite target area so are usually spectators....

Your account of the wedding + reception [for Monte Jr.] was interesting. However there is one Bourjaily wedding I don't want you to attend [Monte Sr. and Norma!] so beware of your irresistible charm. I'm figuring on a silver wedding trip [25th anniversary in 1952] to Lake Louise for you, and the plans can't be changed at this late date.

Wilber surely passed this off lightly as a kind of joke, but his writing it could well have come from an underlying uneasiness about the situation at home. He certainly was not consciously concerned, because, after discussing routine business, he waxed absolutely poetic about Norma, with no hint of doubt.

What a shame to waste time in writing business to you. What I want to talk about is my Norma and her lovely eyes and the perfume of her hair and the softness of her lips. I want to plan hours with her and to recall wonderful days shared with her. She must be told that my love for her is like a golden waterfall in a snowcapped mountain, irresistible, flooding and a rushing power, which is above the strength of man.

Wilber's description of his world on Pavuvu Island went to me.

March 29, 1943, Dear Son — The planes are going "Zoom, Zoom, Zoom," overhead. It is morning before breakfast and the air is very quiet and cool. The palm trees are full of birds and cocoanuts. The birds are waiting to see the sun come up, and the cocoanuts are waiting for someone to walk under their tree without a helmet. Since they are as high as our house they land with quite a whomp. One of the planes is just now coming back in a hurry. We always wonder what he saw or did to make him hurry so. Maybe he thinks, "Gee Whiz, I left the coffee on the stove."...

The sun is coming up now and a whole row of varicolored dragon flies have lined up on each tent rope to get the first rays. They are bright red with black bodies, and some with transparent wings and bodies except for a yellow spot at their tail and a yellow head.... It's nearly noon now and I ... did some digging on my trench both for the exercise and to get a little more room. There still isn't room in it both for me and a bomb. If one falls right in with me, I expect to get out in a hurry. However if one just falls nearby I expect to be as comfortable as a bug in the mud.

Wilber would become much more serious in his letters during the impending close-in combat.

x · o · ø · o · x

Norma by now surely knew she was pregnant and at some point decided against an abortion. To have sought one would have been very tempting because of the great shame attached in those days to an out-of-wedlock pregnancy. But Norma had likely decided to see the pregnancy through for moral and religious reasons, and Monte would have acceded to her strong feelings.

Did they have a plan? Probably. First and foremost was to keep the pregnancy a secret from family and friends and even from Valerie and me because of the disgrace it represented. It was also conventional wisdom reinforced by government announcements that bad news written to overseas soldiers would damage their morale and thus endanger their lives. Keeping the secret from Wilber was essential to his well-being; it was their patriotic duty!

In this letter, Wilber responded to Norma's apparent first seeds of her grand deception. She was, she had written, considering doing some sort of war work.

April 2, 1943 — You ask about Mobilization of Women. I don't know the answer. If you think you should go and can arrange for the care of the children, go ahead.... I could say I want you to stay home but I also want this war to end the right way and as soon as possible. One thing, please remember that you are inclined to take on too much. If you do go into the service of our country in any way, go in all over and don't try to keep up the home work and the other too. What about the F.B.I.?

The children are old enough to understand, and they would be old enough to realize their responsibility too. Remember boys Hale's age work in factories in Europe and girls Valerie's age gather scraps of garbage for food. Whatever you do, I'll not worry.... I love you, My Darling. Whatever you do will be OK with me anytime. Just keep well for me.

This was impressive acceptance on Wilber's part. At that time, working class women were moving into previously male jobs due to shortages of male workers; "Rosie the Riveter" was the prototypical factory worker, but upper class women were still expected to stay home to care for the family.

Nighttime in a boat on the water was always a magical experience for Wilber. Here he was on a PT boat—the kind Jack Kennedy commanded—on a nighttime trip to Guadalcanal that was aborted before they arrived. It was a fast ride in waters subject to Japanese attacks; but it too had poetic aspects.

Apr. 10, 1943, It's Pop again [to Norma] — The ride was a thrilling experience.... As we (two boats) speeded along, the wake seemed all afire with greenish yellow fire. In the general glow, were many little whirlpools and swirls of brilliant glowing spots that danced and brightened to an almost flame-like intensity. The spray beside our bow often came above the rail (if it had been a rail). It looked like a spray of molten silver and the waves out from the bow looked like living essence of moonlight....

[Later on shore] I'm in the tent now. My phone is on a long wire so the phone moves with me, in the tent, out of the tent, under one palm, then another wherever the shade is best. Where I sit is the C.P. [Command Post]. Sometimes the C.P. moves into my slit trench, which now is quite to my satisfaction. I'm down below the surface about three feet on clean coral rock (no mud) with a roof of sheet iron and logs to stop fragments and stray bullets from planes. The logs are reinforced by sand bags and the whole thing [is] camouflaged.

Wilber was well prepared for bombing raids.

Two days later, Wilber wrote Valerie, about to turn 11, vivid descriptions of air raids and nighttime sounds.

April 12, 1943 — Last night the Japs sent a plane over us to look around. It was pretty dark but the moon gave some light. All our lights were out and the men put out their cigarettes and got into their trenches.... In a little while all our soldiers came out of their trenches and went back to bed. Thirty minutes later all one could hear was the guards moving now and then and the telephone operator on night duty answering the phone and a lot of good comfortable and noisy snores. Everyone settled down for a good night's sleep except for two other times later in the night when the Japs came back probably to see if they could see any damage.

On April 15, Wilber received 11 letters from Norma, dated March 1–24; he had previously received three from that period. Norma was saturating Wilber with letters. In her despair (or guilt), she apparently felt a need to remain close to Wilber. Norma often sat in Grace Episcopal Church before and after services waiting for me to finish my choir duties and would write from there as Wilber acknowledged, "Your church letter was one of the nicest yet. I wish I could have walked in and sat beside you while you wrote."

Easter Morning [April 25, 1943] — This Easter morning is cool and fresh. The sun is just up peeping between clouds that showered us last night. The air smells clean and a quiet breeze is drifting thru the palms.... In the south, the bluest sky I have ever seen symbolizes the hope of peace that is in every soldier's heart today.

Norma had planned for all three of us to travel to Washington, D.C., to visit my uncle Paul during the spring school breaks. In fact, I took the train alone at age 12 because Valerie was sick. Paul Bradt, Wilber's brother, was an expert rock climber and a founding member of the rock climbing section of the Washington, D.C., Appalachian Trail Club. On that visit, I was first exposed to rock climbing on Old Rag Mountain in the Blue Ridge, a favorite of that group.

Norma's intense letter writing campaign continued into April. How to conceal her pregnancy, now three months along, from Valerie and me was a problem she needed to face. Sending us to summer camps would be part of the solution.

April 30, 1943 — Your ideas for the children's summer camp sound very practical and interesting. I am only worried about you while they are away. Will you be too lonesome? I don't remember your being completely abandoned by your family before.

Did you know that [Lt. Gen. Oscar W.] Griswold has re-entered my life. He was the commanding Gen. of the IV Corps who asked after me by name in Miss[issippi]. That created quite a bit of consternation in the Bn. then.

He is now our Corps commander again, which is good news. [His questions] will force a very active reconsideration of some views I have proposed [on operating in the jungle]. When I made them, they were smiled away, but now it seems he too does not consider the jungle [to be] impenetrable. It seems now too that a lot of those special reconnaissances of mine [into the jungle] are right down the groove.

This letter went on to assure Norma that life at the front was not, as the news media would have it, all "strenuous, hazardous and glory ridden," but rather, "more commonly a battle against boredom, disease and little annoyances." A few days later, Wilber became introspective.

May 4, 1943 — This is Dopey speaking from a very wet jungle island. No I didn't go somewhere. The rain came today. First it was a cloud burst and now just a good steady rain. I set my two canvas buckets under the tent edge and have both filled with fine soft water. Baths coming up....

It's still raining, and I'm reminded of your hard efforts to give me a good vacation on the Oregon coast once. I'm ashamed of my persistent despondence now. It must have been quite a trial.

This might have been his first admission of "despondence." We first heard of it from Norma in her 1941 (February 3) letter to his parents. This letter implied that a bout of depression might have gone on for some time during that Oregon vacation.

General Griswold's interest in jungle training was having practical consequences, to Wilber's satisfaction.

May 9, 1943 — My CO [King], not being enthused about hiking in jungles and as he said, because of my demonstrated liking for that sort of thing, gave me that end of things. Because it is not my normal duty, I could have declined but I'm glad of the experience so took it on.... We will just get a little mountain and jungle experience.

Preparations for the next advance, an attack on Munda Airfield, revealed a rift in the command structure.

May 12, 1943 — Yesterday ... [General] Barker + Lt. Col. King had been going around + around over some position possibilities [i.e., where to place artillery howitzers] with no progress. Eventually B. blew up and ordered me down to his Hq. It is a two hour boat trip [to Banika Island; Map 7]. So down I went expecting I might get blasted for [in place of] King. No such luck. B[arker] told me what he wanted. I told him what was unreasonable

91

including a reference to King Canute who you recall ordered the tide not to come in. He got the point and asked what I recommended which was fine. "Fine!" "Fine!" "FINE!" It seems I'm one of the only two officers [in division artillery?] who have gone to see what's in the jungle.

This probably referred to plans for emplacing artillery for the Munda operation beginning June 30. The 169th Field Artillery Battalion would be stationed on a jungle island (Sasavele) just off the "mainland." Barker was King's boss and King was Wilber's boss. The army way was to follow the chain of command, and this definitely was not it.

On April 22, the Allies in Tunisia had launched a final offensive on the isolated Axis troops in Northern Tunisia, which were suffering a severe lack of supplies due to increasing Allied control of the air and the Mediterranean. On May 13, the Axis troops in Tunisia surrendered with some 250,000 German and Italian troops passing into captivity; North Africa was in Allied hands.

In the North Pacific, a small American force moved to eject the Japanese from the two western Aleutian Islands they had occupied since June 1942. On May 11, U.S. troops landed on Attu, the westernmost Aleutian island. Fighting continued there through May. On June 8, the Japanese ordered the evacuation of nearby Kiska Island, which was accomplished under cover of fog on July 28. Unaware of this, an American force "invaded" and occupied the island in mid-August.

At the end of May, preparations for the attack on Munda, a month later, were intensifying. Munda was a well defended airfield; the Japanese would not give it up easily.

At the same time, Norma was in her own countdown toward the end of the school year, the separation of the family, and the anticipated October birth of her baby. The letters between Norma and Wilber continued to flow.

May 29, 1943, How'r'ya Toots! — Your encyclopedic letter of Apr. 23 came with a series up to include Apr 27....

King found the flesh was too weak and is off for recuperation, rejuvenation and communion, relaxation and inspiration. He "discovered" that he had high blood pressure and the temptation was too great. Do not quote [this]. Anyway he has lost a lot of weight, not by exercise, and looked pretty bad, so he is on the way to a rear hospital. On the other hand Ol' Man Bradt is still ... free wheeling, so [General] Barker says it looks as if I had a job [as commanding officer of the 169th Field Artillery Battalion].

Wilber displayed some contempt for King's leaving just before the Munda landings, but grudgingly allowed that he could have been truly sick.

Wilber's interest in jungle operations was intensifying.

May 30, 1943, Dear Father — Things here have been on a routine basis since I last wrote. Out of the other duties, I have stolen quite a lot of time in the jungle.... I have learned a lot of things about rates of travel, road building, tactics and artillery possibilities in the jungle, that are not in books.

May 31, 1943, Darling Wife of Mine — Today I took the battery commanders into the jungle on reconnaissance. It was the first time they had been in there.

The soldiers became adept at making rings and bracelets from the aluminum skins of wrecked Japanese and American planes.

June 3, 1943 — It's good to know the "Zero" ring and bracelet arrived and that they were liked. The "ring" industry here is becoming quite a pastime for some of the men. It was quite funny the other day during a rather sad moment when as one of our planes landed on and sank in the ocean near us to hear one voice say "Oh! there go 5000 rings." ... They [the crew] were all saved.

X · O · Ø · O · X

Norma had decided how to maintain the secret of her pregnancy after our summer camps were over: she would place us in boarding schools she had carefully selected. For me, it was St. Bernard's School in Gladstone, New Jersey, 40 miles west of New York City, and for Valerie, St. John the Baptist School in Mendham, six miles from St. Bernard's. They both had Episcopalian underpinnings. Norma had taken us to New Jersey to see our schools in an effort to make us more comfortable with the transition from summer camp to school in September, when she would not be with us.

This would free Norma to participate, she said, in the war effort. In fact, she would instead be nurturing her pregnancy and later her baby and would be unable to work. These arrangements were taking a heavy toll on her, as suggested by Wilber's encouragement.

> Please don't cry Lover about the broadcasts [of the war]. Keep them turned up at the corners. Remember? It sounds like nerves to me. Relax and have a little fun. You can't carry all the weight of this war yourself.

x·o·ø·o·x

Wilber continued to bombard Norma with requests for items he needed, such as the spikes for his shoes, books, batteries, razor blades, and foods, and she dutifully found and mailed them. And Wilber was thriving in his new position as commanding officer.

> June 8, 1943 — Since I've been C.O., I've been sending my officers into the jungles and getting them wised up and toughened up a bit. They seem to like it.... I have said I want this to be the best firing battalion in this theater and there is a chance they can make that a fact. Anyway they will have something to work for.

Wilber aimed high. He wanted intensely to be first in artillery *and* first with Norma.

> June 18, 1943 — We are getting into the groove again and the Bn. is beginning to click.... You should see these officers fire [artillery] now. They get it [the artillery projectile] where it is supposed to go and in a hurry. They are going to give some Japs some very sudden surprises. Barker was, so he said, well pleased and had no suggestions....
>
> The other evening I came back from a conference by boat and saw the most beautiful sunset. The sea was dotted with little palm covered white-rimmed islands toward the west. In the east was our larger jungle covered island [Banika] over which a marvelous moon was rising.

And to Norma, he made his best pitch, and what a beautiful one it was. He started by recalling their first meeting in his chemistry class.

> June 26, 1943 — Today in 1927 you walked into my heart. I can remember yet how fresh and clean and dear you looked. The room [Wilber's lab] had been dingy and dull and it was suddenly a wonderful place to me. Your eyes and lips had a sweetness in them that seemed to be shadowed by something. I wanted then to know how to replace that shadow by a consciousness that someone who mattered loved you. I wanted to matter to you and soon. I still do.... So it has gone all thru the years.... This year is the

94

same. Amid all my worries, fatigue, isolation, and responsibilities, you have been my guiding light, my guardian angel.

Norma would have received this letter after the family had dispersed and as she was beginning her sixth month of pregnancy. It surely would have been wrenching for her. Wilber could reach deep into her heart with his romantic prose.

Then there was a warning to Norma.

> June 27, 1943 — There will likely be a gap in my letters for a while now. We are terribly busy. It will be no reason tho for you to worry, so don't be crediting all the headlines to me. You know I just work here.

The "gap in my letters" message would have been known by now to Norma as notice that his unit was moving on, presumably toward increased danger. In the rush, Wilber found time for his monthly letter to his father as well as one to me and one to Norma.

> June 27, [1943], Dear Father — The thing that concerns me is whether I can do the job well enough. It's a fine artillery battalion with the repeatedly earned record of being the best in this division and I have helped to make it [so].
>
> June 27, 1943, Dear Son Hale — You say you are writing for Nana, that Valerie was washing dishes and Norma hemming Valerie's dress. That sounds as if everyone was doing their job back home.
>
> June 29, 1943 [to Norma] — [As commanding officer,] I now am responsible for a lot of people and their collective efficiency. Good or bad, efficient or inefficient, successful or unsuccessful, all is credited or blamed to or on me. However now being in command I have some control and can exercise command.

Elements of the 43rd Division including artillery made the first landings on Rendova Island in the New Georgia group (Solomon Islands) on June 30 (Map 8). Rendova was the staging area for the attack on the nearby Munda Airfield. Wilber's unit would embark for Rendova on July 3 and land there July 4.

> July 2, 1943, Dearest Norma and children — This is the last letter I will write for about two weeks. Don't be worried if you don't hear from me for a while. It means I just won't be on speaking terms with the P.O. [Post Office] Dept.

Norma, in one last fling of family togetherness and maternal responsibility, organized a music recital for Valerie and me in the Grace Church Assembly Hall. We were the entire program: Valerie singing and playing piano, me on the violin,

R E C I T A L

by

HALE BRADT

and

VALERIE BRADT

Grace Church Assembly Hall, July 1, 1943, 8:00 p.m.

I

Star Spangled Banner.........................Francis Scott Key
Valerie, Hale, and Audience

II

A group of Songs
The Lass with the Delicate Air.........Arne (1740) (English)
When the Roses Bloom..................Reichardt (1790) (Early German)
Dearest, believe (Caro mio ben)......Giordani (1770) (Early Italian)
VALERIE BRADT, SOPRANO

III

Violin Solos
Allegro Moderato, from the Concerto in D........Seitz
Bourree...............................Handel
Berceuse Slave........................Neruda
HALE BRADT, VIOLINIST

IV

Piano Solos
The Nightingale.......................Kullak
Hungarian Carol.......................Folk Song
Scherzino.............................Thompson
VALERIE BRADT, PIANIST

Violin and Piano Duet
Cradle Song...........................Schubert
VALERIE AND HALE
Goodnight

Program of recital by Valerie and me at Grace Church, July 1, 1943, typed by Norma. Norma was the piano accompanist for the songs and violin solos. This was her last hands-on act of motherhood before we three each went off to our separate destinations. [FACSIMILE: HALE BRADT]

and Norma accompanying us on the piano. The recital began at 8 p.m. on July 1, and the very next day I was off to summer camp. I would not see Norma until Christmastime.

The day after that, at 4:45 p.m. on July 3, the 169th Field Artillery Battalion embarked for Rendova Island.

June 1943 came to an end with a major change facing each member of the family. Although bound in marriage and in spirit, Wilber and Norma had each become an independent entity with an independent agenda and challenges. The challenges were all-encompassing and followed from freely made choices: Wilber to enter the service and Norma to continue her pregnancy. Each marched off to carry out his or her duty, Wilber as a seasoned soldier heading into combat, Norma as the commander of a dispersed family on the home front, and Valerie and I as youngsters facing our first year away from home in new schools.

On July 4, Wilber was wounded by a Japanese bomb, before his battalion could fire even one round in combat.

At the end of June 1943, the entire western Pacific and most of Europe remained in Axis hands, but the Allies had begun their long slow march to recover the conquered territories. British and American forces in Africa were preparing for the July 10 invasion of Sicily in the Mediterranean. In Russia, the Germans and Russians were about to engage in an epic battle for Kursk. The next step in the South Pacific, to the New Georgia Island group, had already begun, and Wilber would soon be involved. The war was flaring up on all fronts.

12

"Lovely little shiny bombs"
RENDOVA, JULY 1943

In New York City at the beginning of July, Norma had just sent me off to summer camp and Valerie to relatives and later summer camp. We mailed letters to her at the Hotel Altamont in Baltimore. The Altamont was probably a fictional residence and mail drop point when she was most likely living in the town house that Monte Bourjaily, the baby's father, had rented in the upscale Georgetown neighborhood of Washington, D.C. (He had obtained a high position in the Commerce Department by then.) He and his mother Terkman shared the residence.

Norma could not live openly in Washington, D.C., because Wilber's brother Paul and his wife lived just a few miles distant and would expect to occasionally meet with Norma, and Wilber himself would expect such meetings. Baltimore, only 50 miles away, might have seemed the perfect place for a fictional residence, but managing her correspondence with Wilber through Baltimore would prove to be awkward.

Also, how did Monte explain pregnant Norma's presence in his home to his neighbors and social acquaintances? Did she have to wait until night to leave the row house, or retreat to the upper floor when visitors came? Whatever the circumstances, it must have been very stressful for both of them. She told me much later this had been the only time in 40-plus years that she was without her beloved piano. I find myself impressed that Monte took responsibility for the pregnancy by taking her in.

As a youngster, I was blissfully unaware of the reason for the family separation and went about having a healthy and productive summer at Grace Boys Camp in Bear Mountain State Park, New York. At age 12, I became a confident swimmer, canoeist, and hiker. Valerie, after an extended visit with her Uncle Paul and Aunt Jo in Washington, D.C., attended a camp in Connecticut. She was 11.

In the South Pacific, Wilber's unit, the 43rd Infantry Division, was under the command of the navy's Admiral Halsey. In parallel with Halsey's advances in the Solomons, General MacArthur was preparing to move up the New Guinea northeast coast to the Huon peninsula (Map 2).

The thrust toward Munda Airfield would begin with the capture of the lightly defended Rendova Island a few miles south of the targeted airfield. Rendova would serve as a staging area, and artillery placed there could fire upon Munda. The first elements of the 43rd Division occupied Rendova on June 30 with minimal resistance. Two days later, on July 2, they were stunned by a Japanese bombing raid that resulted in more than 200 dead and wounded [Barker, p. 49].

The day after the air attack, July 3, Wilber was still on Pavuvu Island in the Russell Islands awaiting the sea-going vessels, landing craft, and destroyers that would carry him and his men the 120 miles to Rendova. They began boarding the 158-foot Landing Craft Infantry 65 (LCI-65) that afternoon, which, after an overnight voyage, dropped anchor in Rendova Harbor. It then waited for other LCIs in its flotilla to unload and clear the small beach [Log of LCI-65]. During the wait, Wilber continued the letter to Norma that he had begun on Pavuvu the previous afternoon.

> July 4 [about 11:45 a.m.] — Can you imagine I would ever celebrate the Fourth [of July] on a boat. We are waiting to unload now and have been waiting for three hours. This is a lovely little harbor with little cocoanut plantations on parts of the shore. Back inland, the mountains tower into the clouds. Nearby our artillery is firing on the enemy installations across from us. We have not yet been committed and the men are thrilled to hear their sister unit [192nd Field Artillery Battalion] firing in battle. There are a lot of questions such as "Are they really firing at the Japs?" They can hardly believe that they finally have reached that phase....
>
> I have told you war is mostly waiting, mud, and work. Our work is ammunition. The estimated amount of ammunition we fire in one day's combat is sixty tons. So you can guess at the amount of work our men have been doing lately. They have loaded and unloaded this ammo so often that all they want now is a chance to shove it in the breech of a howitzer and kiss it goodbye.

LCI-65 beached on Rendova at 12:20 p.m. on July 4 and troops and supplies were unloaded. Unfortunately, Rendova had become saturated with men, vehicles, and supplies. The vehicles moving goods on the beaches became mired in the deep soft mud and new troops could not be accommodated. Wilber was ordered to re-embark his troops and equipment and to establish them on a small offshore islet called Barabuni at the entrance to Rendova Harbor. In a letter he wrote to us—Norma forwarded it to Valerie and me—over the next two days, he described what transpired next.

July 5, 1943 [Probably early a.m. on Barabuni Island] — I was told to hold my former ship if possible. You can picture me dashing out into the ocean waving my arms and yelling "Bring that ship back to shore." Valerie would love this war because that is just what I did....

The skipper, a young navy lieutenant from Richmond, Va., named [Lt. Christopher] Tompkins was a bit upset and said he would have to get an OK from the commodore. I gave a few generals as my authority so he started to signal to the commodore about my problems. The answer was "wait" so we did and soon found out why.

Just then from sixteen to twenty four Jap bombers Mitch 97s came over us. They had a formation like this [sketch] and were beautiful silver birds. I could see when they dropped their bombs way up high and noticed how the sun glinted on them as they fell. They looked like little drops of mercury. At first, as I stood on the deck, I thought about a slit trench for me, but they had forgotten to dig any in the deck. Next I considered jumping in the water but decided that was a bad place to be too. All this time (one second) those lovely little shiny bombs were sliding down a steep curve toward the ground. I was quite concerned that they appeared to be headed for our infantry nearby and was wishing them all luck possible. However an instant later I decided they would land on my troops. I was scared to death then at the thought of all those men.... About that time it suddenly dawned on me that I was in the wrong place so far as the bombs were concerned.

So your old man decided to get off the hatch cover he had been sitting on and very efficiently lay down on the deck against a steel bulkhead. The next thing I knew the hatch cover went bye bye and I found I was OK. The first bomb had landed on the other side of my battery [Wilber's troops on the beach], the second one along side my L.C.I. less than eight feet from me, and the others dropped in the harbor.... After it was all over I asked the Skipper what about getting on about our business. He said "Hell! We're sunk." I looked down the hatch and saw it was all torn to pieces inside and half full of water.... It seems I hold a record for this outfit, that of having a ship sunk under me in ten feet of water.

Seriously tho, Norma and Hale and Valerie, I thank each of you for the prayers that saved me from harm. It would only have been Divine protection for I was within less than ten feet of a five hundred pound bomb and only received one minor cut on my forehead. Less than four feet below me a hole six feet across was blown thru the steel side of the ship. My map case which I was holding has a hole thru it where a piece of steel about the size of a pea went thru it [and] thru my maps but failed to go thru the Firing Tables and tore around it and went on its way.

The 500-pound bomb had landed at 2:11 p.m. in the water between the two LCIs, the one Wilber was on (LCI-65), and the one alongside (LCI-24), and blew a large hole in the side of each. A photograph shows the two ships just off the beach listing toward each other. Wilber was hit by a small piece of shrapnel that lodged in his right eyebrow. A sailor on his ship was killed by shrapnel entering his forehead, and two on the adjacent LCI-24 were killed.

I was the only casualty in my battalion, and it has worked out well because I came wading out of the ocean with a bloody head and later a bandage that made me look like Capt. Kidd and went ahead about my business. Mainly I needed to keep going because of the tendency to be shaky. It has paid good dividends tho because the men have steadied a lot. One of the finest compliments I ever received was when one corporal rather shamefacedly said the men wanted me to know that after I was as "calm" as I had been, they would not worry any more about anything. He was a bit confused, but I was very flattered. They have no idea how scared I really was.

We got three other smaller boats that evening, and, when I gave the order to load and move out, the men really hove to. They didn't think much of that place and its Fourth of July fireworks. It's a great life. When we were in those cockle-shells and moving out to sea without a pilot to find an island none of us had seen and after being bombed, they sang "Roll Out the Barrell [sic]", "The F.A. Song" and the others. We landed that evening about dark [on Barabuni Island] and settled down to an all night job of unloading guns, trucks, and ammunition.

The skipper of the LCI-65, Christopher Tompkins, was still alive and well in 1983, at age 74. Thanks to Wilber's mention of his hometown, I found him and called. He told me the whole story of that attack including his memory of Wilber's presence there. The bombing was the most dramatic of his wartime experiences. Regrettably, I never met him in person. He died shortly after his 76th birthday in August 1985.

Wilber's life had nearly ended on that July fourth and could have, had his head been positioned one inch differently. But he carried on his duties, not missing a beat despite the painful head wound.

LCI-24 (left) and LCI-65 after the bombing attack, July 4, 1943, Rendova Island. A 500-pound Japanese bomb had landed and exploded between the two landing craft, penetrating the hulls of each and leading to significant flooding and listing. Three sailors were killed. Wilber was on the forward deck of LCI-65 only about eight feet from where the bomb landed. [PHOTO: U.S. NAVY, U.S. NATIONAL ARCHIVES 80-G-52772]

The landings on New Georgia Island would take place at Zanana Beach, five miles east of Munda Airfield (Maps 8, 9). The infantry would drive westward through the jungle to the airfield. The artillery would be situated on small offshore islands from which the guns could support the infantry all along its drive to Munda.

Wilber's job was to get his howitzers moved the six miles from Barabuni Island (off Rendova) to the small island of Sasavele (just off New Georgia Island), and positioned for firing. His officers had been laying out positions and communication wire on Sasavele during the previous several days. Already on July 5, his howitzers were being moved to Sasavele, one or two at a time in small boats, as Wilber described in this continuation of his July 5 letter.

> July 6 [actually late July 5] — We are still heaving ammunition but today [July 5] [was] a big day. Today I took onto Jap shores [at Sasavele Island] my first howitzer. Her name was Betsy Ann and I walked into the jungle and shed a few tears. This is the last time I make these boys heave this ammunition except into the breech of their guns....

Signal Corps wire crews of the 43rd Division (43rd Signal Company) landing on a New Georgia beach to establish a message center and communication system, July 6, 1943. Note the soldier to the left (arms raised) guiding in another craft. This, given the date, is surely at the tiny Zanana Beach, five miles behind Munda Airfield, where the 43rd Division made its landings over several days. [PHOTO: U.S. ARMY SIGNAL CORPS, SC 185878]

It takes an hour for a boat to travel from this island [Barabuni] to the position area island [Sasavele], so it is slow work. There has been no more bombing in my neighborhood. My head is improving normally. It was quite painful last night but is improving now to the stage of an ordinary headache.

On July 2, the first infantry troops of the 43rd Division had gone ashore at Zanana Beach, which hardly deserved to be called a landing beach because it could accommodate only a few boats at a time. By July 6, with the help of native scouts, the two infantry regiments, 169th and 172nd, were ashore and assembled with the division command post set up. Fortunately, there was little Japanese opposition.

July 6, 1943 [Barabuni Island]. — This is another day of work. My last howitzer is on the boat sailing for my position area, with another day's ammo. The boat I'm leaving here on will carry another and my anti aircraft guns. This is the part not in the movies or newsreels [news movies], but it is what counts in saving men's lives during battle.... [Lt. Earl M.] Payne had laid all our [communication] wire within our area before we arrived. [Capt. Dixwell] Goff had found and selected positions for all our installations and [Lt. Robert W.] Patenge had cut roads thru the jungle for all batteries. All this was done before we brought our troops in at all. They worked close behind the Infantry and of course were in some danger all the time....

My position area [Sasavele] will let me fire on the field [Munda], but that is a secondary mission for us, our primary one being to fire in support of the advance of our Inf. regiment [the 169th Infantry]. I must stop now

Wilber's first real battle was about to start.

13

"The enemy is all around you"
MUNDA ACTION, JULY–AUGUST, 1943

A fire direction center (FDC) for Wilber's artillery was established on Sasavele Island in a protected pit in the ground with telephone and radio connections to the front lines and to the three nearby batteries, each with its four howitzers. Each of the three battalions of the 169th Infantry on "mainland" New Georgia had artillery officers from Wilber's unit with them: a liaison officer and a forward observer. The observers were on the front lines with the foot soldiers. They would spot where artillery shells landed and communicate with the FDC by telephone or radio to make adjustments. Telephone wires had to run through the water and coral separating Sasavele Island and New Georgia. The coral and the Japanese were quick to damage the lines, so maintaining communications was a continuing challenge.

Wilber's operations officer (S-3) and executive officer (second in command), Maj. René DeBlois, ran the FDC, while Wilber was nearly always at the front with the infantry during the month-long drive on Munda Airfield. His letters were sparse during the heavy fighting, but he wrote about it during breaks in the action and later. He was at the front with the infantry almost continuously from July 8 to 25.

On July 7, the 169th Field Artillery began its support of the 169th Infantry as it moved from the trailhead at Zanana Beach toward the "line of departure" two miles to the west (Map 9). On July 8, Wilber went to a 10 a.m. meeting at the division command post on the mainland [169th FA Bn. Journal]. Perhaps it was there, waiting for the meeting to start, that he found time to write us. He would not write again for six days.

> July 8, 1943 — All yesterday and today we have been fighting [the Japs] to get in our L.D. [Line of Departure].... This is still not the attack proper, just the preliminaries....
>
> Right now I am sitting between high, high roots of a mahogany tree. Barker has been here several times to talk with me. He said he wished he had

as much confidence in the other battalions as in us. You have no idea what a man DeBlois is. He is doing a wonderful job…. My head is still improving [from the bomb wound] and I see no reason to be concerned about it.

The two regiments reached the line of departure, launched their attack, and in the next two days advanced southwestward another mile. There they encountered strong Japanese defenses that stalled the advance on about July 10, but intense fighting continued as the Americans attempted to take well-defended Japanese positions in the rolling hills. It was another two miles to the airfield at Munda.

Within those few days, American inexperience in jungle warfare led to severe demoralization in some units. Normal jungle noises were mistaken for Japanese nighttime harassment. Soldiers panicked at real and imagined threats. They wounded and possibly killed their own comrades with undisciplined knifings, shootings, and grenade throwing. Men abandoned their posts in large numbers, including officers and non-commissioned officers [Fushak]. Neuropsychiatric casualties, otherwise known as "combat fatigue" or "war neurosis," or nowadays as post traumatic stress disorder (PTSD), occurred in far greater numbers than in other combat situations, and the 169th Infantry—the unit Wilber's artillery unit was supporting—was the most affected.

In response to the stalled drive, heads fell. The commanding officer of the 169th Infantry, Col. John D. Eason, a good friend of Wilber's, was relieved of his command on July 11 along with other officers. Eason was replaced by Col. Temple G. Holland, a regular army officer. But the fighting continued as the Japanese and Americans fought for control of the local hills.

On July 13, Wilber returned to Sasavele for a brief respite, so brief that by his own account [letter 7/25/14] he did not shave or bathe. While there, on July 14, he learned that one of his forward observers, Lt. Payne, had been killed by Japanese machine-gun fire. He was the officer who had so competently set up the battalion communications in advance of the unit's arrival on Sasavele Island. That same day, Wilber wrote his first letter since July 8, a piece of subterfuge, as it told nothing of his present activities so he could mail it promptly. (He was holding his more detailed letters for later mailing when censorship for this action was lifted.)

July 14, 1943 — You probably have missed some of my letters for mail connections here are not yet very good. However this will probably get thru pretty promptly now. I am well and feeling good. The last two weeks have been pretty strenuous but we are doing our work as well as usual.

On this date, according to the citation for the Legion of Merit later awarded to him, "he supervised the direction of fire on 14 July, 1943, which helped the infantry to seize strategic Horseshoe Hill."

The high command made more changes to revive the stalled drive toward Munda. General Griswold, whom Wilber admired greatly, was brought in as XIV Corps commander on July 16 to oversee the New Georgia Occupation Force, and two regiments (148th and 145th) of the 37th Division were brought in from Guadalcanal to assist the 43rd Division along with the 161st Infantry Regiment of the 25th Division, Wilber's old Washington State guard unit.

The battle-weary 169th Infantry was relieved of combat duties on July 20 and returned to Rendova Island, piecemeal, for rehabilitation and replacement of men and equipment. It would be back in the fight on New Georgia less than a week later. [Ops. Report, 169th Inf. Rgt.; Miller, Cartwheel, pp. 137, 144, 147, 149]. Through all this turmoil, Wilber's unit, the 169th *Field Artillery,* stayed the course on Sasavele Island and continuously supported infantry regiments in the line, the 148th, the 145th, and for a short period, the 161st, as well as the 169th.

Wilber wrote his next letter, this one to me, after a gap of nine days. In it, he described his second wounding. He was still in the front lines on New Georgia. Preparations for an attack on July 25 two days later were nearing completion.

> July 23, 1943, Dear Son — I thought you might like to get a letter written on a battlefield during a battle. Just now things have quieted down right here. However there are some Jap snipers in the trees around me. The men shoot one out every so often. Some fall; some are tied up [in the tree] so they stay. I have a very satisfactory slit trench with poles and dirt over it. I am in it now.
>
> I told you I was wounded by a bomb on the Fourth of July but that it didn't amount to much. On the tenth, I was scratched in the ribs by a Jap bullet. Again it was nothing and is all healed now. I have the bullet for a souvenir. It came in thru my jacket, hit me in the side, and [amazingly!] dropped in my pocket.

(I had this very bullet for some time. It was bent and so had struck some hard object before striking Wilber.) He continued the letter the next day.

> July 24 – [Corps commander General] Griswold was in the next foxhole to mine the other day. I was reintroduced to him as commanding the "finest g– d– artillery in the world," by the infantry commander, Colonel Holland. I appreciated that and said the Lord had been leading me by the hand. He [Griswold] said "I am well aware that you are adding a lot of high technical ability and skill to that. I'm glad you are here Bradt."
>
> The Bn. is doing a great job and I hope we continue to do it. Things are going well with me. I know your and Valerie's and Norma's prayers are pro-

tecting me. Don't let Norma worry about me. I am taking care not to be foolish, and beyond that I am trusting God to do with me what needs to be.

It appears that Wilber really did trust in God. He was also proud that Griswold knew who he was. And his pride in his unit was justified. During the Munda action, the 169th Field Artillery hurtled 28,975 rounds of high explosives toward the front lines [letter 8/5/43 and Barker p. 62], each with great precision. A minor pointing error or a slip in procedure on any one of those rounds could have killed and wounded American soldiers, and this went on day after day and night after night. The gunners, together with the telephone linemen, surveyors, forward observers, and others who constantly supported them, made it all possible.

The next day, July 25, the attack on the Munda defenses with the reorganized forces began. It was slow, difficult going; the Japanese use of pillboxes with overlapping fields of fire, along with the lack of visibility in the jungle, hindered reconnaissance and artillery observations. It would not be until August 5 that Munda would be securely in American hands. Remarkably, Wilber found time to write on the attack day.

July 25, '43, Dearest Norma and children — This is another letter that cannot be mailed until after this action is ended. This is a hot day and is the big push we hope is final. I have been at the front since the sixth except for one day when I returned to the Bn. Goff is here with me and has been most of that time.

This morning was a lot like the movie type of battles. Early this morning the FA began to fire a "preparation" fire. We lay in our hole and listened to the shells whistle over our heads. There were so many that it was a continuous hum. Then the Navy came by and added its share a little farther out from us and the air sent over Liberators with block-busters [large bombs]. Dix said he bet the Japs thought an attack might be coming up....

Once, the Japs came at us thru a narrow valley and Goff went out to the edge of our troops and adjusted our fire so close in to us that fragments were falling over us. He then walked the Bn. fire up that valley and swept it clear of Japs, trees and machine guns and we slept safely another night. Another day [Capt.] Dick Rainey brought down fire on a ridge the Japs held.... We took the ridge without the loss of a single man.

It hasn't been all officers [who have been heroic] either. Telephone linemen have laid and repaired wire under sniper fire and until they could hardly stand. Survey groups have surveyed thru the jungle while being shot at by Japs. Cannoneers have fired all day and thru the night every night for nearly three weeks, stopping now and then to shoot a Jap in their own area....

So you see why I am proud and humble about my Bn. DeBlois back at the Bn. and his Fire Direction Center go on forever and has saved my and scores of other lives both day + night by putting fire exactly where we asked for it. This is the stuff the 169th is made of.

Wilber was writing for the historical record as much as to his family. He knew that un-mailed letters in his possession would be forwarded to his family should he be killed.

In the midst of this drive toward Munda, on July 28, another of Wilber's forward observers, 2nd Lt. Arthur F. Malone of Jamaica Plain, Massachusetts, died in the line of duty. The following day, General Hester was relieved of command of the 43rd Division by order of General Harmon who felt that Hester had exhausted himself [Cartwheel, p. 149]. He was succeeded temporarily by Maj. Gen. John R. Hodge. And on this date, July 29, Wilber wrote his father from a front-line foxhole.

July 29, 1943 — Actually the jungle is far different from that taught in school. We seldom can see [the enemy] from the ground. Anyone in a tree is shot as a sniper. The enemy is all around you and often in your own area. I have stayed awake several nights and watched Japs near my slit trench. Their object seems to be to draw fire so they can wipe out our automatic weapons. We sat with pistols and bayonets and knives through their antics and used the silent methods preferably.

We adjust our fire (F.A.) by listening to the sound and carefully walking the bursts back to our observer. When the fragments begin to fall in front of him he moves it a little farther away and we go into fire for effect. We have had to make some hard decisions and try some very difficult targets such as firing in front of, in rear of, and on both sides of ourselves, or such as firing in a narrow lane through our own troops.

And he found humor in a foxhole, in a letter to me at Grace Camp.

July 29, 1943 — Also a few nights ago I was sleeping in my hole and a big land crab with a body about as big as the palm of my hand crawled across my chest. I knocked him off on to Capt. Goff's feet and he gave it a kick clear out of the hole. It was very dark and we couldn't see a thing but we heard it land and then some soldier in that direction made some very nasty cracks about whoever had thrown a crab on him. Goff and I lay there and nearly burst to keep from laughing out loud.

Another night it rained and we slept in two inches of very muddy water. Whenever one of us turned over there was a lot of splashing, and whenever one turned we all did because there were four of us in a hole dug for two. It's a good thing it's warm here for we are often soaked.

(I often credit this story—of the muddy foxhole—with my joining the U.S. Navy Reserve in 1951 during the Korean conflict, preferring that to the army or marines.)

On July 30, Wilber was ordered to the rear by General Barker. It is probable that his 23 days of nearly continuous service at the front was beginning to wear on him, and Barker sensed that. He arrived back at the relative comfort of Sasavele Island where his battalion was located [169th FA Bn. Journal]. There, he had time to reflect on what he had just been through. He first wrote a letter that could be mailed; it told nothing about the combat. The letters home had been rare, and he was anxious to get that one off to us.

The next day, he wrote a "real" letter to Norma. Recollections of his previous three weeks began to flow. His artillery on Sasavele was still firing in support of the advance toward Munda.

July 31, 1943 [Sasavele Is.] — I am answering your letter of July 9. It is such [a] sweet letter. I came back to the battalion position [on Sasavele Island] yesterday after three weeks [on New Georgia]. It is very quiet here compared to my forward command post. The howitzers pound away every little while and you sit comfortably above ground knowing the shells will land five miles away.

[When I was] forward, I would order fire, hear them wham thru the phone, next hear Ray [DeBlois] say "On the way", wait a few more seconds and the rumble of my guns would reach me across the jungle, and, almost immediately after, the shells will go "whish, whish whish-whispering and whirring" overhead. I take off my helmet and notice their direction and the time they seem exactly overhead, then a few seconds later the sound of the bursting shells comes back to my ears as a series of heavy explosions. I count seconds during that last wait and then calculate how far beyond me the shells landed and authorize the necessary shifts. Sometimes the bursting shells can be seen, but often in the jungle we are limited entirely to sound methods.

It is so quiet here [on Sasavele]. Birds are singing in the trees, lizards go by looking for ants, and an occasional monkey chatters in the nearby trees. At night the jungle noises change and seem to increase. Most of the signals and noise-making terrorisms that the marines credited to the Japs are really perfectly normal jungle noises. I have had reason to be very thankful for the days I spent in the jungle during these past months. When the jungle noises are normal at night, I know no Japs are moving near me. When they change and strange ones start, I know things are cooking.

A couple of weeks ago I heard the Jap whistle that I thought had usually been used by them as a signal to assemble. You know my ability to imitate birds [with] whistles. I gave the signal to disperse (as I thought it was meant).... I had a hunch their plans were a bit confused [by my whistles], for the whistlers gradually receded to a more distant area where they probably tried to decide who had his signals mixed. By the time they came back, my artillery fire was adjusted and the night was handled the American way.

Wilber wrote again from Sasavele, but this time from the fire direction center.

Aug. 2, '43, 9:30 P.M. — This is tomorrow's letter. I'm in the F.D.C. dugout listening to rain outside and news from our front line. This dugout is about six feet deep and is dug into the solid coral rock. Overhead are logs covered with sand bags filled with dirt and covered by a tent. It really is quite a snug place.... It's good to be under a roof during a rain and not in a slit trench in the jungle.

Fire Direction Center of the 169th Field Artillery Battalion in a pit on Sasavele Island. Major René DeBlois, the S-3 sitting at left center, is on the phone receiving reports from his forward observers. The assistant S-3, Capt. Russell Davis, is standing just behind him. The human "computers" for Batteries C, B, and A, are the three soldiers sitting in the rear. The "chief computer," Sergeant Easton, is behind them. They communicated with their batteries via the sound-powered phones hanging around their necks. In the foreground, a journal clerk records the action on a typewriter. [PHOTO: U.S. ARMY SIGNAL CORPS, IN BARKER, P. 106]

We are fortunate to have an Army Signal Corps photograph of the FDC of the 169th Field Artillery Battalion, the very place Wilber described.

> Barker called me this evening to assure himself I'm not up front again. He is right about it. My job there is done now, but I think he suspects I was just up there for fun. Anyway I have received some nice comments for some reason not quite clear to me.... I've met a Col Baxter too and gave him some artillery help in an emergency so he too is a booster for our Bn.... So, when [Baxter's] regiment [148th Infantry] went into the line [against the Japanese] he asked for us. We were already supporting Holland, and they had quite an argument about who got us.

After four intense weeks of fighting, Munda Airfield was pretty well in American hands on August 4, but it was officially captured on August 5. The relief was palpable. Wilber was still on Sasavele when he wrote again.

> Aug 4, 1943, 5:00 P.M. — This is a lovely time of day and I am sitting between two big trees in my jungle C.P. Our part of the campaign is about over.... It was fascinating, strenuous, and sometimes exciting. Because of my having stayed [at the front] in spite of two excuses [wounds] for getting back, I am in a very enviable position in the Bn. The men have decided that I may be a strict + hard boiled Major, but they have also decided I can be relied on in a pinch. I hope the reorganization period when I begin again to talk about sanitation and neatness isn't too much of a shock to them....
>
> This is the quiet night of all quiet nights. No firing tonight. 9:30 P.M.... That probably means the official end of this campaign for us.

The next day, Wilber found time to write separate letters to Norma, me, and Valerie, each with a different tone.

> Aug. 5, 1943 9:00 A.M. Lover Mine — Yesterday my boys shot down two "Zeros" [Japanese fighter planes].... All in all they are pretty pleased with themselves.... I wish I could have kept those letters I buried up front for there is much you mentioned that I have not answered. They were sure welcome. The U.S. mail does go thru even during battle.

Norma, now under cover, still wrote frequently. Unfortunately—in fact, tragically—her voice remains buried deep in the dirt of New Georgia Island in the Solomons and elsewhere in the Pacific, from New Zealand to Japan.

> Aug. 5, 1943, Dear Son Hale — You would like one of my officers, named [Lt. Donald] Mushik. He is a 1st. Lt. He worked for about two weeks conducting our fires from a hill that the Japs could both see and shoot to. Day

after day while he was talking over the telephone I would suddenly hear a loud crash on the phone, then he would say "Gemeny!" and there would be silence for a while, then he would be back saying "200 left. 100 over" which means the last volley we fired was 200 yards left and 100 yards beyond where we wanted the next one to fall. I would guess he was shot at fifty times a day, sometimes by rifles, sometimes by mortars and occasionally by a high velocity dual-purpose gun. He was wounded in the arm and didn't tell me. I was told tho and sent him back to the rear to have it dressed and to get a rest. Two days later I sent for him again and he went back on his hill.... I am going to recommend him for a decoration.

Another of my officers named Bert [Heidelberger] was on another hill for several days. The Japs held a hill that overlooked us and they kept firing mortars and machine guns at us. Just at that time, we couldn't spare troops to capture this hill so Bert would clean them out with our artillery fire.... We called that particular mission "Charlie One" because it was #1 for "C" battery.

Sadly, Heidelberger later became the third observer of the 169th Field Artillery to be lost to enemy fire.

In the letter to Valerie, Wilber talks comfortably with her about his world. He no longer tries to make awkward conversation about her friends and school.

Aug. 5, 1943, 8:00 P.M. — How is the Young American Travel Girl? I imagine you must have had a pretty busy time in Washington. What did you think of the statue of Lincoln? I thought he was really still sending a message to me when I saw it....

The Japs don't like our artillery fire. One day there were a lot of them on a hill where our boys couldn't get at them. Capt. Rainey decided he would help the Japs get closer to us. So he dropped our shells well behind them at first, then closer to us and kept moving them closer and closer to us. Pretty soon a lot of them were running to get away from the bursting shells. They should have stayed in their holes to be safest. However, they got excited and ran toward our soldiers just as if they were attacking us except they had thrown away their guns. As soon as they were close enough our infantry went to work on them, and pretty soon "no more Japs" were there.

The "no more Japs" seemed pretty callous stuff to be writing to a 12-year-old girl. Wilber seemed willing to voice (confess?) to Valerie his depersonalization of human life without fear of reproach. She was his most unquestioning fan.

Here he tells Norma sad news of their Washington State friends of the 161st Infantry.

Aug. 7, 1943 — A nice young corporal, now 1st Lt. [Kenneth P.] French that you may remember and Cris fought their last fight. I know how you will feel about Cris and we felt the same way. Don [Downen] and [Lt. Col. Robert W.] McCalder felt it pretty strongly. McCalder had lived with Cris for quite a while.

Lt. Louis K. Christian had been a close family friend when we lived in Pullman, Washington. McCalder was later killed at Balete Pass in Luzon, in the Philippines, on April 29, 1945.

Don looks tired (this was his first day after the job was finished) but well. He wears a mustache and seems highly regarded by his men and fellow officers. It is just like having a brother here to see him.

The tragedy and horror of battle are chillingly on exhibit here. Donald Downen wrote me in 1981 about how Christian (Cris) and French had died. Christian was wounded by an American mortar shell that fell short. He died of blood loss at the aid station with Don at his side on July 27. Lieutenant French was crushed by a withdrawing American tank that backed over him and three of his men on July 28 during a tank attack. Christian and French were both posthumously awarded the Distinguished Service Cross: Christian for eliminating a concealed Japanese machine gun and French for assisting a tank attack two days before his death. Recall that Lieutenant Malone, Wilber's forward observer, was also was killed on July 28.

(I visited Don Downen at his home in Pullman, Washington, in 1986. He was full of memories of Wilber and their meetings in the Solomons. He was most interested in the Wilber-Norma story. They had been his close friends and neighbors in Pullman 50 years earlier. Don died in 2001.)

On August 10, General Hodge, C.O. of the 43rd Division, returned to his Americal Division and later became a corps commander. Gen. Harold R. Barker, Wilber's superior, became acting commanding general of the 43rd Infantry Division [Barker, p. 83]. It was unusual for an artillery commander and especially a national guardsman to be given command of an infantry division. Barker's aggressive and fearless pursuit of excellent performance must have appealed to Griswold and Harmon. And it was apparently just what the 43rd Division needed; the capture of Munda had not been accomplished with the alacrity the generals had expected. But the artillery performed well.

Aug. 11, 1943, Dear Norma — Barker was very embarrassed the other day when he felt he had to commend his Bn. C.O.s. He hemmed + hawed and said he was no good at saying that sort of thing and ended by saying

Wounded, probably from Munda, being evacuated from Rendova to a PBY Catalina seaplane for flight to a hospital, July 1943. [PHOTO: CHARLES D'AVANZO]

"Anyway you know as well as I do you did a good job." So that was that. I take it "we done OK."

Barker was much more at ease and effective when profanely castigating his officers for their shortcomings and failures.

The capture of Munda Airfield was not the end of combat in the New Georgia group for the 43rd Division. A sudden crisis in the form of a Japanese ambush was now thrust upon the division.

During the drive to Munda Airfield, Allied forces were active in the Mediterranean and in the Soviet Union. The German offensive for Kursk, begun on July 5, was stopped and reversed by Russian counterattacks on July 12 and August 3, which then drove westward some 150 miles to the Dnieper River. On July 10, U.S. and British troops landed in force on four beachheads of southeast Sicily. Two weeks later, on July 25 with fighting raging in Sicily and Kursk, the Italian upper classes arrested Mussolini and began secret negotiations with the Allies, hoping to forestall a German occupation and defense of Italy.

By mid-August 1943, Sicily was completely neutralized. Negotiations between Italy and the Allies continued as Allied forces prepared to invade Italy proper. In the Solomon Islands, on August 15, Allied troops landed on Vella Lavella, northwest of New Georgia and Kolombangara, thus bypassing the Japanese forces on Kolombangara (Map 3).

14

"It was a depressing and unfortunate affair"
BAANGA ISLAND ACTION, AUGUST 1943

The second phase of the Solomon campaign for the 43rd Division was the capture of Baanga Island, a scant three miles west of the now-American Munda Airfield (Map 10). Reconnaissance on August 11 had located enemy troops on Baanga who could threaten the airfield. Company L of the 169th Infantry attempted to land on a beach in a cove on Baanga on August 12. It encountered machine gun fire from several locations and withdrew, leaving 34 men stranded on the beach. Wilber's letter six days later told what happened next.

> Aug 18, 1943 — I'm in business [combat] again. One of our cleanup jobs [Baanga Island] is in process. The battalion was not in that area but Barker and I were. He is acting Division commander now, so he temporarily tossed the [division] artillery into my hands.... We had artillery fire from two borrowed batteries within two hours and eventually worked in another battalion and started to cut some grass [with artillery] for the "doughboys."

On August 14, in an attempt to reach the stranded men, a "depleted" company of 42 men (probably from the same Company L) landed north of the cove and drove west and south (Map 10). Wilber sent Heidelberger and several men with them to provide artillery support. The company encountered resistance and returned to battalion lines the next day leaving six wounded behind. According to Wilber's eloquent oral account after he had arrived home in 1945, the infantrymen had panicked and abandoned their wounded.

Among the wounded left behind were the artillery observer, Lieutenant Heidelberger, and three of his party. Heidelberger and Cpl. Norbert F. McElroy did not survive. Heidelberger was reported missing for some time after his body was found because of difficulties in identifying it. He was not officially declared killed until November.

Other attempts to dislodge the Japanese by the 169th Infantry on Baanga also failed. On August 16, elements of the 172nd Infantry were brought in, and they arrived singing as they marched toward the front. It was a heartwarming and encouraging sound, as Wilber recollected in 1945, "We knew it was going to be OK." Finally, on August 21 the stranded soldiers were reached, a full nine days after being stranded. Only four survived, 20 were dead, and ten others had managed to swim away from the beach. The Japanese finally evacuated Baanga by boat on August 21 and 22. Wilber later [letter 10/22/43] wrote Norma, "I never wrote up the battle of Baanga for you. It was a depressing and unfortunate affair in several ways."

The command of the 43rd Division changed yet again on August 21. Command of the division was assumed by infantryman Brig. Gen. Leonard F. Wing, the assistant division commander, who, as a consequence, would soon be promoted to major general. Wing remained commander of the division, which came to be known as the "Winged Victory Division," through the rest of the war.

Lt. Norbert J. Heidelberger, a forward observer of the 169th Field Artillery Battalion killed in action on Baanga Island, August 15, 1943. Wilber felt his loss deeply. He wrote Heidelberger's mother upon his death and several times later including on the next two anniversaries. [PHOTO: COURTESY OF CARA K. HEIDELBERGER.]

After the Japanese evacuation of Baanga, Wilber recalled more aspects of the Baanga and Munda actions for his father.

> Aug 22, 1943 — The [Baanga] action was particularly interesting to me because Barker was acting as Division commander and I was the only other artillery commander present when things started.... I guess the high spot in the Baanga I. action for me as an individual was the fact that I located, adjusted my artillery fire on, and knocked out the two biggest Jap guns yet found in this area.

Wilber expanded on this event in a later letter to me.

> November 7, 1943 — It was about five in the morning and we [Davis and I] woke up saying 'That firing doesn't sound like ours.' We jumped out

of our foxhole and ran down to the beach [at or near Kindu Point] and saw the flashes from these guns. He had started too early and it was dark enough to let his flashes show. I grabbed the phone and said in it '907-Ten volleys.' Then to another battalion, '905 is 200 right 500 short. Fire at will.' Four minutes later the Jap guns were thru for this war.

Two days later, Wilber went there to see the guns. (Forty years later when I visited, they were still there.) The letter continued with more insight into the Munda action.

Of course you have read the wild horror tales told by the marines of Guadalcanal. I had all the same experiences and found the facts much less vivid.... Sometimes they [the Japanese] show a childish tendency to perform antics. One night one dropped a fish line and hook between the logs over the foxhole where one of my Lts. was sleeping (?). He could have dropped a grenade and the Lt. was ready to shoot if he made any sudden moves.... Anyway my Lt. pulled on the string; the Jap pulled; they repeated this several times until my Lt. cut the string and kept the hook. Mr. Jap left with a few very disgusted jabbers.

Wilber with a coastal-defense Japanese five-inch (naval) gun his artillery put out of action August 17, 1943. This was one of two guns emplaced by the Japanese on Baanga Island to defend the approaches to Munda Airfield. [PHOTO: U.S. ARMY SIGNAL CORPS, 161-43-9009, 8/19/43]

It's a weird war and a lot different from the European type either past or present. The fact that so few prisoners are taken (I have only seen two) is because of a fight to the finish attitude on both sides. No one wants to be a prisoner.... I hope this debunks and explains a bit of the flashy news stories and gives you an idea of what I'm doing now.

Wilber wrote more on this to Norma.

> Aug 24, 1943 — In some ways they [the Japanese] are shrewd; in others they react as a ten-year-old boy would if he found he could run in and out of the enemy camp without being caught. Much of the nightmare stories are based on these antics and a failure to realize what they are.
>
> For example at night I have had single Jap soldiers creep up to my slit trench + peep in. I would be covering him with a pistol + he could drop a grenade on me, but no, he would only be curious + go on. I leave the individual combat to the infantry if I can, and try to stick to my business of artillery.
>
> It isn't all fun or screwy. There are tragedies and mistakes and there is mud and work and sleepless nights and cracked nerves but the best, or rather worst, stories come from the news boys or those who imagine more than they see.... The hardest part for me is to send my friends + men + officers where I know they may die.

Should we believe the stories of Japanese "running in and out of the enemy camp" like ten-year olds? These are dispassionate observations by a mature objective observer. It was, as he said, a "weird war" and "screwy." I choose to accept his testimony at face value. But Wilber also reveals the other reality, that "there are tragedies and mistakes and there is mud and work and sleepless nights and cracked nerves."

Wilber's battalion had moved from Sasavele to a position north of Bibilo Hill, Munda, during the Baanga action.

> Aug 28, 1943 — After a few busy days, I'm back at letter-writing again. We have been in an ideal artillery situation lately. A good bivouac area, sunshine, breezes, no Japs near.... I have the children's winter addresses now. Hope CBS can't get along without you. I take it you now are on the "little job as pianist." Hope you like it + good luck.

Here is our first hint of what Norma was telling Wilber, namely that she had applied for a job at CBS and was now working as a pianist. It was probably all complete fiction. Wilber was beginning to worry about her well-being.

Aug. 31, 1943 — I'm a bit confused about your residence. Do you live at the [Hotel] Altamont? You say it's too far to go after rehearsals. Where do you stay? Don't get yourself too much adrift, so you can get lost by some accident and not be missed.

Valerie and I finished our summer camps in late August. Monte met us and took us directly to our boarding schools in New Jersey, probably traveling from Washington, D.C., to do so. He may not have intended to adopt Norma's entire family, but he certainly was rising to the occasion.

I arrived at St. Bernard's a week or so before school opened and was immediately recruited to help with farm tasks. The students were a rougher bunch than at Grace Church School, so I rapidly learned more about self-reliance and self-defense there. During the school year I was thrust into many new areas: football (reluctantly), caring for cows and horses, scouting, and print shop work. Saint Bernard's School was not as academically challenging as Grace Church School where I had, for example, studied Latin the previous two years. After one month at St. Bernard's, I was moved up from 7th to 8th grade, where I also did well. Each class had 10 or 12 students.

Valerie arrived at her boarding school, St. John Baptist in Mendham, New Jersey, for her first full year away from home at age 11. The school was run by nuns of the order of St. John Baptist, who dressed at the time in the full regalia my generation associates with Catholic nuns. The isolated hilltop rectangular school building and the nuns who ran it could make a forbidding impression. However, Valerie found it a welcoming home.

x · o · ø · o · x

Wilber was far from the worlds of his children. The Baanga operation was barely completed when his attention was drawn to the next island, Arundel, just 1000 yards west and north of Baanga. Wilber's combat experiences in Arundel turned out to be unlike any he had encountered before.

15

"My whispering chorus of observers"
ARUNDEL ISLAND ACTION, SEPTEMBER 1943

Arundel Island (today called Kohinggo Island, Map 10) was probably named by Maine sailors after the town by that name in Maine. It is about ten miles long and five miles wide. Arundel provided an approach to the nearby volcanic island of Kolombangara to the north, a Japanese stronghold, and the location of yet another Japanese airfield on its southern tip at Vila. The airfield was just across Blackett Strait from Arundel.

Since about August 29, the 172nd Infantry had been driving northward up both the east and west coasts, intending to drive the Japanese from the island. Wilber's artillery, the 169th, initially supported this effort from its position near Munda Airfield.

As the advance moved northward beyond the range of the 169th's howitzers, the battalion was moved northward in two sections to keep within artillery range of the action. Wilber's Battery A was placed at Bustling Point on the west side of Arundel with artillery from other units, while Batteries B and C moved to Piru Plantation at Ondonga, a part of mainland New Georgia. The Bustling Point artillery was called the Western Force and the Ondonga artillery the Eastern Force. When firing on Japanese on Arundel, the two forces were firing roughly toward the other, a highly unusual situation. [History Rpt of 169th FA Bn.; see also Barker, p. 100.]

In early September, troops of the 172nd Infantry had reached northern Arundel and were encountering Japanese pockets of resistance. In response, the Japanese sent reinforcements into northern Arundel from Kolombangara Island. By September 10, small units of American and Japanese troops were in contact in the dense jungle of northern Arundel, but with no well defined lines. It was a confusing situation for both sides. American artillery, placed on either side of Arundel—the Western and Eastern Forces—relied on good forward observations so as not to fire on friendly troops. It was the job of the artillery to get observers to these infantry units, not an easy task in the jungle terrain.

Ammunition being loaded onto a truck at Bustling Point, Arundel Island, September 24, 1943. These shells were for the 155-mm howitzers of the 192nd Field Artillery Battalion. Getting the shells to the guns was the hardest part of the job. The never-ending hard work was done by the enlisted artillerymen so much admired by Wilber. [PHOTO: US ARMY SIGNAL CORPS, SC 259147]

On September 13, Wilber accompanied a patrol to bring artillery support to an isolated American infantry unit and ended up at the command post of a completely different regiment and division (the 27th Infantry, 25th Division) at Bomboe Village in northwest Arundel. It consisted of a few huts on a ridge overlooking the volcanic Kolombangara Island three miles distant. From there Wilber directed the Western Force artillery on Bustling Point about one mile to the southwest, while DeBlois directed the Eastern Force at Piru Plantation.

After Wilber's arrival at Bomboe Village, the Japanese on Kolombangara sent reinforcements to Arundel for a few days and later began evacuating them. Wilber's artillery was used to impede both actions, to support the infantry fighting on Arundel, and to bombard Kolombangara. It was a week full of high drama. On September 16, Wilber was in the midst of this action at Bomboe Village and gave Norma only hints of what was going on because of limited time and censorship.

> Sept. 16, 1943 — Here I am on another island [Arundel] again. This is at least a scenic spot. From my bunk (yes I have one), I can see a great tall volcanic mountain [Kolombangara]. I'm glad to report it is an extinct one and beautiful. The white clouds hang around the top of the cone which is a

little over a mile high. The sides are covered by the deep green of the jungle and the base by Japs. So I'm not doing any climbing over there.

Maw, I been shootin' some more Japs again. The old 169th [Field Artillery] just keeps rolling along. Now I'm with a regular [not National Guard] army infantry regiment [27th]. I just happened to come out of the jungle on their side of this island; the troops I had been supporting were on the other side. There [on this side], this Colonel [Douglas Sugg, C.O. of the 27th Infantry Regiment] was, so I introduced myself and was practically "hired on the spot." Gen[erals] Wing + Barker heard I was here + sent word up that anything I said was OK was good with them. So we sowed a few seeds of wrath in the suburbs of the Jap areas and still are. However in this action I'm operating from a nice quiet comfortable rear C.P. with hot meals and a bed.

While I was on this recent trek [through the jungle], the rumor was out that I was trapped so if you hear any such story don't be concerned. As Mark Twain said, "The report ... is very much exaggerated." Your spikes were invaluable again and I thanked you for them several times. It's often the little things that make the difference between continued good health and the possibility of trouble. Being sure footed is a real help.... I feel fine and don't want you worrying about my wounds or health. This is better for me physically than teaching in a U. [University]

Norma was the constant provider for Wilber, Valerie, and me, despite her self-imposed isolation. The various letters report her sending me candy at St. Bernard's, Wilber spikes, film, and pictures.

By the way Gen. Griswold [corps commander] again today told me I was doing a "fine piece of work here." Boy, Am I modest! However I do want you to know that the C.G. XIV Corps has so stated twice now. No raise in pay tho.

Wilber, still in Bomboe Village, wrote again to Norma.

Sept. 20, 1943 — Oh yes, I'm now an artillery Lt. Col. and am very busy being congratulated. Gen. Wing said it had been a long time earned which I thought was one of the nicest compliments I had ever heard.... I love you dearly, My Own. Don't be too lonely because I'm still with you.

Finally, the long deserved—as a battalion commander—promotion had come through. He celebrated his first time wearing the silver oak leaves of his new rank by having his photo taken with two other officers. Here Wilber surmised that Norma was lonely, which was surely the case. Even if she was with Monte and his mother,

Wilber (left), Maj. William N. Bailey, and Capt. Hugh E. Ryan on the occasion of Wilber's and Bailey's promotions (Wilber to lieutenant colonel and Bailey to major), on Arundel Island near the end of the action there, probably on September 20, 1943, when Wilber wrote of the promotion. This was the first time Wilber had worn the lieutenant colonel's leaves. [PHOTO: BRADT FAMILY]

Terkman, she was cut off from personal contact with everyone else, including her children and her own siblings. Although Wilber was unaware of her true situation, he wanted to support her, but he could not spend much time dwelling on it; he was heavily occupied with artillery business.

During the night of September 20 and 21, the Japanese completed their evacuation, but with a large loss of life due to American fire. The battle was over. Kolombangara was the next target, but it would be bypassed. This completed the Solomon Island campaign for the 43rd Division. Wilber remained at Bomboe Village until September 26 when he wrote to Valerie.

> Sept. 26, 1943 — Today I'm going back to my battalion and rest (?) for a while. The Battle of Arundel I. is over and I will go back to the rear until the next one starts. My job during battle is up front but we keep the guns back a good ways and hide them so the Japs cannot find them. Now that

everything is quiet again I'll move them into a good place and let them [his men] settle down for a little sleep.

Back at Ondonga, his troops would have several months of decompression, rehabilitation, and training, and Wilber would have the time to recollect and reflect on the just-completed three months of combat. For example, he drew on a published map the several locations of his artillery during its habitation in the New Georgia group (Map 11).

x·o·ø·o·x

Exactly one month after combat ended on Arundel, Wilber sat down to tell the story of his Arundel adventures in four long letters written on October 20–22. He wrote them on Ondonga Island where his unit was recuperating and on defensive duty. It is, to my mind, a most remarkable account and the single most coherent extended story among all his letters. I call it his "Arundel Story."

The following are excerpts from these letters. The entire account is in the *Wilber's War* trilogy.

LETTER 1, OCTOBER 20, 1943, MORNING

The next morning [September 13], I had seen that DeBlois [managing the artillery at Ondonga] was all set and went over to start Butler [a forward observer] and party in [to join] Naylor [the C.O. of an isolated infantry battalion].... He (Devine) [Executive of the 103rd Inf.] was sending a small patrol around the [Japanese trail] block to lay a new wire to Naylor. It was to be 21 men. They were all men who had been or still were sick. Two officers were along. I looked at Butler with his big grin and all at once he looked just like Heidelberger to me. I remembered it was Sept. 13 just exactly a month since I had sent Heidelberger into Baanga. It wasn't so cheering for he had been the third officer I had sent in not to come out.

Consequently, I said to Butler, "You act as liaison to Devine, and give me your sulfanilamide and First Aid Packet." He did, and I picked up a grenade and away we went across the lagoon. Devine had protested a bit because of the danger, but I felt I couldn't face just then the idea of a fourth officer being killed on my orders. He said it would be individual fighting and every man for himself if we hit the Japs. Anyway I went, and he apparently tried to clear himself of the responsibility by phoning the news back to Division that he advised against it, for it turned out to be considered quite something back there.

125

This scene was amazing: a field artillery battalion commander voluntarily heading into a perilous situation with an infantry patrol because of his fear that one of his junior officers would be lost. This was not his job and could have been viewed as foolhardy and reckless.

The trip to Naylor was a most interesting experience. It was probably not over three miles air line but it took from 9:00 A.M. to 6:00 P.M.... Capt. Haffner [was] in command.... We carried telephone wire [on a large spool] and laid it as we went, also a radio, for Naylor's seemed to be out. This, and the fact the men were not well and the need to go quietly, is why we went so slowly. I stayed near the radio in the file because that was my way to get DeBlois to put fire where I needed it. If we got cornered, I expected to get artillery fire on all sides and let the Japs figure the next move. That meant I had to know where I was all the time. There was no trail, guessing distance was mainly guess, and all I could do was take compass directions to the sound of my guns. Altho that varied a bit, I at least could tell something of my location....

That evening just before dark we reached Naylor, and I think he appreciated my being there.... He [Naylor] had been attacked seven times the preceding day and was low on ammunition and rations but had a local water supply. However he expected a quiet night because the Japs had left booby traps around him. It was a quiet night. We radioed our arrival back to Devine and went to bed in our hole. No noise, no rain, and it was a pretty good night....

Next we were told to join the 27th Inf. [Regiment, C.O. Col. Sugg], which had landed on the west shore of Arundel at Bomboe Village. That was all right except they had a strong group of Japs in front of them and between them and us. Also getting two fighting units together in the jungle without shooting each other up isn't done by the "Yoo Hoo!" method. So it was arranged by radio for us to fire an automatic rifle for ten rounds each fifteen minutes so Sugg's patrol (27th) could find us. It worked too, except all the Japs around found us too, which was OK if we liked it....

The Japs opened up on us a short time later with the heaviest small arms fire I ever underwent. They were on our front and one flank. It was really something to watch and hear. It would have been very comforting to use artillery but of course Haffner was out there somewhere [returning with his party], so that was only a last resort. So I lay there and tried to see the situation as clearly as possible just in case I should suddenly find myself in command. That is one of the hazards of being a Field Officer....

Now we moved to join Sugg.... It was on this move that we went thru a swamp that surpassed all my ideas of swamps. It was deep, slimy, stinking, sticky, sucking mud under about six inches of very nasty water. There were vines and rotten logs to climb over and really every step was over crotch deep. Several times I doubted if I could pull a leg out of the depth to which it had sunk. It would have been a bad place to have the Japs open up on me. However, they didn't, probably because our rear guard kept them busy where they were.

They finally joined one of Sugg's battalions. With Evans, the infantry battalion commander, were two 43rd Division artillery officers, Lieutenant Wild and 1st Lt. Ewart M. Blain, both well known to Wilber.

I found Wild and Blain with [Evans], and we started to do [artillery] business.... When I showed up, Lt. Wild said, "Who is with you?" I said "No one!" He said "Haven't you any party?" I said, "Nope, have you a place for me to sleep?" He did and I did under a bush.... The next morning (Sept. 15) ... I started back by water to the 169th FA Bn, but Sugg kidnapped me. That is the next chapter, and in the meantime I love you Sweet girl of mine.

LETTER 2, OCT. 20, EVENING
Writing under a gasoline lantern, Wilber picked up the story in a second letter.

Yes Dearest I'm back again. I arrived at Bomboe Village about ten o'clock [the morning of September 15] and went up to report to Sugg on what I knew of the forces opposing him.... Bomboe, was truly a lovely spot and must have been something particularly special before the war. I was told a missionary had lived there for years and developed it. However as a C.P., it was a bit public so far as the Japs were concerned and they did shell it now and then according to the reports I received on the way thru.... When I inquired of Sugg about boats, he said, "Oh, but you're staying here, Major."...

The days are a bit blurred that I spent with Sugg so I'll deal more with events than days. The first day or so were used in preparation for a main push and the getting up of supplies. We did some firing of a routine type and I placed officers and parties with all three of Sugg's [battalions].... I put [Mike Butler] on an island we call "No. 1" because it was ... only fifty yards from the Japs. There were other observers on other islands, some also close to the Japs. Each observer whether infantry or artillery had a phone and could report to the C.P. anything he saw. About this time the moon began to be very bright so we could see. Jap planes would fly over at night looking for our batteries and troops....

In the evening I would have all the observer phones and my phone to the Bailey Fire Direction Center [at Bustling Point] connected into a big party line. Just about dark the reports would start, usually in whispers so the Japs wouldn't hear them speak.... We fired at boats when they came out of coves, when they passed points, when they tried to hide in Vila River, when they went to Devil's Island, and then gave them our barrages when they tried to land on [nearby] Sagekarasa [Island]. I'll never forget my whispering chorus of observers....

Once an observer said there was a light on Devil's Island, so I said to Bailey "Put out the light on Devil's Island." Pretty soon four shells landed on D.I. and the light was out. Sugg had never seen artillery used to put out lights before.... Barker said, "It used to be the tanks, then boats, now planes. What's next for artillery?"

By such means we stopped the Jap reinforcements, and after two nights had Blackett Strait under control....

It's ten o'clock now Lover and I must get to bed. I love you, My wife.

LETTER 3, OCTOBER 21, EVENING

Wilber continued the story in a third letter. Japanese troops were still on the mainland of northern Arundel on September 16, as well as on the offshore island of Sagekarasa (Map 10).

Darling of My Dreams — Its seven again after supper, and I'm thru for the day....

The night before the first attack by Sugg's regiment was a busy one for me. I was up all night controlling and directing fire against boats, etc. It was my second such night, and Col. Sugg was worried about me and had planned for me to sleep during the day [but I didn't].... So I went back up the lagoon [by boat] with Sugg that A.M. It was lovely and quiet and peaceful, and the sun and water were fresh and clean and cheerful. We thought (and correctly) the Japs didn't know we had tanks nor that we expected to attack that morning.

It had always been Wilber's practice to stay near the action and the infantry commander so he could rapidly adapt his artillery to a changing situation.

The six tanks moved out with their machine guns and canister firing. All the machine guns in our lines started mowing down the bushes ahead of them and Tommy guns, auto rifles and M 1 rifles started searching for Japs. Our men ignore the tanks and fire at and around where they are, because the marines inside the tanks are safe, and fire close to them protects the tanks from any Jap trying to slip or throw mines under them.... The Japs had broken and taken to cover. As soon as their fire stopped, our men moved in and the Japs left. They don't face tanks, especially surprise tanks.

There were also tank attacks on the two following days, September 18 and 19. On the 18th, two American tanks were disabled by Japanese antitank gunfire [Estes, p. 52].... The Japanese battalion commander facing the Americans was Col. Seishu Kinoshita, whom I interviewed in March 1983, shortly before I visited Arundel, as I recount in the following Interlude (page 151).

The next morning [9:00 A.M., September 20] we hammered again on the door [of the west end of Sagekarasa Island] and it practically fell in. They were weaker all right. Ammunition was practically gone and so were a good many Japs....

It's 10:30 P.M. and I must stop. I hope this is interesting to you. Tomorrow or soon I'll wind this up. There "ain't" much more.

LETTER 4, OCTOBER 22, 1943, EVENING

It's evening again Darling ... Continuing and winding up the Arundel story.

By Sept. 19 the Japs were trying to get out of Arundel. The Sagekarasa route was closed to them but they could go out on a long peninsula which based [had its base] on the east side of Arundel and extended NW toward Kolombangara. Col. Ross ... was holding that side of Arundel, and [Sugg's] 27th Inf. and Naylor's battalion from the 172 Inf. [were] driving the Japs against Ross....

Such was the general picture. On my side I was still putting in sleepless nights and chasing around the various fronts in the day.... I had been ready to fire a preparation for the attack when [Senator Henry Cabot] Lodge, [Admiral] Halsey and a lot of brass [including corps commander Griswold] came in on the Bomboe Village C.P. I was low on ammunition and was tempted to proposition Halsey about [getting] a few more boats but thought better of it....

Griswold came over and said "Bradt it wouldn't hurt to have quite a little firing while we're here, if you have any targets that would justify the ammunition." I said "General, I'm awfully low in ammunition but I've plenty of targets so I'll do what I can."... And the shells whispered over while the celebrated guests discussed. We also started a fire or two on Kolombangara on the side and blew up a Jap ammunition dump at the same time. I announced each item of interest to G., and they were casually introduced in

From left, Adm. William Halsey, Jr. (area commander), Gen. Oscar Griswold (corps commander), and U.S. Senator (Massachusetts) Henry Cabot Lodge on a visit to forward areas of the New Georgia Island group, September 1943. This was taken the very day, September 19, of their visit to the 27th Infantry command post that Wilber described so humorously. Note the fancy overhead fringe on their well-appointed "admiral's barge" and the protective craft following them. [PHOTO: U.S. ARMY SIGNAL CORPS, SC 186140]

the conversation. When they left, G. looked over and nodded, quite pleased; I was really low on ammo for the next couple of hours....

When the Japs evacuated, all their Artillery opened up on us [to protect the evacuation]. But we outguessed them. We did not fire back at them except with one battery. With the other two, we just kept shooting at boats as if it was a nice quiet night. Some Fun. The next night, Sept. 22 [Sept 21/22], I slept all night.

"Some Fun"? Wilber expressed a different view in annotating his copy of an article about the Arundel action in the *Infantry Journal* (September 1944, p. 20]. At the description of Japanese "massed artillery fires" that night, Wilber wrote, "Not Fun."

The next day [September 22] we knew the job was done.... The prisoner said the Jap regimental commander [Colonel Satoshi Tomonari] was killed by a shell burst on his first day on Arundel.... I think I saw Col. Tomonari's grave. The Japs had built it up with coral and flowers into an unusually imposing mound. No name post was placed on it.

So ends the battle of Arundel as seen by your Old Man.

The American artillery killed the revered regimental commander of the Japanese 13th Regiment and two of its battalion commanders. The loss of the highly regarded Colonel Satoshi Tomonari was a grave and dispiriting blow to the Japanese. Kinoshita, the final commander, was proud of the fact that he and his troops never surrendered. They spent the rest of the war isolated in the mountains of Bougainville and were taken into custody by the Australians only after Japan capitulated in 1945.

x·o·ø·o·x

Combat for the 43rd Division in the Solomon Islands was finally over. For his service in the Solomons, Wilber was awarded the Purple Heart with cluster in recognition of his two wounds and also the Legion of Merit, a high-ranking medal for exceptional service.

He and his unit were further recognized by a personal letter of congratulations from Colonel Files, the executive officer of the 43rd Division Artillery. He noted that Wilber's battalion supported six different infantry regiments (169th, 172nd, 145th, 148th, 27th, and 161st) during the campaign, when one was the norm. Wilber's battalion also received unit commendations from the commanders of the 148th and 145th Infantry Regiments of the 37th Division. Wilber also received a personal commendation from Colonel Sugg, the commander of the 27th Infantry Regiment, for his work with that unit on Arundel.

Wilber's battalion, in fact, performed well above the average in several measureable ways. The 169th Field Artillery Battalion saw more combat, fired more rounds, and suffered more casualties than any of the other three field artillery battalions in the division. Purple Hearts, given for a wound, were awarded to 15 of his men compared to four, one, and none in the other three battalions. In addition Purple Hearts were awarded posthumously to four of Wilber's men.

The casualties indicated that Wilber had indeed been an aggressive commander, as Colonel Files noted. Was he overly so? He always claimed to weigh the risks against the benefits of his own personal choices, which he certainly did as well for his own men. Wilber took the loss of his men to heart and blamed himself especially for the loss of Heidelberger. The ultimate benefit was, of course, the saving of infantrymen's lives, and his artillery did that in abundance.

The number of war neuroses (akin to today's PTSD) in the 43rd Division during the Munda action was unusually high compared to those in other units under comparable circumstances. Many of the cases developed in the first days when the 169th Infantry was first exposed to the nighttime jungle sights and sounds. The causes of these problems were varied and systemic, according to a 1999 study of the 43rd Division's experiences by a student at the U.S. Command and General Staff College [Fushak, 1999]. According to Fushak, major lessons of the past, from the very beginning of military history, about the value of unit cohesion and neuropsychiatric casualties were simply forgotten or neglected. Fortunately, the experience of the 43rd Division led immediately to improved training and better care of these casualties.

Wilber was with the 169th Infantry during those early days, and his letters showed little sign of the discouragement and setbacks that the regiment must have felt. (In contrast, he did allude to such problems in the Baanga action.) I gather from this that despite the problems, all was not despair and gloom. Wilber and most of his infantry colleagues swallowed the setbacks and continued to move ahead as best they could. The 43rd Division earned its spurs at Munda and performed creditably throughout the rest of the war, apparently without excessive neuropsychiatric casualties.

X·O·Ø·O·X

As the New Georgia campaign ended for the 43rd Division in late September, Valerie and I were adjusting to our New Jersey boarding schools; it was our first extended time away from home. At the end of the Arundel action, Norma was only a few weeks shy of her due date.

Italy surrendered unconditionally to the Allies on September 3, 1943, the same day Allied troops came ashore in Calabria, in the boot of Italy. On September 9, British and American troops landed farther north at Salerno, on the west coast south of Naples. The German response was to occupy Italy, take Italian soldiers prisoner, brutally put down any resistance, and most important, to resist the Allied landings. The Salerno beachhead was in danger of being overcome by the Germans in the first week, but Allied air and naval support carried the day. It would not be until October 1 that the Allies would enter Naples and begin the slow drive up the Italian peninsula toward Rome against strong German defensive positions.

In the USSR, by September 30, the Russians had secured five bridge-heads across the Dnieper River. The summer campaign was a disaster for the Germans, and as winter approached the conditions would again favor the Russians.

The tempo of the bombing of German cities was increasing. The bombing of Hamburg by the British late in July 1943 led to a "firestorm" that killed 23,000 of its inhabitants. Industrial areas were the prime targets, but the bombing of civilian areas as a means of impacting morale was becoming common in the campaign against Germany. This practice had been initiated in Europe by the German raids on London in 1940, and was notably unsuccessful. American bombers of the Eighth Air Force in England were joining the British in the bombing campaign. German resistance to these raids with anti-aircraft fire and fighter planes was fierce. A raid by 229 B-17 bombers on a ball bearing factory in central Germany on August 17 led to the loss of 36 of those planes.

16

"Swan doesn't polish those insignia very much"
ONDONGA, NEW GEORGIA, OCTOBER–NOVEMBER, 1943

With the end of the Arundel combat, the different components of the 43rd Division moved to defensive positions on the New Georgia and Russell Island groups. Wilber's outfit remained on Ondonga, but Battery A stayed on Bustling Point in the Provisional Battalion under the command of DeBlois, Wilber's executive officer. His absence at Ondonga gave Wilber a heavy additional workload. The 43rd Division's objective was initially defensive as well as

Wilber on the phone in his "office" at Ondonga. To his right was his "command car."
[PHOTO: CHARLES D'AVANZO]

rest and rehabilitation of the soldiers and equipment. With time, as the threat of attack receded, the focus of attention became training for the next combat.

Wilber's letters told of a promotion party, and he began to reflect on the past three months.

> Oct. 3, 1943 — It's Sunday + I am giving, with our Doctor [Charles D'Avanzo] who is also just promoted, a little party to my officers and Downen.... It's our first chance to sit down together. Time 3:00 P.M. this afternoon. I wish you could be the hostess....

Officers of the 169th Field Artillery Battalion at the promotion party hosted by Wilber (at head of table) and Charles D'Avanzo, the battalion medical doctor, at Ondonga on October 3, 1943. The large canvas tarpaulin in the background was probably where Wilber and Captain Rainey lived. If so, the canvas covered two smaller tents [letter 10/30/43]. These were the officers who carried the 169th through three months of Solomon Islands combat. [PHOTO: CHARLES D'AVANZO]

I wear my insignia in combat so the infantry enlisted man will know the artillery is really right with them. It's heart warming to see the look of appreciation on the face of a tired, dirty and maybe discouraged private who is on the way forward to possible blackout [death]. However I must admit Swan doesn't polish those insignia very much, and I haven't complained at all.

(Snipers tried to identify officers as the more valuable targets.)

X·O·Ø·O·X

Norma, now within weeks of her due date, apparently had written Wilber a reassurance he did not know he needed. He responded with poetic fervor.

I know you will never leave me. You haven't a chance if you tried. You keep reassuring me, and I "ain't" even worried. You're hooked, Lady, for the duration. You are my most solid rock and I'm counting terribly much on you to be there when I come back. It is the most wonderful thing I ever knew to have you with me thru this war. The war seems so trivial beside your love for me. It gets noisy now + then, but the music of my Nana sounds clear + pure thru the noise + confusion to me.

Norma, it appears, was casting her lot with Wilber, not with Monte, and wanted Wilber to know it should he learn of her pregnancy. She must have feared that Wilber would leave her if he did.

X·O·Ø·O·X

In his October letter to his father, Wilber provided additional insights into jungle warfare.

Oct. 4, 1943 — For September, the 169th went into business again on Arundel I. There we practically eliminated the Jap 13th Inf., which was rated as one of Japan's best two regiments.... They may get me pretty soon, but I have already credited myself with a Jap regimental commander and two Jap battalion commanders of the 13th Inf. and also the complete destruction of the C.P. of the Jap 229th Inf. [on Baanga Island]. Consequently even if they do catch up with me, I'll feel the score is still in my favor....

I don't know if this interests you or not, but I'm sure a lot of hokum gets in the papers from some of our returned "heroes." My predecessor [Lt. Col. King] is one. He, it now seems, is home because of a severe

136

wound received in Guadalcanal. Actually he was wounded by the rumor that we were going into Munda. Anyway he has since been released from the Army and is making many speeches on "Slow Starvation in the S. Pac" "The Horrors of Life in the Jungle" "Jap Jungle Tactics," etc. All get into the paper and come back here.

This was pretty devastating commentary about his former commanding officer, but seemingly justified if the facts are correct.

Once on the Munda job I went without [sleep] for six days and nights. More recently on Arundel, I slept for five days and nights only between 3:00 A.M. and 6:00 A.M., thereby confusing a lot of Japs and amazing the infantry I was supporting. So I feel fine but tired now.

Indeed, he does look tired in an identification photo taken at Ondonga October 10.

A surprising opportunity presented itself to Wilber. He was offered the position of executive of an *infantry* regiment, with the likelihood of being its commander within six months, which would merit a promotion to full colonel. He turned it down.

Oct. 17, 1943 — I'm still an artilleryman and expect to stay so. The C.O. 169th Inf. growled at me about it, but I said I'd be up front with him anyway [as his artillery commander], to which he agreed. I finally decided I was too tired to tackle a new field this late in the war.... So I didn't take it. If I can come home Lt. Col. of F.A. in good standing, I'm going to be content and won't even wonder if I could have been Col. of Inf.

There are some compensations to being in the 169th FA Bn. One officer in the 43d Div. Arty and the General are to have two weeks leave in New Zealand as a rest. It is a reward and recognition too of outstanding service in combat. Barker offered it to me. I declined and asked for the chance to name one of my officers....

I have felt bad about Cris and French too. Both died within two hundred yards of me [during the July 25 attack toward Munda Airfield]. The old group is diminished. Those two are dead, Langley transferred, Hudleson evacuated with rheumatism, Faler with malaria, Lamont with machine gun wounds, but Don and McCalder are still OK.

Wasn't Lake Louise [British Columbia, Canada] wonderful]? ... No. We stayed at L. Louise two days and one night. Papa was counting his finances and stayed two nights and one day at Sicamous [BC] for half the price....

October 22, 1943 — It's evening again Darling. I'm just thru with a dish of ice cream. The CBs [Construction Battalions] have an ice cream machine,

Official army portrait of a tired-looking Wilber, taken on October 10, 1943, shortly after the end of the Solomons combat. His right eyebrow showed no sign of the shrapnel lodged in the bone there. He wore his newly acquired lieutenant-colonel insignia, the silver oak leaf, on his right collar. On the other, he wore the crossed cannons of the field artillery.
[PHOTO: U.S. ARMY]

and they have twice helped us give our men some for dessert. Believe me, that's a real treat here.

An airfield at Ondonga peninsula was completed on October 23. Its defense was the mission of the 161st Infantry (Wilber's Washington State outfit), which was supported by Wilber's artillery battalion. The army was not forgetting Pearl Harbor.

The next day, planes of the Royal New Zealand Air Force flew in and then onward to support landings at Torokina, Bougainville.

x·o·ø·o·x

At the end of October, Wilber wrote Norma with an enthusiastic pertinent greeting.

> Oct. 29, 1943 — Today Lover is Norma Day on this Island. I wake up thinking how much I loved you, spent the day interrupting my work to recall your sweetness, and after supper read your four letters dated the twelfth, and now am ending the day to you. So today was Norma Day. I'll have others too on other islands.

It truly was Norma Day! On this date Norma gave birth to Gale Alice Bradt in the Georgetown University Hospital in Washington, D.C. The birth certificate recorded Norma and Wilber as the parents. Unknowingly, he continued describing his current situation on Ondonga intermingled with reflections on the past combat.

> We are still reveling [sic] in peace and freedom from Jap shells. It's wonderful. We even have lights at night and can read. Of course the bombers come over once in a while but we don't expect them to be very accurate and so far they aren't and the boys bet on them and enjoy it....
>
> You see, in combat I work like this. Everything travels [sic] along the line ... [forward]. My forward observers use it + lose it. The liaison observers replace it and ask me for more. They take my coat, my compass, field glasses, radios, telephones, maps, watch and canteens. Everything moves to the front except calls for more artillery fire and those go back.... Nearly any outfit can shoot, but to keep the stuff at the front makes the shooting more continuous.
>
> We had a bombing the other night, some "near misses" but no damage. It was funny because before breakfast the next morning, practically every one of my men was doing a little improvement on their dugouts. It's very reassuring to see how they react to Jap bombs – no excitement – just in their holes or flat on the ground until it's over then a big argument about how close they landed.

Wilber wrote Valerie, the only daughter he knew.

> Oct. 30, 1943 — I live with Capt. Rainey in a pair of small wall tents that leak. We put a large tarpaulin over them to shed the rain and built a

139

board floor so we are very comfortable too. The double canvas makes it cool. Rainey says it looks like a Mongolian yerk [sic]. Since I don't know what a "yerk" is nor how to spell it, you will have to tell me. [It is "yurt."]

Here, Wilber reflected on what Norma was likely telling him about her piano playing for remuneration. He of course is unaware of the new baby.

Oct 31, 1943 — You seem awfully busy. I do hope you aren't getting yourself well run down for the winter. It's too bad there are so many business details for you to do. I know how depressing bills are too. Don't let them get you down. I wish you could be comfortably settled down doing the things you enjoy. I know you enjoy playing but to play a concert for $10.00 seems too bad. Why don't you give the concert free if you want to play there?

Norma had apparently revealed her discouragement to Wilber, disguised as financial worries. It was doubtful she was playing commercially at all in those last weeks of her pregnancy. She continued to write up to within days of her delivery. He responded to some of them.

Nov. 10, 1943 — Your letters of Oct 23 + 25 just came with assorted letters from Evie, Gerry J., + Irene Bray. Yours are the nicest, of course. We had pork + beans for supper – good too.

The Armistice Day will be a religious service for our dead who are in this island. It will be a sad Armistice for us for Lts. Payne and Malone and Heidelberger will be there in the cemetery [at Munda] from the 169th [Field Artillery]. However each was doing a grand job when his time came.... It doesn't help much to know that each was where I had sent him but of course that is one of the aspects of the commander's responsibility.

A week later he wrote about the service to Valerie; it is one of the most poignant scenes in all his letters.

Nov 16, 1943 — We attended a religious and military memorial service on Armistice Day in honor of our dead comrades. We stood at salute while the firing squad fired a volley for each battalion or regiment that had one or more men killed. For us the speaker said "For 1st Lt __, the first to fall in the 169th F.A. Bn. and his brave comrades that followed." Then the volley was fired. It was a beautiful spot that had been made into a cemetery and the service was lovely but so, so sad. I hope too many more don't "follow" in the next year.

Norma was still using the Baltimore post office box address while living in Washington. It was not clear how Norma and Monte managed this. I doubt they

Munda Cemetery, New Georgia, July 8, 1944, a year after the battle began. These graves were moved either to the Manila American Cemetery in the Philippines or to the U.S.A. after the war. [PHOTO: U.S. ARMY SIGNAL CORPS, SC 526385]

drove to Baltimore to mail a letter because that would have expended valuable rationed gasoline. The train would have been practical but time consuming; mailing a letter could have taken a half-day or more.

Nov. 24, 1943 — In your letter of Oct 28, you assumed I was on the move again. Poor Nana, all full of worry. You should relax.

Norma was still writing Wilber on October 28, the day before she gave birth. I can picture her, uncomfortably pregnant, at a typewriter beside a south-facing upper window of the Q Street row house, with the sun streaming in, working away on a letter to Wilber, pondering what to say when she could not mention where she was and what loomed so large in her life.

On Thanksgiving day, Wilber was thankful for few or no short rounds that kill and injure one's own troops and for turkey provided by Uncle Sam.

Nov. 25, 1943 [Thanksgiving Day] — Uncle Sam did very well by his boys for Thanksgiving Dinner. He furnished turkey generously and the "makins" for dressing, cake and fruit. The boys were just as happy as kids. Afterward they lay on their bunks trying to out-groan the others. We made ice cream and got the CBs to freeze it for us. Fifteen gallons for 150 men. There were no complaints. So far as I know, the 169th was the only outfit of the 43rd [Division] that had ice cream. Pretty soft!

Nov. 28, 1943. Little Snow Maid [Norma] — How is the weather for you Sweet Heart? I'm sorry you had a cold. You have been holding out on me, no word of a cold except that it's about over. I knew it tho because of the gap in my mail so I worried anyway. It's wonderful to have such a nice girl to worry about, and dream about and think about and to love. Do you still have the little crease marks on your arms?

Actually, the "cold" was the delivery of baby Gale in Georgetown University Hospital. Wilber was just then getting letters written by Norma after Gale was born—Norma had picked up her letter-writing duties quite promptly.

Today I wrote to Mrs. Norbert J. Heidelberger of 1111 Whitesboro St, Utica, N.Y. about her son Bert who was a 1st Lt. in the Bn. He was missing in action and had been so reported until we had all the available facts collected; then he was reported killed in action. It was a hard letter to write because I could say so little that would be a comfort to her. He was a fine boy who had done a wonderful job everywhere he worked.

(I talked to Heidelberger's brother by phone in 1981 and shared this letter with him.)

In Russia, the onset of winter and rapidly strengthening Russian forces, aided by supplies from the U.S. through "Lend Lease," led to solid advances on all fronts. At the same time, Hitler, fearing an Allied invasion of France, halted the shipment of troops from France to the Russian front. Kiev on the Dnieper River was captured by the Russians on November 3, 1943.

On November 20, 1943, army and marine troops landed in the Gilbert Islands (Map 5), on Makin atoll and Tarawa atoll respectively. The former was captured quickly, but in the several days of intense fighting on Tarawa, the U.S. Marines encountered fierce Japanese resistance that resulted in about 3000 marine casualties. This was the beginning of an island-hopping campaign in the Central Pacific by Admiral Chester Nimitz. The advance toward the Philippines and Japan would be two-pronged, with MacArthur directing the drive up the New Guinea coast toward the Philippines.

17

"Poor Nana"

ONDONGA, NEW GEORGIA, DECEMBER 1943–JANUARY 1944

After two months, Ondonga Island was becoming like home for the 169th Field Artillery. As the front became ever more distant, preparations for future combat began to take precedence over defense. Meanwhile, Norma was adapting to her new baby and telling no one of it. Wilber was increasingly aware that Norma was withholding the details of her life, and his frustration was growing.

> Dec. 2. [1943], Dear Mother of Hale + Valerie — Do you realize that I'm the boy that you had asking you to be the mother of his babies some wonderful years ago? You did say "yes" and you did give me such wonderful children. I'm so happy about your loving me Dear....
>
> I'm wondering if you still are working on the morale circuit. You may not realize it but your letters have certainly lost all geographic significance. Don't you ever eat? Or go to shows? Or sleep anywhere? Or see anyone you know? Mysterious Norma. If you have joined the FBI, I should at least get a receipt for one very nice wife, slightly used, value priceless.

Norma's letters, mailed from Baltimore, lacked the little day-to-day items she would usually recite and often displayed postmarks well after the date she wrote. Wilber was growing very concerned, but also was sharing the local scene.

> Dec. 5, 1943 — I'm thinking of you again. It's a day so like many we've shared; cool and rainy.... Nana Mine, the inspection turned out to be a major celebration. Gen. Ross who is now assistant division commander and who formerly commanded the 172d [Infantry] was the inspector. The men were as clean + well shaved as if they were starting home. They sirred him and saluted him and did reporting to perfection. The vehicles were all on the line, all freshly painted and all in spotless condition.... Records were

143

OK, kitchens spotless, not even one fly showed up, tents were spick + span and areas were tops.

Dec. 9, 1943 — At last some letters came thru from you. Two letters came, one dated Nov. 4 and one Nov. 8. Both were mailed Nov. 16. You must have been sick for some time to hold them so long. I worry about you much more this year than last and that makes letters seem farther apart too.

I wish you weren't so isolated. You never mention meeting any friends, nor what you do on off days (I assume you cannot discuss your work.), nor [do you] even seem to have a place to spend Christmas. Poor Nana, this is being a lot harder on you than on me. I wish I could do something about it. You speak of not enough money for carfare to go see the children. Please Lover, don't be silly about trying to save too much…. I'm not going to say any more about paying off the debt on the house or buying bonds.

Wilber's anguish was nearly palpable. He could only provide money, when he wanted to do much more. He knew it had been his own choice to join the active army, which took him away from his family, and he was suffering the consequences of that choice. But it is likely his suffering would have been no less had he been back home while his former comrades were fighting in the Pacific.

About this time, Mrs. Heidelberger wrote Wilber. Her generosity of spirit was admirable, although her heartbreak was evident.

December 13, 1943, Dear Lieutenant Colonel Bradt — I cannot begin to tell you or thank you enough for your lovely letter to me today. Whereas in our respect it was the saddest day in our lives because of what it confirmed; it was a great comfort to us to know just what really happened to Norbert…. Please do not blame yourself for anything that happened to Norbert. I am sure he is proud of you because he did his job so well.

Wilber apparently had shared with Mrs. Heidelberger his own feeling of responsibility for sending her son into a bad place. She was consoling *him*!

Perhaps sensing that he could well be losing Norma, Wilber's letters were becoming more solicitous and tender. He reentered the romance mode, which "he could do so well," as Norma told me many years later. Nevertheless, he started this next letter with a bit of reproach lightly masked in black humor.

Dec 15, 1943, Hello There Sweet and Lovable — How's your handwriting today? I haven't seen any samples recently so still wonder if you really are finally ready to discard your old man….

The other day I decided that when I come back to you, I will court you all over again. That would be so you could be sure I really loved you.

Besides I never had any more fun in my life then when I was making you love me. Do you remember, Dear. The moon has never been so bright as it was those days. The air was always so soft and you were so charming and sweet that I could hardly believe I was really awake. I'm so glad you decided to love me.

Dec. 17, 1943, Dear Wife, Today is another day that I love you... – Hallelujah! Letters from Nana just came. I'm so relieved. So relieved. Now I know you have just been too busy to write and I can stop worrying. They were dated Nov. 18 and 20, were mailed Nov. 27 and arrived Dec. 17. Not so good as it might be "but good." "I'm eatin' it, ain't I?" At least you don't say you have been sick. I notice tho, you don't say you weren't sick either, so maybe it isn't so good. You sure have a knack for not saying a word about yourself. Don't you ever buy a new dress, or eat a special dinner, or see a show or a dog fight.

Not being under the pressure of combat gave Wilber time to fret. Norma probably had no idea he would be comparing postmark dates with her letter dates or that the absence of personal details would be so revealing. The covert life was not her strong suit.

Answering your 18th of Nov. — No, Wife of Mine, I'm not going to come back with a lot of the conventional mental scars. I'll just be tired and lazy and cantankerous and in love with my family.

On this date, December 17, at St. Bernard's School, I sang a solo (soprano) as one of the "Three Wise Men." It was part of the last-night festivities before Christmas vacation, which began the next day and ended on January 3. It was to be a real treat for Valerie and me because Norma came to New York City to be with us. It was our first time together since June.

This was Wilber's second Christmas in the Pacific. He captured the scene on Christmas Eve in this letter to Norma.

Dec. 24, 1943 — It is a quiet night here now. I am sitting in one of my new chairs that Swan made for me. Capt. Davis, [Chief Warrant Officer] Gagner + Major Rainey are sitting beside me around Dick's gasoline lantern. Davis + Gagner are reading my Sat. E.P. [Saturday Evening Post magazine] and Dick is writing. Outside a motor is thrumping to charge a battery. My radio is singing "In the Gleaming" and I have within reach a bottle of beer and some peanuts. In the distance the Protestant service is in progress. They are singing something by Gounod, the Messiah, and some other lovely selections....

I wonder if you + the children will be at Grace Church tonight. Wherever you are I pray God to watch over you and to keep you safe (all of you) in 1944.

Norma had probably written that she would see Valerie and me in New York. I only barely recollect that Christmas. We may well have attended the Christmas Eve service at Grace Church with its wonderful music reminiscent of my two years in the choir. Wilber later heard from Norma that we visited Valerie's former school in Greenwich Village [letter 1/12/44].

A few days later, Wilber had the privilege of seeing one his officers receive a very high-ranking medal for his exploits as a forward observer in Munda.

Dec 27, 1943, Dear Hale — Today General Barker came up to my island [Ondonga] to give Lt. Mushik a Distinguished Service Cross. It was quite a program…. Afterward the band played a concert, the photographer took a lot of pictures and congratulated Mushik. The men looked fine as they marched by the reviewing stand. We are all proud of Mushik….

Dec. 29, 1943 — It's a Norma night here tonight, warm, bright stars, night noises making a Silly Symphony that isn't at all silly….

Gen. Barker just called and said he could send two officers to New Zealand for a leave and would I go if he named me. No I would not go unless he ordered it…. I'll buy a bond with that money and sleep on my own cot on my own island instead of being lonesome in someone else's city.

This was the second time Wilber had been offered and had declined leave in New Zealand [letter 10/16/43].

Wilber's unit and others were on a number of different islands in the Munda area. This led to a lot of boat use.

Jan. 6, 1944 — The coxswain of my boat is the son of a Reg. Army Colonel of the Air Corps. He is quite a character; very small, talkative, has been wounded, and either seen a lot of service or lies well. His crew is named "Junior" and Junior is not letting this war bother him at all For example, yesterday I told the coxswain, "I want to go to_____ next," ____ being about three miles away…. Next the bilge pump stopped working and the boat began to fill…. So Junior climbs up in the bow and we ease into the shore. The cox says, "How's it look, Junior?" Junior just looks + keeps quiet. The cox says, "Well is it OK to go in, Junior?" Junior doesn't commit himself. So we go on farther in when Wham, Scrape, slide, scrunch and with a jolt we stop on a rock. The cox says "Junior, you should ought to tell me about those." We back off the rock with a lot of unpleasant scratching noises and the cox remarks to me, "These old boats are getting worse every day."

Farther on I ask the coxswain what about beaching the boat + he allows as how maybe he can make it home. Since the last three mile stretch didn't have any convenient islands I picked a beach + told him to pull in to it. So Junior takes the bow + away we go. On the way in the cox pleads with Junior for signals + words to guide him in. Finally Junior relents + says, "I kain't see nothin so just give'r the gun + we'll know if we hit something." So we did and didn't.

Wilber reported to his father that swimming was now in favor.

January 15, 1944 — We, also being on an island [Ondonga on New Georgia], push swimming. This is particularly important because of our always being in amphibious operations where the most critical times are ship to shore periods. After these boys had gone over the side of a transport a few times they didn't need to be urged to learn how to swim.

They were becoming at home in the tropics. When the division was first in the Solomons, Wilber wrote [letter 3/28/43], "Sharks, barracuda, rays, dolphins and tuna-like fish have all been seen. The enthusiasm for swimming is a little low."

Jan. 15, 1944, to Norma — My tent floor is a great luxury and now my life is complete for I have a broom. Two were issued the other day and there are only two floors in the Hq battery so I sent word that I would like one kept at my tent. The supply Sgt. sent me word that he had issued one and was using the other himself but that he would try to get another for me. Corp. Swan told him to send one down to my tent and then to try to get another one for himself. Apparently Swan was convincing for I now have a broom and Swan no longer sweeps with a clothes brush....

Jan. 18, 1944, Sweet Norma — It didn't rain quite so much today.... Civilization is catching up with me; tailors, exchanges, refrigerators are all beginning to appear....

I wrote to Don [Downen] yesterday and to Col. Eason whom I haven't seen since he was relieved [from Command of the 169th Infantry] on the Munda Trail. He + I had spent a pretty nasty week together and I had come to like him very much. He is in the States now.

The "pretty nasty week" was Wilber's only acknowledgment of how badly things had gone for the 169th Infantry in the early days of the drive on Munda.

X · O · Ø · O · X

147

Norma's plans after Valerie and I finished the school year were revealed in this letter to Wilber's father. Now that she was no longer pregnant, she could show herself to Wilber's brother Paul. But she could not reveal the baby's existence!

Jan 13, 1944 — I am trying to locate in Washington to be near Paul and Jo. I have some prospects for work there. The children wish to be near Paul in the summertime, so as soon as I locate some work and an apartment there, I will move [from Baltimore].

And Wilber's concern about Norma was becoming almost frantic as he continued his letter of January 15.

I wonder if you are worrying too much [about me]. I know now you don't tell me when you are sick and have relapses and have to go back to bed, so I wonder all the time if no mail means you are sick. Please don't hold out on me. The one thing I asked for when we were married was to carry part of your load. Now you are believing the propagandists instead of me, and I hear afterward you have been sick. Would you prefer for me not to tell you of my illnesses + wounds? Please?

Nevertheless, Norma continued supporting Wilber with letters and shipments while caring for her newborn, but she could not bring herself to share her secret burden. Both husband and wife were trapped by their human nature, the war, and the norms of the day.

x·o·ø·o·x

On January 22, the 43rd Division received good news. It was alerted to a move that would begin January 26 to Guadalcanal and then on to New Zealand. This likely necessitated a great deal of preparation as well as joy because of the ultimate destination. This was Wilber's last letter from Ondonga. In it, in apparent anguish, he pleads for Norma's understanding and with great emotion acquiesces to a shift in their relationship.

Jan. 25, 1944 — Please try to realize my situation, Darling. I like letters. I don't care for them except as they help me keep in touch with my family. All my life I have wanted to be the kind of husband and father that did know what went on in his family. The war, I knew, would make this difficult but I was determined to overcome that difficulty. However, I guess it is too long and the war wins....

Dearest Wife, don't mistake my words for my thoughts and intentions. That one important thing is my love for you. All the things I say poorly or

148

fail to say are still an effort at the expression of my love for you. You are having a hard time there and I realize it is harder for you than for me. I was at home too during much of the last war, so I know about it. You don't want to worry me, I know, and I appreciate that.

From now on I won't say anything about these things. You can write as often or seldom as your situation requires and I will understand that it is OK. If there is a reason why I should be told so little about you, that too is all right, and I will be sure you are doing what your judgment requires.... You can consider me as a consultant rather than as a co-administrator from now on. Don't forget tho that I'm still your very-much-in-love, altho difficult, husband. That is one thing I won't stop doing even to win war.

Typically, Wilber then finished a difficult discussion by switching abruptly to a lighter topic, this one about flies.

In one of the published orders by higher headquarters was the following: "It has been observed that flies are prevalent around latrines and kitchens. The latrine flies often go to the kitchen and the kitchen flies to the latrines and vice versa. Corrective action will be taken immediately." This isn't an exact quotation but it's no worse than the exact one. Since then one of the local news letters came out protesting the injustice of such an order and pointing out that some kitchen flies go [to] the latrine for pleasure but that some "have to go" and further that the latrine flies certainly were reasonable in [making] their trips to the kitchen at meal time. Morale is up ten points.

The defensive mission of the 43rd Division on Ondonga thus came to an end. On January 26, 1944, the first detachment of the 169th Field Artillery Battalion, including Wilber, departed on an LST for the overnight trip to Guadalcanal. Four weeks later, they would board large ships for Auckland, New Zealand.

X·O·Ø·O·X

Wilber's wife and children had settled into their independent post-Christmas routines. Valerie and I were by now quite at home in our New Jersey boarding schools, though I was a bit blue and even teary as I rode the train on a gray rainy day back to school after Christmas. But once there, I settled into the routine of classes, working in the print shop, and passing scouting tests. Valerie soldiered on with her nun-teachers and classmates. Norma had returned to her life in Washington with baby Gale. She was probably working at her writings and possibly piano practicing if a piano was available.

While Wilber was at Ondonga, the advance up the Solomons toward the strong Japanese base at Rabaul on the northeastern tip of New Britain continued without the 43rd Division. Landings on Choiseul Island and the Treasury Islands on October 27 and on the large island of Bougainville on November 1 (Map 3) made possible the establishment of airfields, radar sites, and PT boat bases that would serve to support further advances. The western end of New Britain itself was invaded at Arawe (Map 2) on December 15 and at Cape Gloucester on December 26. Rabaul would eventually be neutralized (March 1944) by landings beyond it in the Admiralty Islands (Map 2) and by further advances up the New Guinea coast. In the Central Pacific, the next step in the drive toward Japan was the occupation of the Marshall Islands. Landings on Kwajalein (Jan 31) and Eniwetok (Feb. 17) led to their captures in a few days.

In Italy, the Allies had been slogging their way up the Italian peninsula since the early September landings at Calabria and Salerno. In December, they were stalled by a defensive line at Cassino, well short of Rome. An Allied landing at Anzio behind the German lines on January 22 was contained by the Germans for several months because Allied resources were being husbanded for the planned invasion of France the following June.

The Russian Army had made advances across its entire front and had finally broken the German siege of Leningrad on January 19. The siege had gone on for a full thousand days causing great hardship for its Russian inhabitants.

18

Interlude 1983, Japan and Solomon Islands
MARCH AND MAY, 1983

In the winter and spring of 1983, I spent a sabbatical leave at Japan's Institute of Space and Astronautical Science. During March of that year, I visited Hiroshima, the site of the first offensive use of the atomic bomb, and also visited Col. Seishu Kinoshita, a surviving senior Japanese battalion commander of the Munda and Arundel campaigns in the Solomons. In May of that year, I traveled to Australia to carry out astronomical observations. En route, I stopped in Luzon, the main island of the Philippines, for one week to search out the sites and people Wilber had written about. On the return trip, I took another week to visit the places he had been in the Solomons. The following year, 1984, while en route again to Australia, I stopped for a week in New Zealand and found the people who had treated Wilber so hospitably after the Solomons combat. In essence, my travels in 1983 and 1984 were a condensed form of Wilber's own three-year Pacific odyssey.

I was driven to visit these sites by my intense curiosity about my parents' story. My attraction to these sites was compelling. I was surely searching for my father, and in certain ways, I did find him, particularly in the village of Bomboe on Arundel in the Solomons, the town of Pakil in the Philippines, and in the small town of Carterton, Wairarapa, New Zealand.

I recount these visits in three Interludes in this volume. My accounts draw heavily on the journals I kept on these travels. Here, I write of my visits in Japan to Hiroshima and with Colonel Kinoshita and then of my visit to the New Georgia group of islands in the Solomon Islands.

HIROSHIMA AND COLONEL KINOSHITA, MARCH 1983

Visiting Hiroshima was, for me, a very emotional experience. The use of the atomic bomb by the U.S. was a major step for mankind—in a dangerous direction according to my thinking and that of many of my physicist colleagues, some of whom had participated in the bomb's development. On the other hand, I knew that its use helped bring about the end of the war without a costly invasion of Japan and very likely the loss then of my father.

I spent several hours touring the Peace Memorial Park at Hiroshima and its exhibits, and was deeply moved and saddened by them. The Japanese exhibits made real the agony of that day, but downplayed Japan's role in bringing about the Hiroshima bombing by its own history of conquests and atrocities. I was, frankly, put off by the one-sided presentation. Yes, it was a terrible event, and I did and do grieve for the 80,000 innocents who died that day.

X·O·Ø·O·X

A Japanese military historian, Hishashi Takahashi, at Japan's Center of Military History told me that a senior officer of the 13th Regiment still lived on Kyushu, namely Col. Seishu Kinoshita. Wilber knew of Kinoshita as one of the Japanese battalion commanders on Arundel Island. He believed, according to his notes, that Kinoshita had been killed there.

I visited Kinoshita at his home in Kurume, Kyushu, on March 21, 1983. He lived in a small house with a pretty vegetable and flower garden outside; gardening was his hobby. I was served tea and sweets on "this special holiday upon which we honor dear friends and relatives." I met his wife, son, and daughter-in-law. I set up my tape recorder on the table, as did his son. An English teacher served as translator (a military man) so Kinoshita could tell his story quite freely in Japanese.

He excitedly pulled out his maps of the battle places in the Solomons. All of his official maps had been confiscated by the Australians, so these maps were drawn from memory on large poster sheets of paper and were sometimes vague or in error. He spread them out on the floor and got on his knees and excitedly told his stories as he pointed to geographic features. He was the battalion commander who fought immediately opposite the 27th U.S. Infantry Wilber was with at Bomboe Village. He also participated in the defense of Munda Airfield.

At Munda, he said many of the Japanese soldiers were new to combat and badly frightened by American artillery and planes. After the first American attack with tanks on Arundel (Sept. 17, 1943), he said, heroic efforts were made to bring forward an anti-tank gun from Kolombangara to the Arundel "mainland" where the tanks had attacked. It was the last anti-tank gun of the regiment, and there were only ten shells for it. He described how, in the next American attack, the first shell destroyed one of the tanks and another damaged another, and that this had cheered the Japanese soldiers. In the tank attack the next day, he thought his days were numbered. Later when the Japanese were attempting to evacuate Arundel in the

General William Naylor (left) and Col. Seishu Kinoshita examining a map in 1984 as they discuss their wartime experiences on Arundel Island. Each was an infantry battalion commander, and the two units were in direct conflict. Naylor arranged the meeting after hearing about Kinoshita in a talk I gave to the 43rd Division Association in August 1983. They met at the National Defense College in Tokyo on April 16, 1984. Their meeting was recorded but not advertised. Both are now deceased. [PHOTO: WILLIAM NAYLOR]

midst of American artillery fire, the boats would become grounded in the shallow water when loaded. Kinoshita, now the regimental commander, helped push them off standing in water up to his chest.

Five months later, I described this visit in a talk at a reunion of the 43rd Division Association. The former 1st Battalion commander of the 172nd Infantry, William Naylor, who had fought directly opposite Kinoshita's battalion at Arundel, was present and questioned me about it. Shortly thereafter, in April 1984, he went to Japan, and the two commanders had an unpublicized meeting at the Defense Ministry in Tokyo, where they reviewed their mutual experiences for history. Both are now deceased.

Was it filial duty that led me to visit Wilber's adversary? Did I need to atone for Wilber's artillery that probably killed Kinoshita's revered regimental commander and fellow battalion commanders? Or did I instead feel the need to fill out the story by getting Colonel Kinoshita's view of those times and hearing about his later life, a life Wilber never had? All were probably at work in my head.

SOLOMON ISLANDS, MAY 1983

Two months after visiting Colonel Kinoshita, I visited the Solomon Islands. To get to Munda Airfield on New Georgia Island, I traveled through New Guinea and the world-famous island of Guadalcanal.

Guadalcanal's airfield is the renowned Henderson Field around which the fame of Guadalcanal revolves. The U.S. Marines landed there in August 1942 and defended it heroically from Japanese attempts to retake it. Now it is a little relaxed airport with no bank for changing money, a source of some difficulty for me then, as the only bank on Guadalcanal was closed on Sunday and I had no Solomon dollars.

This was my one day (afternoon and evening only) on Guadalcanal so I used the daylight hours to visit some of the battle areas in a rented Avis car. First I drove a few miles to "Beach Red" where the Marines had first landed. There I saw a terribly corroded 3-inch gun on the beach pointing out to sea; it could have been American or Japanese.

I then was directed to a little dirt road leading to "Bloody Ridge," aka Edson's Ridge, where I was told there were Japanese and American memorials. This is where the U.S. Marines desperately defended Henderson Field from aggressive Japanese attacks only a mile from the airfield. As the road became ever narrower with tall grass obscuring it, I stopped and asked directions from a little old man who was working in a field. When I told him my dad had been there with the Americans, he lit up and offered to take me himself. His name was Jason Alaikone. He had been a scout for the Americans, he said. He climbed in the car, machete and all. The road in some places had grass as high as the car's hood and was very steep in one place.

We found the U.S. memorial, then drove on to the Japanese memorial. Both were very simple. The U.S. memorial was a white four-sided pyramid about ten feet high with a base about ten feet square set on a square base of rocks about three feet high. The Japanese memorial was a simple vertical wooden post about eight inches square in cross section and about ten feet tall with painted inscriptions on it. A nearby small stake, painted white with inscriptions, indicated recent visitors. The successful defense of Henderson Field on this unpretentious hill was a turning point for the Americans; thereafter they began to take the offensive against the Japanese on Guadalcanal.

I had heard that there were war relics on or near the beach just opposite Henderson Field. With the guidance of a young boy, Salia, age 11, we found relics of airplane parts, two different landing craft rusting in the jungle not far (30 m) from the beach, and wrecked metal wharves.

I then drove into Honiara, the main town on Guadalcanal. My hotel, the Honiara, was simple and clean. I had supper and then walked about one mile into town to the fancy Hotel Mendana. On the walk, I chatted with another native "Charlie" who was walking my way. He was very talkative and interested in conversing with an American. These islands were British until independence in 1978 so most people knew English.

At the Mendana, I had ginger ale as I looked out over the dark waters of "Ironbottom Sound" and mused on the destructive naval battles that had taken place there. Then I got a taxi and had the driver show me the downtown monument to the American dead. Then back to my hotel, to bed and up early (again) for the flight to Munda. This was the end of my touring Guadalcanal. Time was precious.

X·O·Ø·O·X

My flight to Munda on Monday, May 23, was in a small propeller plane of Solaire Air. We flew at low altitude and it was a beautiful clear day. (I was in the copilot's seat with absolutely no qualifications for it.) We flew over the Russell Islands, and I could see the characteristic outline of Pavuvu Island there that I knew so well from the maps. Then Rendova Island came into view, the 43rd Division's jump-off point for the Munda landings. The harbor where Wilber wrote his pre-landing letter on July 4 and was wounded by a bomb was easily identifiable. This was no map; this was the real thing. I was transfixed.

As we made the approach for our landing at Munda Airfield, I could not believe I was coming to the hard-won objective of the 43rd Division's month of combat in July and August of 1943. By this time, Munda had become almost mythical to me. But there we were, and here I was standing on New Georgia Island. At Munda, I was now walking, figuratively and literally, in Wilber's footsteps.

Immediately after my arrival at Munda, I met Alfred Basili—to whom I had been referred in previous correspondence—and saw his canoe, and was relieved to see that it had an outboard motor; I would not have to paddle as I had thought. It was a long canoe (30 feet) so went very fast. I was staying at the Munda Rest House, a simple set of motel-like rooms facing the water. A small dock near my end of the motel had boats occasionally coming in and young boys swimming off it. It was a relaxed Caribbean-like scene.

I asked Alfred if the big naval guns were still on Baanga, and he replied that one of them remained but was damaged. When he asked where I wanted to go first, I immediately said Baanga, which I knew was nearby. That was where Wilber's artillery had disabled two Japanese naval guns and where one of Wilber's forward observers, Heidelberger, had been killed.

We got into his canoe and buzzed over to Baanga in about 15 minutes. It was a beautiful sunlit day, maybe 85 degrees. We beached the boat and walked into the

155

jungle—THE jungle! And it wasn't spooky, creepy, full of mosquitos, or dense with vegetation. It was pretty, with dappled sunshine coming through the tall trees.

After a 20-minute walk, we came to one of the guns. What a moment! I have a picture of Wilber alongside one of them just after its capture, and for many years I had kept the telescopic gunsight he had given me. This was one of the same two guns! The long (approximately five meters) barrel was on the ground—the result of someone salvaging the brass bearings—with large recoil springs and other parts nearby. The main stand was still solidly upright. Despite Alfred's denial that there was a second gun, I went looking for it and found it a bit down the beach. It was in similar condition.

We then visited the beach where the men of L Company, 169th Inf. Rgt., were stranded for nine days. Knowing the story gave that innocuous little beach a whole new visage. We never tried to explore the swampy region where the attack north of the cove ran into trouble. I was feeling quite adventurous, but deliberately walking into swamps didn't seem necessary. We then returned to Munda where I had a nice cool beer.

Then we were back into the canoe to go eastward about five miles to Sasavele Island, where the guns and Fire Direction Center (FDC) of the 169th FA Bn. had been established during the drive to take Munda. On the island, we were followed around by some two dozen school children who loved being photographed; I was like the Pied Piper. The village is today on the same (northeast) end of the island as the 169th FA Bn. had been, but the village was established after the war.

At the village there was an old vehicle dump with some six or eight abandoned U.S. Army vehicles, still complete with rubber tires. They could well have been 169th FA Bn. vehicles. We also saw Zanana Beach, so small as to hardly qualify as a "beach"; it was maybe ten meters of sand wide and only three meters deep. Bringing in the invading troops in small boats from Rendova must have been a slow, cumbersome operation.

On our second visit several days later, an old man showed us a garden where there had been a large pit with sandbags when the villagers first settled there. That was most probably the FDC, the nerve center of the 169th FA Bn. as it fired some 29,000 artillery shells in support of the infantry advance on Munda Airfield. We then took the canoe back to Munda in time for supper and bed. What a day this was: I woke up on Guadalcanal, flew to Munda, toured Baanga Island to the west, then toured Sasavele to the east, all before supper.

The next day, Tuesday, May 24, Alfred and I circumnavigated the island of Arundel in his canoe, a distance of about 50 miles. We went up Wanawana Lagoon on the west side of Arundel (Map 10). There were lots and lots of tiny islands and coral rising up to the surface. It would have been very easy to become stranded.

Left: Coastal gun mount of one of the two Japanese 120-mm coastal guns on Baanga Island, and me, May 1983. Right: Fifteen foot barrel (tube) of the same gun. Two such guns were put out of action on Baanga by Wilber's artillery on August 17, 1943.
[PHOTOS: HALE BRADT]

Alfred's canoe drew very little water and really moved. It was a beautiful ride past green jungled islands, over green and white water sometimes only six inches deep.

Bustling Point was on the west side of Arundel Island about a mile southwest of Bomboe Village. This was where the "Provisional Battalion" of artillery was located while Wilber was at Bomboe Village directing its fires. The gun positions were still there: dirt and coral built up in a circle around the gun pits. Albert W. Merck, one of Wilber's officers, had been there a few months earlier and showed them to Alfred.

We then carried on in the canoe to Bomboe Village (pronounced "Boboi") where I saw about two dozen houses and could identify the low "ridge" where Sugg's tent [the Command Post] probably had been. This was the very site where Wilber sat in Colonel Sugg's tent night after night controlling the artillery at Bustling Point as it supported infantry attacks and fired on boats and a seaplane with the help of his "whispering chorus of observers." I could picture the ghosts of Admiral Halsey, Senator Lodge, and General Griswold sitting and conversing in that tent, all three drinking spiked orange juice.

Alfred Basili and me in his canoe after several days at Munda; I was completely relaxed by then. The 30-foot canoe with outboard motor really moved along. [PHOTO: CLAUDE COLOMER]

We sat in the shade under one of the raised houses and talked to the villagers, two of whom (Igolo Koete and Moses Sesa) had participated in the rescue of John Kennedy when his PT boat was sunk by a Japanese destroyer in nearby Blackett

Strait. They told us there was an American tank in the jungle to the east. So, of course, I asked if we could go see it. We left the village in Alfred's canoe with a local guide, Peter Evan. After motoring perhaps a mile to the east, Peter led us into the jungle, hacking bushes and vines and plants with his machete as he went. Finally, we found the tank. It was in fine shape; the jungle had not succeeded in rusting away any of its thick armor plate, its basic armor. All of its hatches still opened and shut, and the rubber treads on its tracks were still largely intact and not rotted. I even climbed down into the tank.

We found two or three neat little holes, about one inch diameter, in the front armor plate down low where the shells from the Japanese anti-tank gun had penetrated the 1.5 inches of steel plate! This, then, was clearly one of the two tanks Kinoshita saw destroyed. "I myself was standing beside the gun," he had said. This was one of the tanks Wilber had seen attacking the day before. Again, I was walking in Wilber's footsteps; he had walked around this smoking battlefield with Colonel Sugg and General Griswold.

We then went back to the canoe and, returned Peter to Bomboe, and continued our circumnavigation of Arundel with the mile-high Kolombangara on our left. As we proceeded down the east side of Arundel, we passed Piru Plantation (Ondonga) where the "Eastern Force" of artillery had been located and where the 169th FA Bn. subsequently was on defensive duty. A large Japanese fishing station was now located there. The Japanese economic needs were being met peaceably in 1983, unlike in 1943!

U.S. Marine tank in North Arundel jungle. It was disabled in an attack on September 18, 1943. [PHOTO: IAN WARNE]

Our canoe then took us down the west side of Baanga. We passed by the location of the naval guns, but we couldn't see them, and arrived at Munda at about 5 p.m. for a much needed beer, swim, and supper.

So ended my second day at Munda.

On Wednesday, I relaxed in the morning and in the afternoon was driven in a carryall down the Munda Trail, a narrow dirt road, to Zanana Beach, in the reverse direction the 43rd Division had taken as it fought its way toward Munda Airfield. On the way back, we stripped to our shorts and swam in a clear, clean pool of stream-fed water of the Barike River under the tall jungle trees with dappled sunshine filtering through the leaves high above, a jungle paradise and a far cry from the 1943 scene.

After the swim, we continued toward Munda and stopped and climbed Horseshoe Hill where the Americans had been held up for about two weeks. There, we saw what looked like a scarecrow in a garden. It was a pair of crossed sticks with burlap for a cloak, and an old rusty G.I. American helmet on top that seemed to be looking off toward Munda. It was a potent symbol of what had occurred there. (G.I. was slang for the regular soldier, as if he were another piece of army "General-Issue" equipment.)

Our return to the Munda Rest House concluded our third day at Munda.

Scarecrow constructed of a cross of sticks, burlap, and a rusted American G.I. helmet, in a garden on Horseshoe Hill, New Georgia, May 1983.
[PHOTO: CLAUDE COLOMER]

X · O · Ø · O · X

The next morning, my last at Munda, we took Alfred's canoe eastward toward Zanana Beach and stopped on Nusa Banga where we saw a newly made war canoe of the type used by natives of the western Solomons in their head-hunting raids on the eastern Solomons—before missionaries put a stop to that. We then visited Sasavele again, where we found the location of the fire direction center pit as recounted above.

That afternoon, Thursday, I departed Munda on Solaire for the ten-minute flight to Ringi Cove (Vila airfield) on Kolombangara. It was the beginning of my trip back to modern civilization. I spent the night in a private home there. After a movie, late in the evening and under a full moon, my host took me to the waterfront where I looked out over Blackett Strait toward Arundel. On that peaceful scene, I super-imposed Japanese barges, lights, frantic reinforcement activity, and artillery shell explosions. I could feel the excitement and fears of the Japanese as they looked out onto that same scene.

The next day, Friday, I had a beautiful tour of the northern Solomons as we flew at low altitude in another Solaire flight northward to Kieta via Gizo and Ballale, both wartime Japanese-built airports. Kieta is on the east coast of Bougainville. High jungle-covered mountains rose up inland from the coast. Our jet plane to Port Moresby headed westward over these huge mountains immediately after takeoff. Thanks to my careful attention (!), our plane did indeed clear the peaks of Bougainville without deviating one bit from its straight-line rising flight path.

Port Moresby; I made it on time for my flight to Japan!

Thus ended my week tracing Wilber's footsteps in the Solomon Islands. It was an adventure into another world and time. Legends from the war came alive for me. Soldiers of two nations were there again as were their struggles, sufferings, deaths, and pride of accomplishment. Looking back on my visit now, in 2016, that week in the Solomons and indeed my entire month-long Pacific adventure seem like a dream.

1944

My Darling Daughter,

Happy Birthday to you, My dear.
I can't tell you how glad I am to
have you for my girl. You are just
the very particular girl I would have
picked if I had gone shopping in
heaven and selected the nicest baby they
had. I wish that this will be a
really nice year for you and hope
you can make it nicer too for all
your friends. Don't forget you have a
Daddy that loves you dearly. On your
birthday I'll pretend I'm having a "Round
and Round" with all of us together again.
Please pretend with me and maybe it
will come true sooner.

Je t'aime,

Wilbur.

PART IV

REST AND REHABILITATION

NEW ZEALAND
FEBRUARY—JULY, 1944

Wilber (left) and Russ Davis on leave in Wellington, New Zealand, March 1944, in a photograph taken by Olive Madsen. [PHOTO: OLIVE MADSEN]

19

"Our plan is to get away from soldiers"
GUADALCANAL & NEW ZEALAND, FEBRUARY–MARCH, 1944

On January 26, 1944, the first contingent of the 169th Field Artillery Battalion sailed for Guadalcanal on a Landing Ship Tank (LST), an overnight trip. The next morning, Wilber wrote Norma from the ship.

> Jan. 27, 1944 — It's a lovely sunshiny day and I am thinking how nice it would be if you were with me.... This sea is as smooth as a Maine lake and is so restful and blue....
>
> I feel sad about leaving Malone + Payne + Heidelberger here. It still seems impossible that they are gone. Sometimes I think they are still part of the battalion and are by their examples still leading us in combat....
>
> If I were to tell you how it rained all the time we were loading yesterday and how muddy it was and [how] wet I was, it would just remind me of a trip into Yellowstone and how well you cared for me when I had a cold there. That was so nice that I'll never forget it. I was so all in and fagged and discouraged that I didn't want to do anything. You made the decisions, did the work, and I never felt so wonderful about anything in my life. Since then I've learned to lean on your sweetness.

This was another of the few times Wilber frankly admitted to low periods. How he would respond to a forthcoming leave in New Zealand was an open question. The next day Wilber wrote exuberantly from Guadalcanal.

> Jan. 28, 1944, Hello Nana! — Your old man is back on land again. Yesterday we arrived here about noon.... The men are busy setting up kitchens, tents, caring for equipment, ditching, cutting away brush + grass and generally getting settled....
>
> I know you have been worrying about me + trying to keep my morale up. I don't intend in any way to try to run your life and if you have really

decided you want a home life instead of a career, I'll be very happy about that.... Furthermore as I said before, I don't expect to worry about it anymore.

Norma was apparently wrestling with her feelings and uncertain future. She defended her independence, but expressed the desire for a "home life." Norma was now flooding Wilber with letters, and some brought up the notion of Monte's role in their relationship.

Jan. 30, 1944 — You do try so hard to spoil me that I'm embarrassed. Today I received seven letters. It was fun too but you don't need to do it you know....

It's nice of Monte to still keep in contact with the children. He has the knack of doing the things for them I would like to do. I liked him very much and wish we could have had more time together. He is certainly interested in you and I feel sorry for him in a way.... It is a peculiar situation but in a way I'm glad he is standing by in case I'm liquidated.

Wilber was wise enough to know and admit that he could well be "liquidated" and that Monte would be a safety net for the family. Norma surely realized this too. It was the wild card in Wilber's and in every soldier's hand in wartime.

Norma finally located an apartment in Washington. Wilber first heard of it indirectly.

Feb. 7, 1944 — I see by a letter [from you] to D'Avanzo's wife forwarded [here] to D'A that you now have a Washington, D.C., address. That is once I found out in spite of the distance. WB.

The apartment at 1754 Q Street NW, a mile from Monte's home, gave her a respectable address. She could have moved there with baby Gale, but more likely she used it only as a pied-a-terre for her daily mail and for her children's expected spring vacation visits.

Wilber, after recounting a humorous scene, gently told Norma that her descriptions of her life were somewhat wanting in consistency.

Feb. 10, 1944 — Yesterday I fell flat in a mud hole of black mud + water about a foot deep and the watch came thru fine. Incidentally I was on the way to a meeting of the commanders of the division. One item taken up was that there was no excuse for wearing dirty uniforms. The Chief of Staff looked a bit dazed at me but went thru with his exhortations. It was quite funny because I further mystified him by neither explaining nor apologizing, just acted as if it was my usual afternoon dress....

These last letters are wonderful. They take me right with you and show me yourself and I think you're lovely.... You still seem to feel that I am critical of you and I feel badly about that. I've tried so hard to let you see I was worried by the dual factor of having no address except a P.O. Box and by the fact that your last letters said you had been ill. You also say, "Maybe I had talked too much about the places we played, etc., plants [factories] in and near Baltimore." To me that is startling news for the only thing I have received was a statement that you could not tell me those things.

Feb 14, 1944, Happy Valentine's Day Darling — You can't be mine this year for I asked Valerie. Of course my heart takes a big flipflop every time I think of you....

I sent Mrs. Heidelberger the First Lts. bar [insignia] Bert [Heidelberger] wore in his last combat. He didn't hide his insignia. She must be a very nice mother. Unfortunately two of the three officers I lost by death were the ones I would have picked as the very nicest and cleanest of all. It almost looked as if they were too good for this business and the Lord took them away before their souls could be hurt.

It had been 18 months since Heidelberger had been killed in action, and Wilber had not forgotten him or the others. Note the value he placed on an officer not hiding his insignia in combat. The risk of being identified as an officer by an enemy was outweighed by the encouragement your presence gave to your men.

Don't worry about Mother + me. That was bound to happen no matter who married me. I knew it, but really couldn't believe she would cherish resentment so faithfully.

This left little question that Wilber's mother was not writing because of festering resentment. It had been three years since the bitter dispute about money owed, and she still was not writing.

Feb. 17, 1944, — We are doing no training at present and the days are dull. It is usually too wet to walk and our equipment is not available now for training. So we give the men an hour of exercise in the morning and take them swimming in the afternoon.

The division was about to board ships to New Zealand.

Feb. 20, 1944 — We are having a big police [clean up] today, and the men are burning a lot of surplus junk. It is necessary to do this every so often in order to have room to live. I must stop now but will write again in about a week. In the meantime you will be constantly in my thoughts.

I love you Dear One. Don't ever forget that you are my precious wife and that I want you all to myself after this war is over. No choirs, no organs, no [National] Guard, nothing but things we can do together. Hand in Hand Nana. Please.

This appeal to Norma may have been Wilber's last letter from Guadalcanal.

On this same day, Norma wrote to her father-in-law, revealing an awareness of her own contribution to the long-standing financial misunderstanding. She wrote from her new Washington address.

Feb. 20, 1944, Dear Father — I hope that all is well with you. If you think it would do any good to write a letter of apology to Mother, I would be glad to do so, as I really and truly now feel that I should apologize for my disrespect. I do not ever expect her to receive the children and/or myself in her heart, but do hope and pray that soon she may feel differently toward Wilber and write to him. He is in such mortal danger all the time, and I know that his heart aches for word from her.

On the morning of February 22, 1944, Wilber's battalion, the 169th Field Artillery Battalion, boarded the USAT Willard Holbrook for their seventh voyage. This was another older ship; it had served as the President Taft during the prewar years. It departed Guadalcanal at noon that day en route to Auckland, New Zealand. (Map 12) The departure must have been a great moment for these troops. They were returning to western culture after a 15-month absence.

x·o·ø·o·x

The Holbrook arrived in Auckland at 5 p.m. on February 27, and the 169th Field Artillery Battalion reached its base in Papakura (Opaheke) about 20 miles south of Auckland at 11 p.m. Liberal leaves were granted during March, and many men, including Wilber, availed themselves of the opportunity to see New Zealand, which led to a little romance for Wilber.

Feb. 28, 1944, Dearest Wife — I'm living with the staff in a real house. We are planning to buy a few chairs and rugs to make it nice. And tonight I'm writing in front of a cozy fire in a fire-place. Will wonders never cease!... Good night Dearest. I was up late last night [getting settled here] but I still love you.

Mar. 1, 1944 — My vacation is practically in effect now.... Half of my boys are on vacation now, and Ray [DeBlois] + I hope to get away next week some time. He is going with Downing and I go with Davis. Our plan is to get away from soldiers. Ray + Downing plan to fish and will probably sit in the canoe back to back so they will not need to see any soldiers.

Mar. 2, 1944 — Yesterday René [DeBlois] and I went to the city [probably Auckland] to check on vacation tours and fishing points.... I'm in a real depression trying to figure out something I'd like to do. Probably if I fish for a week or so, I'll welcome combat again.

Mar. 5, 1944 — Your letter mailed Dec. 16 came today as fresh and clean as if mailed last week. It was a sweet letter about our last Christmas in Bangor with love in every word. I felt so happy after reading it.... I'm sleeping long hours and can't seem to get too much of it.... Maybe I should go to a town where there is a good library, movies, and hotel and read + sleep for a week.

This was Wilber's last extant letter to Norma until the end of April, except for one on April 6, and there were only a few in May. They could have been misplaced, and Wilber admitted to some gaps in his letter writing due to his vacation travels. There are, in contrast, letters from him to me, Valerie, his father, and his brother during this period. The first to his father started with a scenic description followed by this overview of his men's activities.

March 5, 1944 — Now we are in a real rest area and our men are getting passes and trying to get drunk on the local beer and making the usual advances to the local girls. In some ways, as the C.O., I think I prefer the active combat when the men who make mistakes are evacuated or buried and don't get dumped on my doorstep.

On March 8, Wilber left for an 18-day vacation on North Island, New Zealand, and then on to South Island, with Capt. Earl Russell Davis. They traveled mostly by bus [letter 3/1/44] and were required by army regulation to be in uniform while in public.

March 10, 1944, Dear Hale — I am having two weeks vacation and this is my third day. Yesterday we drove very leisurely thru mountain country and sheep meadows. There are certainly a lot of sheep here and they are very pretty against the green hills.... It, so far, has been a wonderful rest. I had been a bit jumpy and very tired but now am feeling much better already....

I'm glad you are getting a chance to live with other boys and to have men teachers this year. It is important for each of us to decide what type of things we will and will not do.... Every man must set his own standards and must be true to them.... I am sure you will choose a good way to live. I love you son.

This fatherly advice, greatly shortened here, was admirable in that it avoided defining specific do's and don'ts. He left the boundaries up to me, a smart strategy when dealing with a 13-year-old.

On this date, I had begun my spring vacation (March 10 to 20) from St. Bernard's School. I went by train to Washington, D.C., where I stayed with Wilber's brother Paul and his wife Josephine. I saw little or nothing of Norma, who was hospitalized after being hit by a car in Dupont Circle. I went hiking with Paul and Jo and was aggressively toured all around Washington, D.C., on buses, trolleys, and on foot by Aunt Jo's father, Mr. Irey.

My reconstruction of Wilber's New Zealand vacation itinerary from souvenir photos he annotated has him visiting the Egmont, Whanganui, and Tongariro National Parks, all on North Island, about 200 miles south of Auckland. Visiting national parks had been Wilber's habit in the United States, and he continued it in New Zealand. On March 14, Wilber and Davis were in a hotel "in a large city," which probably was Christchurch on South Island. He wrote Valerie about the earlier week on North Island.

> Mar. 14, 1944 — Yesterday and the day before I was traveling in a car among pretty green fields over high steep hills and thru wooded ravines. The plants are different than ours and one often sees giant ferns which are taller than I. The names of some of the trees are native, for example the Wheki tree....
>
> Sunday [March 12] I visited in a little town and a man took me out to the bowling green for the afternoon. There was a tournament being played and it was very interesting. I had never seen outdoor bowling before....
>
> That evening we went to Evensong at St. Andrews, Church of England. The service was almost the same as ours and it was the first time I had heard a pipe organ since we were together. They chanted more of the service but in other respects were quite low church.
>
> Today [Tuesday], I'm in a large city [Christchurch], sitting in a hotel room listening to my little radio as I write. All this is a real rest from being in the jungle. I love you Darling.

It is likely that the church Wilber and Davis visited was St. Andrews, in Plimmerton, a seaside resort about ten miles outside Wellington and home of the Plimmerton Bowling Club. From published shipping schedules, it appears that they sailed for Christchurch the evening of March 13. In Christchurch, they stayed, I learned later, at the rather expensive and historic United Service Hotel. Souvenir picture cards of Christchurch locations in Wilber's collection suggest that they may have spent a day or two seeing the sights of the city.

Souvenir photos with Wilber's notations place him and Davis on the west coast of South Island at the Franz Josef Glacier. En route there, they most likely spent a few days in Queenstown hiking and boating and then bussed northward the 220 miles to the glacier areas of Westland and Cook National Parks. Mt. Cook is New Zealand's highest mountain at 12,316 feet.

By the time this next letter was written, Thursday, March 23, Wilber was "on the way back to work." He and Davis were due back at their camp early on Monday morning; their leave was coming to an end. This final letter to Valerie was probably written as they awaited the ferry to Wellington possibly at picturesque Picton at the north end of South Island.

> March 23, 1944 — The other day I went climbing on a glacier [Franz Josef Glacier]. It was the first ice & snow I have touched since my last leave in New York in 1941. The guide cut steps in the ice and we climbed up the steep places wondering if our shoes would slip. In the crevasses were lovely blue colors where the light had reflected. One ice cave about as big as our living room was so lovely I'll never forget it. It felt good too to be cold again. All about us were great rocky snow capped mountains with little white clouds playing hide & seek among their peaks....
>
> I'm nearly thru my rest now & am on the way back to work.

Wilber and Captain Davis arrived in Wellington late Thursday or early Friday, stayed at the St. George Hotel, and returned to Auckland by train, a roughly 15-hour trip, two days later on Sunday, March 26. The Wellington visit wrapped up a marvelous grand tour of New Zealand, which was actually not as relaxing as Wilber had hoped. Unmentioned in these letters so far was a bit of romance that Wilber found during this trip. He will allude to it in his final letter to Norma from New Zealand.

X·O·Ø·O·X

About this time, Wilber found time for another letter to Valerie, anticipating her forthcoming birthday (age 12, April 18).

> ca. Mar. 28, 2016, My Darling Daughter — Happy Birthday to you, My Dear. I cant [sic] tell you how glad I am to have you for my girl. You are just the very particular girl I would have picked if I had gone shopping in heaven and selected the nicest baby they had. I wish that this will be a really nice year for you and hope you can make it nicer too for all your friends. Don't forget you have a Daddy that loves you dearly. On your birthday, I'll pretend I'm having a "Round and Round" with all of us together again. Please pretend with me and maybe it will come true sooner. — Je t'aime, Wilber

20

"I'm taking over another battalion"
MATAKANA, NEW ZEALAND, APRIL–MAY, 1944

As Wilber returned to his unit in the Auckland region on March 27, Norma was struggling with what to do when Valerie and I finished the school year at our New Jersey boarding schools. Should she stay in Washington, D.C., with baby Gale and keep us in school, or should she reunite the family, possibly in Bangor, Maine, where we owned a home and where Wilber's job as a university department head awaited him? In either case, explaining a new family member to neighbors and friends would have been more than awkward. The social pressures of the day might well have driven Norma and Monte to consider giving up Gale for adoption, a thought that gives me the shivers, even today.

On his first day back on the job, Wilber was greeted with news of a brand new assignment. He wrote to Jo, his brother Paul's wife.

> Mar. 27, 1944 — I'm taking over another battalion [152 FA Bn.] in a few days so have a big job ahead bringing it up to the level of the 169th. I asked the General [Barker] if the shift was due to any failure on my part. He punched me in the ribs + said, "I don't need to tell [you] but I will say it again. The Division commander, the Assist. Div. Commander + I all consider you the best Arty. Bn. C.O. in the Div. That is why the shift." So I'm stuck and afraid he'll find out I'm a phony too.

General Barker apparently felt that the 152nd needed a strong commander.

The 152nd Field Artillery Battalion had been Wilber's outfit in Bangor, Maine, before it was inducted into federal service. This move to the command of a different battalion of the 43rd Division was a lateral move; it did not merit a promotion. The 152nd was stationed about 40 miles north of Auckland at Matakana (Warkworth). In action, it would support the 103rd Infantry Regiment, also from Maine; see Chart 2.

In his monthly letter to his father, Wilber was unusually candid about his situation and condition.

4/1/44 — Several things have happened. We moved back to civilization some time ago and I was given 18 days rest. It was nice but I was disappointed to find I still haven't rid myself of a tenseness and nervousness that developed in the "Islands." It isn't serious, but bothers me.... It was all very pleasant and expensive but I don't vacation easily.

The other event is the fact that I am taking command of the 152d FA Bn. today. I'm depressed about leaving the 169 [FA Bn.] but realize it's a war. The 152 is my home unit from Bangor, and I am glad to be back home. However I made this 169 famous all over the So. Pac. and really feel it was mine. Now I'm starting all over to try to do the same for the 152d....

The final recent event designed to make me feel old at the age of 44 is the fact that I am in the hospital myself for a general check up and minor repairs.... I think I told you I don't expect to live thru this affair [the war], but the fact doesn't particularly dismay me. In fact it enables me to do things in combat that I would otherwise not be able to do.

Wilber had succumbed to a discouraged and somewhat fatalistic view of his role in the war, clearly abetted by his being in the hospital and thus being inactive. He had yet to dig into the job of bringing the 152nd Field Artillery up to his standards.

Next came a big letter from Wilber to me about sex, the counterpart to his father's 1918 letter to him about morality and in particular, smoking! He wrote it from the hospital.

April 3, 1944 — Norma tells me you are taking girls to dances now.... This sex business is pretty powerful stuff when you get a little older and can give you either a lot of fun or a lot of trouble. The thing to remember is that it is one of the most powerful instincts we inherit, just as that of self-preservation and therefore can't quite be treated as a bad habit....

I know now that it is wrong to do anything that would harm either the body or spirit or reputation of another person. Doing anything, which a girl or you would look back on as being cheap or that would make either of you ashamed afterward, would be wrong. Since sex is based on a powerful instinct, you will see girls who will attract you that way.... it is therefore up to us men to see that our girls don't feel sorry for anything the next day or month. If an unmarried girl has a baby, people make life very hard for her and for her baby.

Neither he nor I realized how close to the bone he was cutting here. I must have sent this letter on to Norma; it was in one of the collections I obtained from her.

It doesn't do to feel that these situations won't happen to you. I have never lain with any woman but Nana and never will, but there have been women who were attractive to me that way.... After one is married, it is legal and normal and there is nothing to be ashamed or embarrassed about it. It is really just another way to express your love for each other, is fun and rather wonderful to know you both enjoy it.

Only one thing more – some boys as you probably know think a lot about sex and get into bad habits because of it. This may show up with a tendency to play with the penis, which is called masturbation.... In general try to be moderate in your habits.... I hike and climb, go to church, study every day, and work on the battalion duties each day. That keeps me on a fairly well balanced keel and I don't get my mind too much on anything.

Wilber was telegraphing here how he kept his own life in balance. The entirely voluntary statement "I have never lain with any woman but Nana" assures us yet again that Wilber's sexual experiences had been solely with Norma. I am impressed with his gender sensitivity and that he did not demonize masturbation. But he still displayed the male chauvinism typical of the era: the men should take care of the (helpless) girls.

By late April, Wilber was out of the hospital and settled in Matakana with his new unit, the 152nd FA Bn.

April 28, 1944 — I'm sitting at 10:00 P.M. in my hut beside my oil stove, thanking you for my warm pajamas with every shiver.... No one else will do, and I'll be glad when I can get back to the jungle and won't be seeing couples together and children playing in yards or lighted windows. Don't you hate single beds?...

I would never run a battalion like Whitney did this one. He had 2d Lts doing jobs for 1st Lts and vice versa, junior officers above their seniors and gave everyone the highest ratings officially even in cases where he said the officers were N.G. [no good].

A few weeks later, nevertheless, he would write some very positive comments about Whitney's command.

April 29, 1944 — This afternoon I spent all my free time studying the records of my officers. The information I gathered was quite encouraging.... I told Wing to watch this Bn. during the next combat and that I expected to make it the best in the division. He said that would be no surprise.

May 3, 1944, Hello Bright Eyes! — Next week we go into the mountains for a month of exercises. That means fewer letters, I'm afraid, so don't draw any heroic conclusions. It will likely be a lot colder there than here but it is a volcanic area and I may settle down in a nice warm geyser and refuse to come out to play with the General.

The divisional exercises were to be in the Rerewhakaaitu range outside Rotorua, some 120 miles south of Auckland (Map 12). Rotorua is famous for its hot springs. But southward and higher elevations meant colder weather. In May, the New Zealand winter was settling in.

Two weeks later, Wilber was in those mountains and wrote to me and Valerie.

May 18, 1944, Dear Son — For the past two weeks I have been on the firing range with the Bn. It is a lovely area with a volcano on one side that erupted in 1880 and a lake in the impact area. We find gun positions in valleys behind high hills and shoot out into a large rough plain. All the battalions here have been doing the same thing and we shoot at the same targets, so it is interesting to watch and see who comes the closest to the targets and which Bn. is the fastest. In three exercises, the 152 [Wilber's unit] has not only been the most accurate but also the fastest.

May 21, 1944, Dear Valerie — This is a nice brisk morning and I am just thawing out from a very cold night. Frost was thick everywhere when I got up.... You must have had quite an adventure on your way back to school.

Valerie had spent her spring vacation with Norma in Washington, D.C. She still remembers her return on Sunday April 23. The trip did not go at all well: she left her purse with money and instructions in the taxi taking her between train stations in Newark, and then got on a train going in the wrong direction, though she managed to straighten it out. Upon finally arriving in Morristown, she was relieved to find the school station wagon ready to take her "to the school that [she] would come to call home."

For Wilber, Sunday provided a break in the intensive training and testing. In addition to the above letter to Valerie, he sent one off to Norma.

May 21, 1944 — It's so nice to have a talk with you again. The past week has been very strenuous for me but a triumph for the 152. Our firing has been far superior to our friendly competitors.

The final days of the 43rd Division's month in the mountains would terminate with intensive graded artillery tests.

On the next Sunday, Wilber wrote again to Norma even though the firing continued. He also found time to relax and establish rapport with some of the officers of his new unit.

May 28, '44 — Last evening, six of us (Maj. Fish, Capts. Mushik, Ackerson, Green, + Lt. Landers) went to a hotel for dinner and to a [movie] show later. I didn't realize it at the time but it developed later that the previous Bn. C.O. had never done such a thing.

The results of the final artillery tests were reported to his father.

May 31, 1944, Dear Father — I've just finished a rather strenuous month in the mountains of [Rerewhakaaitu]. We are not in combat but have been training our replacements, working with our infantry, and doing the tests required of all artillery units in the States before they sail. It has been a very gratifying month. On our tests, the scores for the four Bns. involved were

[Battalion]	Test 1	Test 2	Test 3	Av.
Bradt's [152]	Sat	95.5%	100%	97.5
McCormick's [103]	Sat	70%	94.5%	86.7%
DeBlois' [169]	Sat	57%	72.5%	64.7%
Nichols' [192]	Sat	52%	54.7%	53.4%

You will note the mathematics of the scoring board is a little weak, so it may all be a mistake.... Anyway the 152 was away out front and I hope it means they get the hot point in the next push. I've asked for it, but of course it is a matter affected by the mission of my Infantry, the 103d [Inf. Rgt.].

(I would venture to guess that the other battalion commanders were not volunteering for the "hot point.")

As you see by the news, Admiral Halsey has moved to a new assignment because the So. Pac. [phase] is completed. I regret our no longer being under him and will always be proud to have served under him.

The 43rd Division was now, or soon would be, under General MacArthur's Southwest Pacific Area command (as distinct from Halsey's former South Pacific Area command).

On April 22, MacArthur's forces had advanced westward 580 miles by sea to the central New Guinea north coast in landings at Aitape and Hollandia (Map 2), thus bypassing the Japanese 18th Army. However, since the landings isolated the 18th Army from its sources of supply, its survival depended on the elimination of the new Allied positions. The 18th Army began a westward land-based movement toward Aitape; a major battle was anticipated.

On May 18, MacArthur's troops moved 100 miles farther west in New Guinea to the Wadke Islands. By this time mopping-up actions at Hollandia and Aitape were well in hand and airfields at each site were operational, but the Japanese 18th Army to the east of Aitape remained a threat. Landings at Biak Island (Map 5), another 200 miles westward, took place on May 27. MacArthur had promised the Filipinos that he would return, and he was driving toward that goal.

21

"I've asked for the point of honor"
NEW ZEALAND, JUNE–JULY, 1944

The battalion was back "home" in Matakana, north of Auckland. It was mid-winter, and the men were given some days off to compensate for their extra work in the recent exercises. This gave Wilber time to write about a tongue-tied general, the next action, and his homebody inclinations.

June 1, '44, Hello Wife of Mine — We have just returned from our field exercises and tests.... However, my luck was with me for the Bn. really went to town.... We are trying to act modest but it is hard.

Barker called me in and complimented the Bn. very highly, excusing himself by saying "He had to go by the figures." I assured him we weren't 97% perfect but that I would rate the Bn. at about 85%. That cheered him immensely and he admitted I probably knew weak spots they did not know of. I reassured him that such was the case, but that I proposed to take care of matters. Before we changed the subject, he felt better, having been convinced I wasn't going to retire from active training.... In the meantime maybe the 152 can get in a few more rounds with the Japs. I've asked for the point of honor in the next action so we may get a chance. This Bn. did a lot of sitting around in N. Ga. while the 169 had business.

June 2 – This is Fr. [Friday] P.M. and nearly everyone has left for town. Only the "duty officers" for each battery and one for the Bn. will be staying – except for me. Maj. Pierson and Maj. Fish still worry about my not going social each weekend. They have observed that I have a good time with people so have decided I just need encouragement.... I consistently agree that all their proposals for moving into the private home of "lovely people," or having a date with a "wonderful girl," or spending a weekend at the races, or with the navy would be lots of fun; then [I] point out that I would prefer a quiet week-end minding my own business.

On June 6, the Allies finally took the war into the heartland of Europe with a massive invasion of the Normandy beaches of France.

> June 6, 1944 (Invasion Day!) — Invasion Day! I've hoped so long for it. Darling it's another step toward the end. Thank God for an Administration that gave our men training and equipment before asking them to cross the [English] Channel. Many will die but at least they had a chance and that is worth much.
>
> June 9, 1944 — It's another rainy night (6:30 P.M.) and I'm sitting in my hut with a cozy oil stove beside me. On the stove is heating my bath water. On the walls are my maps that you sent me showing the dates of our advances in the different theatres....
>
> Last night I was invited over to Mr. + Mrs. [Olive] Croker's house for tea. Three other officers went with me. It is the third time I've been there. They have some of our men over nearly every night and officers about once a week. The Crokers are dairy farmers and are very nice, hospitable people. If we ever come here together I will want you to meet them; Mrs. C. serves a mean table. It is a meal such as one seldom sees. I never eat breakfast after I've been there and should fast for a whole day afterward.
>
> I'm glad you are getting our [Bangor] house in shape again. It probably needs it badly. Your idea of being with the children pleases me too.

Norma had decided to return to Bangor, Maine, with Valerie and me; baby Gale would remain in Washington with Monte and his mother. Being separated from her baby would certainly become a severe test of her ability to conform to the proper life demanded by the times. Come September, I would be in ninth grade, one grade ahead of my former classmates, and Valerie would be in seventh.

The closing exercises of the year at St. Bernard's School were held on June 14. I graduated from eighth grade after a spring term interlaced with print shop work and scouting. Norma was at the graduation. We went directly from there to Bangor by train as we had no car.

x·o·ø·o·x

In New Zealand, the 152nd Field Artillery Battalion was preparing for its next move, to New Guinea.

> June 17, [1944] — Our inspection was quite a complete affair with division officers from Arty, ordnance, survey, signal, motor vehicle and supply branches – 12 in all. Altho I haven't received the written reports yet, they all left amid a barrage of favorable comments.

On July 3, the move to the ship in Auckland was imminent, but Wilber did not mention it in this next letter; lacking any confidential information, it could be mailed immediately.

[July] 3, 1944 — I'll have to make this letter short because I've quite a few things cooking just now.... Since I've come here, I've obtained 18 Bronze Stars for the 152 men for acts performed in New Ga. They didn't see as much action nor as hot action in the 152 as the 169 boys did.

Later that same day, Wilber began a vivid description of the hurried move of his battalion of 500 men to Auckland for the boarding of the transport ship, USAT Sea Devil. The battalion was 40 miles north of Auckland, the ship arrival and loading schedule was quite uncertain, and the supply of trucks was limited. Wilber vividly portrayed the stresses, strains, and hard work of such a move. These letters would not be mailed until the move was history. Here are excerpts.

July 3, 1944, — This is the first of a series of letters that will not be mailed until our censor says we can say we have moved. Today I am in our camp at Matakana, N.Z. We have just received word we are to move and in a hurry. I've sent Maj. Fish and four staff officers to Auckland to take care of things at the port and on ship, also Burns to Div. Arty. as a liaison officer. We have loaded all our trucks with impedimenta and sent them down to the area assigned to us until the wharf is free....

About 1100 [hours] Fish called and said everything was quiet, no ship had come in and that we could relax. At noon he called again and said Hussey's battery [Battery B] should get down (70 miles) as soon as possible and that he would have quarters for them. They were to be a loading detail to load the ship. They have gone just now amid much perspiration.

The 70-mile distance given by Wilber suggests the heavily loaded trucks took the long route westward through Helensville to avoid the ferries; the current Harbour Bridge and Upper Harbor Bridge were not built until well after the war.

July 4, 1944 — This is a fair morning with hope of sunshine.... At 1000 [hours] Fish and Burns call with the report that no loading has started, with a lot of details to be checked, and say Div. Arty. is sending us more trucks from Nichols's and McCormick's Bns. We send out all our trucks again loaded on the general idea that what is gone won't have to be moved later.

At 1130 Fish calls again and says to rush McIntire's battery [Battery C] down. Loading is under way and division is in a mood to rush. He needs more men. Our borrowed trucks arrive just in time to be loaded + started back with orders to check with Fish before returning. We relax a little for we've no trucks so can't do anything even if we do receive orders.

The letter continued on July 5, with the remaining events of July 4 [152nd FA Bn. Journal].

July 5 – At 1300 Fish calls again + says everything is under control, our trucks are started back and it looks like we might be here a week yet. I tell him to release half the borrowed trucks (McCormick's) and to send the others up to me to stand by overnight.

At 1500 he calls back and says the ship has suddenly decided to load vehicles that night, that he needs more stuff. I decided to move the rest of the Bn. down starting at 2000 [8 P.M.] and tell him to send me every truck he can spare from the loading.... Between 1500 and 1700 there have been three changes of decision as to where the Bn. will go.

It's cold on the way down and I notice it more than usual because we had ice cream for supper.... However Ruhlin had kept reserved for me for the past week a room [in] an officer's rest camp and I find good accommodations.

Fish has all hands working and word comes from Pierson that the Bn. is on the road [at 2000 on 4th; 152nd FA Bn. Journal]. I go to bed. And dream of my dear ones, of trucks, of our house, ships, changes in orders, [and] combat, and spend a rather active night so far as dreams go.

The balance of the battalion arrived in Auckland just after midnight on July 5, according to the battalion journal. The battalion apparently rested easy on July 5, a Wednesday, after the strenuous move of the day before, as there were no further journal entries for July 5.

July 6, 1944 — Here is that man again. I get up late (0830) [July 6] and purposely sleep thru breakfast so I'll get plenty of rest. I think of how you would approve and thank my stars for two such field officers as Fish and Pierson. By 0900, I'm at the wharf and discover I'm the commander of all the troops on board....

I go on the ship [USAT Sea Devil] + contact the ATS officer on board. He is a captain and seems to have a personal feud with the skipper, which doesn't simplify my problems at all. At 1100 we assign the ship's details (totaling about 500 men) to the various units, make plans for embarking the men and getting them fed as soon as possible.

At 1150 [General] Barker shows up and takes me to lunch. I eat oysters on the half shell, fried oysters and steak. Barker underestimated me so I had to help him pay for the dinner. He was much embarrassed.

Oysters were a favorite of Wilber's. He evidently did not hold back on how many he ate; see below.

> By 1300 I was back at the ship to watch personnel go aboard. My Bn. is first. They go on quietly and rapidly.... At 1730 [the mess officer] started feeding the men on board but we are still loading personnel. That is finished at 1800. I place a guard around the ship.
>
> At 2330, I go to my stateroom. There is only one on this ship and I share it with the Div. chaplain, Fr Connelly (Rom. C.).... I decide I'll sleep late again and let Rainey work at Troop Hqs. without me until after a late breakfast.

The ship was finally loaded with its 2400 soldiers and ready to sail; Wilber could relax. The next day, he described the ship's departure.

> July 7, [1944] — Ye olde man slept thru breakfast this morning on the theory that the six-dozen oysters [!] he ate yesterday would sustain him for a little longer....
>
> It is a cool cloudy morning and the ship is nosed away from the wharf about 1000 and out into the stream.... The pilot is dropped at 1100 and I enter in my record book: "Lv. Auckland on [USS Sea Devil] 1100 July 7, 1944 WB," so it's official. We are really off and on our way back to the combat area. The harbor is beautiful as we pull out. A[uckland] is really a lovely city. I'll show you some day.

Norma never made it there, but I did.

> Before we leave the N.Z. subject there are some people here to whom I wish you would write if you have time. First Mr. + Mrs. Sidney (or Sydney?) Smith, Matakana, N.Z. He is the local butcher. Matakana is just a crossroads town of a dozen homes. The people here are nearly all country people and I have never known people anywhere try as hard for so long (five months) to make us feel at home.... I gave Mrs. Smith a pin of novelty jewelry, a black boy dancer.
>
> Another is Mrs. (and Mr.) S(?) A(?) Croker.... The emphasis on the Mrs. is because Mr. never says a word. He just sits and smiles and answers all questions by one word. Mrs. C. has more or less organized all the entertainment (local) for my men. For example, she specialized in fine and fancy cooking.... These evenings [at her home] consisted of tea (our supper) which is a good substantial meal of soup, salad, vegetables, meat and dessert and, about three hours later, supper (!!!) which is your departure snack. It consists of tea, about eight kinds of cakes, cookies, sandwiches, patties,

scones, puddings and "trifle." One eats some of each and is assisted to the car. Usually one such event is all the human system can stand in a week.... Please also mention the Jones girls. They are numerous and are practically her Lieutenants.... Mrs. Cs address is also Matakana, N.Z.

Wilber was full of gratitude for the kindnesses of these people and wanted Norma to help him return his thanks. He was also creating a record of names and addresses that would survive him should the worst occur. I looked up some of these people when I was in New Zealand in 1984. It was here, as he continued, that we finally learn about his romantic episode.

There is only one other letter and it isn't so important. That would be to Miss Olive Madsen, Wairasa [Wairarapa], N.Z. That isn't the complete address but I think it is OK. If I find the rest after we reach my trunk I'll correct this. She + her mother I've mentioned before as part of my vacation contacts. [That letter is among the missing.] I met them on the boat going to Christchurch, N.Z. from Wellington and liked them. I found she was taking her mother on a vacation, the main purpose of which seemed to be to meet some N.Z. aviator. On one of his duty nights, I took her to a movie and then on my return to Wellington ten days later, we (Davis + I) were invited out to their farm. We couldn't go, so the daughter came into town and spent the day with us. In fact she nearly walked me to death. That was that and OK, but I never saw the farm.

Wilber would have done well to drop the subject here, but in fact he went on with more (incriminating?) details!

As I said above, this letter isn't urgent. I think I paid for dinners etc. to settle that aspect of things. In fact I sent her a corsage [!] and learned later she ran a florist shop. It should be a lesson to me. She wrote a few times and I finally wrote that I would only have time to write you and suggested she end the correspondence. She wrote one more letter, which I haven't and won't answer in which she said "of course she would never want to do anything which would hurt my family." Since she rather accurately read my mind, I was a bit ashamed and felt a bit embarrassed. If you write and say you appreciate her kindness and her mother's kindness to me, they will know I hadn't felt she had any designs on me. I could write that, but I don't want to get involved again in a morale building correspondence.

A corsage. How romantic! Was this a complete account of his meetings with Olive and his feelings about the meetings and correspondence, or was there more to it? The extended details and the boyish awkwardness of this "confession" make clear

Olive Madsen wearing the corsage given her by Wilber in Christchurch, New Zealand, March 1944. She is pictured here at the modest Ambassador Hotel where she and her mother stayed. She gave me this photo on my 1984 visit. [PHOTO: OLIVE MADSEN]

the importance of this encounter to Wilber, but also suggest that there was little else to tell. I did meet Miss Madsen on my 1984 visit to New Zealand, and she completed the story for me as I recount in the next Interlude (page 187).

To finish my July 7th record, the rest of the day was spent in issuing plans + orders for the troops, feeding, recreation, sanitation, discipline, security for a trip thru the [censored; Coral Sea]....

I love you all three. These letters are for all of you and are just the story of how I left the South Pacific.

The 43rd Division was off on a new mission: landings at Aitape, New Guinea, on the north central coast, to the west of the Japanese 18th Army, to reinforce American units already there. The shipment of the 43rd Division to Aitape was hurried because of indications that the bypassed (and trapped) Japanese 18th Army was preparing attacks westward in an attempt to dislodge the Americans and capture American supplies and the American-held airstrips.

In the Central Pacific, the Allied advanced on June 15, 1944, to the Mariana Islands, the next closest group to Japan. The Allied occupation was made secure with the end of Japanese resistance on Saipan July 9 and the capture of Tinian and Guam Islands on August 1 and 11 respectively. Also on June 15, B-29 bombers based in China made the first air raid on Japan (Kyushu) since the Doolittle raid two years earlier.

The naval Battle of the Philippine Sea (June 19–20, 1944) took place west of the Marianas while portions of the fleet were still supporting the Saipan landings. The battle effectively destroyed the Japanese naval air arm. Of 430 Japanese carrier planes; only 35 survived the two days of battle. [Morison, Vol. VIII, p. 319]. American air losses were minor in comparison, and no American ships were lost.

On the India-Burma front, the Allies repelled a major Japanese offensive. After months of bitter fighting from March to June, the Japanese, without supplies and decimated by disease, retreated back to the Burmese plains. Fighting farther north and in China continued.

Throughout the spring, the Russians had been advancing westward in Europe. A renewed attack began on June 22. On July 3, in the north of the Russian front, Minsk fell, and on July 8, the nearby surrounded German Fourth Army surrendered. The Russians were outside Warsaw, Poland, by August 1, 1944.

In Italy, the Allies had broken through the Cassino defenses in May, and entered Rome on June 4. The Germans retreated over the next two months, June and July, to the "Gothic Line" near Florence, which they would hold through most of August. In the meantime, of course, the Normandy landings in France had occurred on June 6. The battle to break out of Normandy lasted until early August. On August 15, the Allies established another front with landings on the southern coast of France.

All in all, the Allies were on the move, but as the Axis forces were pushed closer to their homelands, their supply lines became shorter and fighting intensified. Exacting the greatest possible cost from the Allies with the greatest possible delay was the goal of both Germany and Japan. If the Allies became sufficiently dispirited, perhaps an armistice could be obtained that was more favorable than the outcome demanded by the Allies, which was unconditional surrender.

22

Interlude 1984, New Zealand
NEW ZEALAND, OCTOBER 6–13, 1984

In October 1984, I was scheduled to again join my young colleague, Ronald Remillard, to conduct astronomical observations at the Siding Springs Observatory in Australia. I took that opportunity to visit New Zealand for the week prior to our work, as I had done in May 1983 with my visits to the Philippines and the Solomons. My journal provides much of the following material.

THE JONES GIRLS AND SMITHS

Upon arriving in Auckland the morning of October 6, after 32 hours of air travel, I drove to Matakana (1.5 hours) where the 152nd FA Bn. had been quartered for five months in 1944. Matakana had a main (essentially the only) street with about 20 houses and a butcher shop. Since Wilber's letter mentioned Sidney Smith, the butcher who gave him free steaks, I immediately went to the house across the road from the butcher shop where the butcher's truck was parked (it was Saturday). It turned out to be a different butcher, but his wife, Dawn Jones Penney, was one of the Jones girls (there had been six of them) mentioned in Wilber's letters as helping with all the dinners put on by Mrs. Croker for his men and officers.

I had a lovely chat with Dawn (she was 59 then), was given 1940s photos of the Crokers (deceased), the Smiths, and the Jones girls. She took me to the farm (Whistler's farm on Port Wells Road) a few kilometers away, where the 152nd Field Artillery had camped. I met the farmer, saw his cows being milked, and walked among the remains of the camp—only a few concrete tent bases were left. She also showed me the former Croker home where the sumptuous meals had taken place.

A battalion of 500 men suddenly arriving in the midst of this tiny town must have made quite an impression, although this camp had been used by other troops at other times. Dawn told me about the dances and dinners, but she did not remember my father specifically. The entire visit gave me a strong sense of Wilber's experiences and, in general, a sense of how small towns all over New Zealand had handled the influx of American soldiers. There must have been many of those overwhelming tea suppers and, in return, many shared American goods.

The next afternoon (Oct. 7), I drove down (about 1.5 hours) to see Sidney and Minnie Smith in Devonport and found both of them nimble and alert despite Sidney being quite ill. They remembered my father well, the first people to remember him in my Pacific travels. They had an autograph book with his inscription, "To a good neighbor with a real wish for a reunion some day at 204 Broadway, Bangor, Maine. Wilber E. Bradt." Reading this now (2016) brings tears to my eyes.

Minnie still had the little "black-boy" pin Wilber had given her [letter 7/7/44] and showed it to me. They told me about entertaining the men in their home. Wilber may have eaten in their home a dozen times and they ate at the camp about half that number. "Wilber loved to come and sit in front of the big open fire. Some of the men smoked cigars and played blackjack," they said. More than once, Wilber had arranged for the Smiths and others to get some scarce groceries or delicacies, like sugar and sockeye salmon, to compensate for their expenses in feeding the men in their homes.

On a subsequent visit to New Zealand with my wife two years later, we looked up Mrs. Smith and had a nice visit. Mr. Smith had died in the meantime.

OLIVE

After a brief visit to South Island where I saw Mt. Cook and spent an afternoon in Queenstown, I flew to Wellington, the capital city of New Zealand, where I hoped to find Olive Madsen, the woman Wilber had admired. My previous queries had not located her. From my Wellington hotel, I asked telephone information for the phone number of an Olive Madsen in the Wairarapa district. Immediately, I had her number and then her voice on the phone. She was delighted to hear from me, remembered Wilber and invited me to her home. We arranged to meet the next afternoon.

At about noon the next day, I was off to Carterton, Wairarapa, about two hours to the north, to see Olive. I drove in my Avis rental over a beautiful yellow-flowered mountain: lots of hairpin turns I had not expected and then into flat warm sheep country. I loved it – what a tour!

The visit with Olive Madsen was an absolute delight. I was warmly welcomed and spent several hours chatting with her in her sitting room before returning to Wellington. She was 69 (b. January 10, 1915) and very perky. She had had cancer 18 years earlier and a stroke 18 months before my visit, of which I could see no evidence. She never married and had lived with her mother for years. She operated a flower shop for 16 years and then a ladies clothing shop for another 16 years. She had moved to her present home in 1972. Her story of her meetings with my father vividly filled out his versions. More or less, it went as follows.

I met your father (Wilber) and Davis (the officer he was traveling with) on the ferry from Wellington to Christchurch on South Island. I was on holiday with my mother. In Christchurch, Mother and I went to our modest Bed and Breakfast hotel (the Ambassador), and Davis and Wilber went to the expensive United Services Hotel. The next day, while I was out, flowers arrived from Wilber with an invitation to go to the movies. The flowers were orange to match my frock – it was nice he remembered. I was in quite a tizz, being a country girl (age 29) with a Lt. Col. (age 44) paying attention to me. (My mother was unusually attractive, and it was she who usually drew the attention.)

I think Olive herself had also been quite attractive, according to a photo from that time.

We went to the movies and it turned out that he had previously bought the tickets and inspected the reserved seats to make sure they were OK. When he took me back he kissed me goodnight, but other than that never made a move for me, unlike most of the many other G.I.'s I had met. Wilber had told me he was married, but never discussed his family or job. That was that for Christchurch. Davis and Wilber continued their tour and we our vacation.

About ten days later [on Friday, March 24], I received a call from Wilber from Wellington; he and Davis were returning north. They had very little time and so Wilber asked me to come down to Wellington for the evening and following day. He would pay for my hotel room in their hotel (St. George). Ordinarily, I would never accept such an invitation, but since he was so perfect a gentleman, I accepted and took the bus to Wellington.

That evening, Davis, he, and I had supper together. Your father and Davis were like brothers. We then spent the rest of the evening in the hotel lounge with a charming group of New Zealand and American people. Later Wilber spent 1/2 hour with me in my room, but nothing serious occurred. We sat on the side of the bed and chatted. At one point I leaned across his lap to reach for something and he kissed me lightly on the neck. He remembered that later in a letter he wrote.

The next day, we ate breakfast together [with Davis probably] and walked around Wellington with Davis. Wilber made no attempt to exclude Davis. As we passed a bookstore, Wilber romped into it in a little boyish way and bought me a book of poems that I still have here [which she showed me]. We then went over to see a cricket game at Basin Reserve at Courtney Place by tram [trolley]. I tried to explain cricket to them, probably not successfully.

189

Olive Madsen, 1944. She gave me this photo on my visit in October 1984.
[PHOTO: OLIVE MADSEN]

We stayed only about 1/4 hour. We then walked to Oriental Bay to see the boats, expensive houses, etc. I took a photo of Wilber and Davis there. Then, back to St. George's Hotel, and then I got the bus for home.

Wilber wrote to me at most two times and I wrote two or three times. He had asked me to 'please write'. I no longer have his letters. The whole episode must have meant a great deal to me if I can remember so many details of it now.

I asked her if she had hoped that he might come back, that perhaps he had been her "lost love" for whom she stayed forever single?

I knew he was married, and goodbye was goodbye. I had a number of other American correspondents. I was very leery of marriage—possibly because my parents were quite unhappy—and my close association with my mother probably didn't help. (A slight tone of regret here.)

She showed me photos (1940s and 1980s) of her American correspondents, and told me that some of the marines who had been stationed near her town were later killed in Tarawa. She came up with some remarkable mementos of Wilber: the book of poems, the negative of the photo she took of Wilber and Davis at Oriental Bay—a photo I had known but not its provenance—which she gave me, and a Lt. Col.'s silver oak-leaf insignia Wilber had given her, a not inconsequential gift. Olive offered it to me, and I suggested that it would mean more to her than to me. She agreed and kept it.

After leaving Olive and Carterton, I returned to Wellington and visited the St. George hotel where Olive, Wilber, and Davis had stayed. The small staircases up to the rooms surely dated from the 1940s or earlier as did the rather narrow halls and solid wooden banisters.

I can feel viscerally the bedroom scene in the hotel as if it had been me: the mixed feelings of romance, chivalry, and physical desire combined with timidity

Olive Madsen and me at her home in Carterton, New Zealand, October 1984. She died in 1989. [PHOTO: HALE BRADT]

and nervousness about whether and how to proceed. Olive's candor in recounting these details gave me confidence that her story was complete in its essentials, including that the relationship progressed no further. Olive and Wilber were two ships passing in the night of war.

For her part, Norma took Wilber's descriptions of the encounter as a clear indication that Wilber had had a sexual affair with Olive, or so she told others. Her belief may indeed have served as justification for her own actions—and as a bolster for her own sanity.

Beyond the romantic drama, Olive's story was rich in the details of ordinary facets of Wilber's and Davis's tour of New Zealand. They stayed in the better hotels, they had no vehicle and so mostly traveled by bus, their tour of Wellington that day was on foot and tram, and they routinely wore full uniforms. I communicated with Olive for several years after our meeting. She died in 1989.

My week in New Zealand was up; on October 13, I departed Auckland. It was quite a shock to re-enter 1984 as I at last flew to Australia and met Remillard for our astronomical observations.

Wilber E. Bradt, Lt. Col.
No. 0182711, Hq. 152nd F. A. Bu.
A. P. O. 43, c/o Postmaster
San Francisco, Calif.

U.S. ARMY POSTAL SERVICE
4
SEP
1
1944
A.P.O.

AIR 6 MAIL
CENTS
UNITED STATES OF AMERICA

Wilber E Bradt

Miss Valerie E. Bradt
204 Broadway
Bangor
Maine

PART V

COMBAT, NEW GUINEA

AITAPE, NEW GUINEA
JULY—DECEMBER, 1944

Studio portrait of Norma Sparlin Bradt, November 1944. [PHOTOGRAPHER: UNKNOWN]

23

"I'm back on the Jap business again"
AITAPE, NEW GUINEA, JULY–AUGUST, 1944

Norma, Valerie and I, aged 38, 12, and 13 respectively, were together again at our prewar home at 204 Broadway, Bangor, Maine, in July 1944. Valerie and I remained unaware of Norma's baby (Gale) who was in Washington, D.C., with her father and grandmother. It was to be a relatively relaxed summer for Valerie and me, with no significant commitments other than helping around the house. I recall long hours reading on the porch. My violin practicing and lessons, totally neglected during my year in boarding school, resumed that summer.

My memories of life in Bangor that year are rich with varied experiences. I enjoyed the freedom a bicycle gave me for the first time since our summer in Hattiesburg, Mississippi, two years earlier. I bicycled the three-quarter-mile trip to Garland Street Junior High (now the Cohen School) with scores of other students, as did Valerie. And I continued my riding all winter, through snow and ice, much to my Bangor friends' amazement. I became adept at repairing my bike and learned the hard way that one does not take apart the coaster brake with its multitude of tiny parts and ball bearings on a grassy lawn!

A friend and I would ride our bikes into the countryside and shoot at crows with our .22 rifles, though we never hit one. We had better luck shooting rats in the city dump. I was active in scouting, helping to run our small troop, which put on a war trophy show in the high school. I took my schoolwork seriously, including algebra and French, but not overly so. I played in the school orchestra; we played loud marches with great gusto and little precision. I was beginning to find girls attractive. However, I was barely able to muster the nerve to ask Sue Chase out for the only date I had that entire year. I took her to a movie matinee, but that was a bust romantically because another of her admirers came along with us!

X·O·Ø·O·X

It had been nine months since the men of the 43rd Division had last seen combat. Wilber's troops were now, on July 8, 1944, en route on the USAT Sea Devil from New Zealand in the midst of winter to the warmer climes of New Guinea (Maps 2, 5), in theory refreshed, trained, and fully staffed. It was a voyage of ten days. Despite the presence of many replacements who had never heard a shot fired in battle, the division was nominally a seasoned professional outfit. As noted, indications in June that the Japanese were moving westward and thus threatening Aitape led to the July 7 embarkation of the 43rd Division in Auckland for Aitape. Wilber described the voyage to Norma.

> July 11, 12, 1944 — This is morning now and a soft breeze blows and it promises to be a hot day. I've enjoyed the heat and the freedom at night from all the blankets I used a week ago. Our men have pretty well adapted themselves to the ship's routine.... Most of the big gamblers have learned to control their ambitions. It stopped quite suddenly when I confiscated about $75.00 [roughly $1000 in today's dollars].... The inspection yesterday showed a spick + span ship. As the boys say, if we are here long enough, we will clean up every ship in the Pacific....
>
> Dearest, since I'm going back to the jungle, packages are in order again at your convenience. This is a request for lobster, mustard, oysters, cheese, coca cola syrup, olives and any other items that do not cost ration coupons and that might make good sandwiches. (No Vienna sausage please.) ... I'll send a request [required by the postal service] about once a month just to remind you husbands + daddies are some trouble + like to be spoiled.

On July 10, one week before the arrival of the 43rd Division at Aitape, the Japanese 18th Army under Lt. Gen. Hatazo Adachi attacked westward at the Driniumor River in the vain hope of capturing Tadji airfield 15 miles to the west (near Aitape, Map 13) and thus acquiring American food supplies. It broke through one segment of the U.S. lines but was driven back. Subsequent sporadic fighting took place well into August. The Japanese were suffering "increasingly heavy casualties from combat, starvation and disease; they had no artillery support and could obtain none." [Smith, *Approach*, p. 195]

The USAT Sea Devil arrived at Aitape on the morning of July 17, and the battalion was ashore by mid-afternoon [152nd FA Bn. Journal]. This was an extremely busy time for Wilber. His battalion was initially stationed on the Tadji Plantation at the mouth of the Raihu River. Their mission was to defend the Tadji airfield several miles to the east. The battalion saw no organized combat for about three weeks. Interestingly, Wilber now revealed that he was on New Guinea. And he continued to worry about his relationship with Norma.

July 19, 1944 — I'm back on the Jap business again. You can be sure it is a welcome change. Just now I'm sitting under a tent beside the ever-present palm tree. This palm tree is in New Guinea but it looks familiar just the same. So far I haven't fired any shots in anger but other people are, so I have hopes.

July 25, 1944, Dearest Norma — Apparently something I have said about your writing and music has worried you. Dearest I didn't mean to hurt you. Please know that. Also when I spoke of wanting you just to be a wife to me, I realized that is out of the question. Things will work out OK, Dear. I'll be trying to be an understanding husband when I come home. This being apart is hard on each of us and my first prayer is that afterward we can find something as fine as we knew before the war.

Wilber was becoming more realistic about his relationship with Norma. It was not to be all roses and sex. He then responded further to some of Norma's worries.

July 29, 1944 — I've three grand long letters from you, each written when you were too tired on June 25, July 2, and 7. Thank you.... Your letter doesn't sound dreary. It sounds tired and maybe lonesome.... Sparlins do get so "perterbated," and my stumbling letters never seem to picture my thoughts correctly. In fact most of my difficulties started in my letters.... Your declaration of independence is noted.

Norma was insisting on her independence, but had willingly returned to her former domestic life. She was not free of the norms of the times.

I was out on an infantry patrol today and am pretty tired tonight. It wasn't dangerous so don't be worried about me. René DeBlois was wounded yesterday. He caught a bomb fragment in the fleshy part of his leg just above the knee.

There were no Japanese aircraft in the area then! According to Wilber's former subordinate, Capt. Howard Brown, DeBlois was wounded by a practice bomb or bomblet dropped by a U.S. plane for target practice. Friendly fire was a consistent threat, as Wilber, in a rare admission, then revealed.

We get in the news a lot but this, so far, is a pretty sedate battle for me. I've only been scared once and that was by our own mortars.

On August 10, Wilber's battalion moved about 18 miles east to the mouth of the Driniumor River. The battalion gave artillery support to aggressive patrolling east of the Driniumor River, which encountered pockets of resistance. Forward observer and liaison parties from the artillery battalion accompanied these patrols

Wilber (left) and Capt. Frank J. Burns adjusting artillery fires in New Guinea [letter 9/16/44]. [PHOTO: PROBABLY U.S. ARMY SIGNAL CORPS]

and brought artillery fires onto Japanese strong points. Small aircraft were also used to carry out artillery observations [152nd FA History].

Two days after the move, Wilber wrote to Norma, about an exploit of his executive officer (second in command), Major Waldo H. Fish.

12 Aug. 1944 — [Note on the side of the page:] Don't worry about this combat. It's really tame. Numerous Japs are surrendering. WB

Fish just came in with his prisoner and he was his prisoner that he captured himself. The whole Bn. is thrilled about it. This is probably the first Jap ever captured by an artillery major. Fish said the Jap was bathing in the ocean and was wearing a loincloth and carrying a grenade. He looked at Major Fish and threw the grenade out into the ocean. He had a can of our rations and came up to Fish holding his hand out and grabbed and shook vigorously Maj. Fish's hand. Then he offered Maj. Fish a cracker out of the can. When Fish declined, he took a bite and looked like it was very good and ran his hand up + down in front of his stomach as if it were a big fat one. Next he took some Jap rations out of a cloth he had on the beach and smelled it, then made an awful face and threw it toward the Jap lines.

Fish put him in the car and started off and the Jap began to sing. He bowed and bowed toward the Jap lines, held his arms up to the sun and looked at it, and whenever he passed U.S. soldiers he waved and waved at them. Next he tried to choke himself by pulling his rag tight around his throat. He pulled it so tight his tongue and eyes stuck out but when Fish didn't seem to mind he decided not to commit suicide. Later he kept looking very inquiringly at Fish and drawing his finger across his throat, apparently wondering if he was to be killed that way. Waldo gave him some more food and he relaxed.... We call Waldo "Bring 'em Alive Fish." He is sure being kidded a lot....

Aug 15 – I can easily see why you would need a rest.... Is it hot in Washington? It was a good idea to have a [medical] check-up.

Norma apparently visited Washington, D.C., in late July, almost certainly to see baby Gale, but under some other pretext. Was affection for Monte a motivation for the trip? I prefer to think not, but we will never know.

Wilber's next letter to me enhanced our view of his life on the Driniumor River.

August 20, 1944 — My battalion is in position on a nice beach, and when we are not firing, the men who are not busy go in swimming. There hasn't been much action for us altho we have worked in three different divisions [43rd, 32nd, and 31st; WB Journal]. You know me - just being helpful.

By this time, the Japanese 18th Army, initially consisting of some 50,000 men, had endured thousands of casualties and had ceased to be an effective force. On August 25, the Aitape operation was declared ended by General Krueger, commander of the Sixth Army, of which the 43rd Division was a part [Smith, ibid. p. 204]. The Japanese survivors retreated eastward toward Wewak and eventually into the mountains south of Wewak (Map 2). After the surrender of Japan in August 1945, they exited into captivity. General Adachi was later convicted of war crimes and sentenced to life imprisonment. On April 27, 1947, he committed suicide.

Wilber found time on Thursday, August 31, to write several letters, one to me with grim news, passed on rather lightly.

August 31, 1944 — This isn't a bad war here for I've seen a lot more dead Japs than wounded Americans. However two of my best friends were killed, so it is still a war with all its bad aspects.

On August 7, five officers and nine enlisted men of the 2nd Battalion, 169th Infantry, had been killed or fatally wounded and another 11 wounded by misplaced mortar rounds fired by the battalion's own mortar company. The battalion-sized TED force was carrying out a nine-day probe behind enemy lines through thick, hilly jungle when these tragic events took place. The wounded had to be carried on jungle trails for two days before they could get medical treatment [Smith, p. 199; Higgins, p. 39.] The deceased officers of the 169th Infantry surely included Wilber's two friends. Wilber had worked directly with the 169th Infantry Regiment in the Munda campaign. (See Ockenden, Chapters 19 and 20, for a vivid first-hand account.)

On September 2, the 152nd Field Artillery Battalion ceased its support of the 103rd Infantry and the next day returned to Aitape, probably to Tadji Plantation. The division was to be primed with intensive training for the next advance.

x·o·ø·o·x

At home, late in August, Norma rented a cottage for a week on Phillips Lake, in Lucerne, Maine, some 15 miles outside Bangor. I find it surprising that she would take the trouble to do this, given the work needed to fix up the Bangor house. She would get into her head an idea that something would be good for her children, and then she would just go ahead and do it.

The Allied armies in France had finally broken free of Normandy in early August and were rushing across France toward Germany. They were soon to be joined by troops that had landed on the south coast of France on August 15. They entered Paris on August 23.

On September 15, landings at Morotai (Indonesia) west of New Guinea and at Peleliu in the Palau Islands (Map 5) would bring the Americans to the doorstep of the Philippines. In Europe, the Russians began an offensive in the north, also on September 15, which led to the capture of Riga on the Baltic coast on October 13 and the encirclement and isolation of the German Army Group North.

24

"Running on and off ships"
AITAPE, SEPTEMBER–NOVEMBER, 1944

With the end of action in Aitape, three months of training commenced. On September 15, MacArthur was directed by the Joint Chiefs in Washington to proceed to Leyte on October 20. The 43rd did not participate in that operation, though for a time it was a possibility. In late December, the 43rd Division would depart for the invasion of the main Philippine island of Luzon.

> Sept. 16, 1944, Dear Son of Mine — It is fairly cool tonight and I am sitting in my tent with Major Fish. He is working on his radio and I have a Nestles choc. bar. I'll use the last piece for bait in my rat trap. We have caught five this week but decided not to eat them as the Japs sometimes do....
>
> I went fishing the other day and caught – nothing. BUT I got dumped out by the surf and really was soaked. Fun!

Penciled notations by Norma on this next letter suggest she was not in Bangor sometime after receiving it. She may have been visiting Washington, D.C., perhaps for Gale's first birthday on October 29.

> Sept. 20, 1944 — The other day I went to the G-2 office to ask if it was safe for me to go to Y __ [probably Yakamul, about six miles east of the Driniumor on the coast]. They gave me the horse laugh and said, "Why do you ask? In New Georgia you went where you pleased without even telling where you had been." I seem to have some very loyal + inaccurate friends. – It was safe + I'm back OK. I still love you.

As usual, Wilber's monthly letter to his father revealed practicalities of the war that he may not have shared with his immediate family.

September 25, 1944 — We have had a strenuous but not particularly hazardous month. A little local combat broke out in my area and we heard a few rifle bullets go by too close, but all in all it was pretty mild. The battalion did a good job, rushed back from the perimeter and spent a period in amphibious training (running on and off ships) with all our equipment and vehicles.

Training could be as strenuous as combat. The ships were anchored well off the beach, accessible only by small boats. Getting aboard required booms and winches for cargo and climbing nets for soldiers.

Wilber again turned to serious advice for me, his son, this time on dating. In his efforts to be a good father, he mistook my yearning for some connection with my female classmates for actual activity. He was blunt and direct in his advice. I was not quite 14.

Oct. 8, 1944 — In several of your letters you have mentioned interest in girls.... Except for special occasions, I want you to stop any social twosome dates until you are in the upper two years of high school. I want you to learn to like and make a practice of choosing your recreation with either boys or mixed crowds. This doesn't mean at all that I don't want you to have girls among your friends. It does mean that I will be very disappointed to have you hanging around some girl's parlor at this stage in your life.

In fact, I did all my biking, hiking, scouting, and shooting in and around Bangor with male friends. My dating life that year, as noted, was non-existent.

The planned move to the Philippine island of Leyte took place on October 20, 1944, without the 43rd Division. Wilber wrote Norma the next day about some mischief making.

Oct. 21, 1944 — DeBlois' Service Battery achieved a combination of renown and notoriety the other day. Three of his men stole a truck out of the motor park, speeded past one of General Wing's staff majors so fast he couldn't catch them and drove down the beach to the front lines.

That didn't mean a thing to them because the infantry had already picked up the souvenirs there, so they went on thru the U.S. Outpost line and found a new road previously not known to our troops. They drove farther into the Jap area than any of our infantry patrols have gone before or since. Finally they came to a hill and climbed it and saw a lot of Jap cooking fires all around them – "hundreds of them" so they decided "to get the h--l out of there." Just then some Japs jumped them and they killed one or two, captured a Jap Medical Captain complete with instruments + kit and a Jap Lt. of a new kind of Jap unit not yet known to U.S. G-2s [intelligence branch]. Then they loaded Jap pistols, rifles, and a saber, field glasses and other junk in the truck and came home. Results: 1. The G-2 section wants to decorate them. 2. The G-3 section [operations and security] issued orders that passes are required to get outside the main U.S. bivouac area. 3. The Div. Ordnance Officer wants to court martial them for damage to the truck. 4. The Provost Marshall wants to try them for speeding.

It's DeBlois' problem and I'm glad. I love you Sweet Heart.

On two occasions, Wilber had to face investigations of his battalion.

Oct. 27 — Night before last wasn't so pleasant for me. We were firing into the jungle when the phone rang with the cheerful tidings that we had fired into some [Allied] troops and wounded four. When these things happen, it is always interesting to see who has confidence in you and expects it to be an erroneous report, who just expects to make a thorough check-up to find the truth before acting, and who immediately assumes you guilty and hastens to point out that the Bn. CO is responsible. Of course the Bn. CO is responsible and he knows so many different men could make mistakes and cause things like this. He is confronted with the necessity first of determining for himself if his Bn. is guilty or innocent and next of establishing that innocence so definitely that no one can question it. That means outside officers checking the laying of the guns, the records of the fire, the charts and points of impact. These are the things that lead to exoneration or the "Board" [court martial].

So our firing stopped about 8:00 P.M. and the evidence was collected and a preliminary hearing held at about 9:30. Fortunately (Thank God for a good Bn!), I could prove all my rounds were falling at least a mile from where the men were wounded. That still left the fact that there were casualties unexplained. Since they were Allied troops [probably Australian], there were a lot of generals excited about it. I was sure glad I was in the clear this time, altho eventually something like this may land on my doorstep. The next morning it developed that the four soldiers had been trying to disassemble a dud mortar shell for souvenirs, so our Allies were no doubt glad they had been courteous the night before.... These are the things that put grey hair on artillery commanders' head[s].

The checkup on me when Gen. Krueger [Sixth Army commanding general] said I was firing on his airport was even more thorough. Berry + Barker + Files [all of divisional artillery headquarters] were practically petrified because they couldn't conceive of Krueger [a four-star general] being even questioned. In fact I received the impression it would be discourteous to prove that I hadn't fired on his airfield. I'm not so easily impressed and did have a personal interest in the case, so I insisted on clearing myself.

General Krueger's postwar memoir mentioned this event [Krueger, p. 73]. On July 23, 1944, he had flown to Aitape from Hollandia "but [our plane] was unable to land at Tadji airdrome because of our own artillery test-firing from within the perimeter, which for lack of radio contact we could not stop."

Wilber's attention turned again to his father, with news of inspections and his unit's readiness for combat.

Oct. 27, 1944 — This has been a strenuous month for me, but the hazards have been of the diplomatic and administrative type. We have been attached to two different Armies and made a part of two different Corps. All four of these headquarters very properly wanted to know how good we were and proceeded to deluge us with inspectors. I couldn't get a haircut without an inspector checking on the barber. We've adopted the "latest" modes in tents, truck parks, shops, dispatch systems, urinals, mess halls, [and] incinerators four times. One inspection crew liked soup so we had soup on our menus until the "stew" proponents came along.

Two days later (on little Gale's birthday), Wilber wrote 12-year-old Valerie, a most poetic letter.

Oct. 29, 1944 — This is Sunday morning and I have just gotten back from church. Our chapel is called St. Andrews and the men built it....

Last night was cool and I drove about 20 miles along the beach + thru jungle trails. Along the beach the starlight and car lights made the surf mysterious and depressive, almost ominous. The waves would come rolling in dark and seem to grow and grow in height then all at once they would break with a deep boom and thud as if they were dropping explosives to tear away the beach. The backwash of the previous wave would meet the incoming one and they appeared to struggle for supremacy. High columns of water and foam spewed up into the air as in gestures of anger and hatred. In contrast, the beach in the car lights was all silver and diamonds. The foam left by the receding wave made thousands of little bursting bubbles each one glistening like jewels. Hundreds of big and little crabs frightened by the light skated sidewise along the beach and across the beach. Each one appeared ivory white. The contrast between the beach and the sea was absolute; the one was a fairyland while the other suggested Beowulf and Neptunic strife.

On the way down to this position area to which I was going, I traveled an old jungle road. Along one side was a swamp, which occasionally became a lagoon. It was as noisy as an Indiana pond in June. The air was full of fire-flies, katydids, mosquitos. Snakes were crawling across the road. We have pythons here but the ones I saw were pale green. Big green frogs hopped along in the car lights and one jumped on the radiator and rode almost a half-mile. He was a tree climbing variety because he climbed up right in the middle of the windshield and stuck on there like an incubus. (I wonder what an incubus really looks like.) Bats with wingspread up to two feet were upset by the lights and flew around the car, sometimes so close I could reach them with my hands. Fallen trees in places arched over the road and everywhere an almost solid mat of vines and palms made it an almost complete tunnel. I didn't see any Jap bones, but I knew they had been there when we fought along this trail not too long ago for I saw them then. You have no idea of all the noises of the night jungle....

Physically the ride was an endurance contest. I'm still lame, but it was a different page in my Jungle Book. I love you Dearest.

Then on Thanksgiving Day, Wilber wrote to me about thankfulness and to his father.

Nov. [23], 1944 — We have a lot to be thankful for this time, don't we?... I'm thankful too for good health, for good officers and men, for a chance to fight for the things for which my country is fighting, for a good tent, for my chairs, for all the interesting things I've seen and done, for the beautiful things I've seen, and more than anything else for the family waiting for me in Maine.

Nov. 23, 1944, Dear Father — We have really been busy lately. I go around with my tongue hanging out and wondering just what I'm not doing that I should be doing.... It's a great life, but one always has the feeling of being just one jump ahead of some mishap or omission. I'll be glad when it's over.

Wilber clearly felt the burden of command in busy times. The pressure was now on in full force for the unit's embarkation for its next phase of combat a month hence.

On October 24–26, a series of naval actions—the historic Battle of Leyte Gulf—arose from an all-out Japanese attempt to defeat the Allied land-ings on Leyte. Allied occupation of Leyte would isolate Japan from its conquered territories and its oil supplies. Although there were serious

Allied blunders and losses (three light or escort carriers, two destroyers and one destroyer escort), Japanese naval losses were huge: four carriers, three battleships, ten cruisers, and perhaps 11 destroyers. Japan's attempt to block the invasion had clearly failed.

Thereafter the surviving Japanese heavy warships were rarely deployed because of oil shortages. In this action, the Japanese first introduced suicidal "kamikaze" air attacks wherein piloted planes carrying torpedoes or bombs would strive to crash directly into Allied ships. Kamikaze attacks became a major threat to U.S. ships in later encounters.

On November 24, Tokyo was bombed by 111 B-29 bombers based in the recently captured Mariana Islands. The conquest of Leyte Island in the Philippines was proving to be a difficult task in the face of determined Japanese resistance in mountainous country. On December 7, an additional American division landed on the west coast at Ormoc. That quickly brought the campaign to a close, with organized Japanese resistance ending late that month.

25

"You can be sure we'll take care of Mother"
AITAPE, DECEMBER, 1944

The buildup to the invasion of Luzon, the principal island of the Philippines, dominated Wilber's last month in New Guinea, but he also had a new concern, placed on him by his sister Mary. On November 20, Mary had written Wilber a V-mail letter (now lost) notifying him that their father had had a heart attack on November 11 and was seriously ill. On November 25, she wrote an update, "The doctor says he is 'not out of the woods' yet," which Wilber would not receive for several weeks.

On December 1, the Australian 6th Division relieved the 43rd Division at Aitape [Barker, p. 141; Williams, p. 342]. Intense preparations continued for the departure in just a few weeks for the Luzon invasion.

> Dec. 5, 1944 — Day before yesterday, [Major] Fish + I and Lt. Col. Devine (Inf) went out to dinner on a ship [USS Fayette, APA-43]. We were the guests of the Captain and the Commodore, named respectively [Capt. J. C.] Lester and [Capt. D. L.] Ryan. It was nice to eat off a linen tablecloth with silver and ice water and napkins. It was a good dinner too, fresh potatoes (fried), steak, fish, and ice cream + coffee.

This was the ship on which Wilber's unit would sail 20 days later.

On the third anniversary of the Pearl Harbor attack (and my 14th birthday), Wilber wrote that he had received a portrait photo of Norma, which pleased him greatly. Later that day, he received Mary's letter with the news of their father's illness. Wilber then wrote his father a letter that began with an awkward attempt at humor. President Roosevelt had just been elected to a fourth term.

> Dec. 7, 1944, Dear Father — I'm sure you are taking the Roosevelt Reign too seriously.... Seriously tho I'm more sorry than I can tell that you are

having trouble. I hope that by the time this letter reaches you that you will be back on your feet and feeling fine. Remember I'm counting on seeing you after this war and that will be some time yet....

Please Father take care of yourself and fight this thing thru until you are OK again. However if it is too much trouble, you can be sure we'll take care of Mother.

Sadly, my grandfather had died on December 3 at age 73. But Wilber would not learn of this until several weeks later.

The news of his father's illness surely was responsible in part for the depressed mental state Wilber revealed quite candidly in a letter to his friend Prof. Irwin Douglass, the acting head of the chemistry department at the University of Maine.

Dec. 12, 1944, Dear Doug — Today we are having one of the movie-type tropical downpours....

My morale still seems to keep up to normal (for me) and only suffers twinges when I allow myself to remember I've been out here over two years now. Physically, I'm probably better off than if I were at the U.... Psychologically, I find myself extremely unstable varying from a condition of absolute terror to that of extreme optimism, from interest to the ultimate of boredom but most of the time typified by a mottled-gray attitude. That, I think, accurately reports on the present status of one Bradt.

Norma added some complexity to the family dynamics in the wake of her father-in-law's death. She typed a rather impolitic letter to Wilber's brother Rex nine days after the elder Hale had died. She wrote from our home in Bangor, Maine.

December 12, 1944, Dear Rex — We address you, as you were kind enough to write Hale such a nice long letter about Father's ideals of duty, justice, and all. We agree that Father is one of the most remarkable men of our time....

Hale was very worried about your remark, that, due to your remaining in chemistry instead of going as a soldier, you would probably not have a job after the War. You said that you could have gone, and wanted to, but learned it was your duty to stay here in ordnance work. I am sure that you have done a very fine job and [made] a great contribution. You said of course you would not have the parades, medals, bonuses, nor all the glory of the soldier, but ... etc. The children were much puzzled, as their values were suddenly assailed. If you will ponder, you will see why. You had just sent on Wilber's Legion of Merit medal. Valerie hotly contended that Daddy did not go to war for the Parades, Medals, and Bonuses. She said "Didn't Daddy get this medal for bravery?" Hale and I both said certainly yes, and I had to explain about you, and about Wilber.

The indignation here was largely Norma's. Neither Valerie nor I would have had the sophistication to make such arguments. Rex was clearly sensitive to not being in uniform. She went on with a good description of her life in Bangor.

> Right now, with the housework and the children at home, I keep up my skill by writing all during mornings on radio scripts and books, I practice [piano] all each afternoon, begin cooking, etc., at 4 [P.M.] and work on until 12 at night on washing, ironing, mending, bookkeeping, etc. It is the only way I feel safe. And I do not mind it at all. There is no time to be bored and my writing and music are such joy that they compensate. The best radio programs are at night while I do my housework, so that is fun.

Norma had indeed made a nice home for us. I remember how I loved the wonderful smell of baking Syrian (pita) bread wafting up to my bedroom late one night when I was sick and quite miserable with a painful earache.

In the palm groves of New Guinea, Wilber found that training was not without its misunderstandings.

> Dec. 13, 1944 — Another day nearer to the end of this war and what a day. [General] Harold [Barker] came out where we were training and flew into quite a rage so I closed up the firing and ordered the unit back to camp. Boy was he mad! I wasn't any less so, but not so demonstrative if you know what I mean. He haled [sic] me over to his Hq and slapped a pamphlet in front of me and wanted to know why in __ I hadn't followed the instructions therein. My answer – "I've never seen it before." More fireworks. Big investigation of records to show where I had signed for it. Very embarrassing because they show I had never received it. Much rage at his message center. More rage at his staff, rage all around for everybody.
>
> Next he hauls out [a] training memo and unfortunately it directed we do what we were doing. Not so noisy now. "Bradt do you have any questions?" Boy did I have questions; most important in my mind was "How long is this war going to last?" However I contented myself with, "Yes. What do I do now?" More earthquakes, blood all around, monkeys fainting and falling out of cocoanut trees. To make a long story short the poor staff got a harangue on how could Bradt know what to do if no one informed him and why did he have to do all the coordinating. Lord, spare

me from too much coordination. After the storm, "Now Bradt why don't you stay for dinner?" I didn't say why but I didn't stay. So went the 13th of December in New Guinea.

Wilber finally did get word of his father's death, three weeks after the fact. He then took on the role of oldest son as best he could from such a distance. He was extremely busy, with embarkation for the Philippines less than a week away.

Dec. 21, 1944, Dear Mother and Mary — I've just heard of our loss [Father's death].... I wish I might be there and try to comfort you. You used to say, Mother, that my shoulders were good for crying. Spiritually I offer it [sic] to you now.... [Marginal note:] I'll write you [Mother] within one or two days of the first of each month as I did to Father except when we are restricted by the tactical situation. Please do answer.

The plea to his mother, "Please do answer," was heart rending—and this, from an outwardly tough wartime commander of 500 men!

Wilber had received from Norma a copy of her unfortunate letter to Rex. Wilber's response to it targeted beautifully the underlying issue, but with sensitivity to Norma's feelings. He wrote her on Christmas Eve.

Dec. 24, 1944, Dearest — Your letters of Dec. 8 and 12 came today. It sounds as if you and the children were on a pretty strenuous schedule. I should have enjoyed Hale's play and can just imagine how nice Valerie's Christmas Card design was....

Your letter to Rex disturbs me quite a bit. I'm sorry you wrote it. You must realize the people who are not in the service now are on the defensive in their own minds. It is very important that they justify to themselves their decision. I have always felt that we who were in the Service could afford to be generous in this matter and had promised myself to try to remember to be so.... I'm sorry about the medal [Legion of Merit] having occasioned this trouble and wish I had not received it, if it becomes the cause of misunderstanding.

Please don't feel badly, Lover. I know your motives were of the best and that it is natural to want to strike back. I love you, My Wife, and wish I could be with you now. This Christmas Eve, I'll be praying for you. Keep your courage a little longer and I'll be home to take a lot of worries off your soft white shoulders.

The next day, Christmas Day and the eve of his boarding ship for the invasion of Luzon, Wilber set aside all concerns about the army, his father, his widowed mother, and Norma's letter to Rex, and wrote "final" tributes to Norma, Valerie, and me. It would be a long (2500 miles) voyage, half of which would be through Japanese waters. Despite the impotence of the Japanese fleet, land-based Japanese planes with suicidal intent (kamikazes) were plentiful and a mortal threat. Transport ships full of soldiers were high-priority targets. Yet again, Wilber knew that these could well be his last words to us.

> Christmas Day. [1944] — Merry Christmas from New Guinea! I have had a very nice Christmas, thanks particularly to you and also a good dinner, thanks to Uncle Sam.... Everything is as peaceful here as a Christmas should be everywhere.

> Today Hale I want to thank you for being such a young man about our home and for being as fine and honest as you are. I see so many boys here whose sons are getting in trouble at home and I know how terribly they worry because they can't be there. I predict that you will be a fine man like your grandfather. So now I wish you a very very happy New Year and know you will help others to have a happy 1945 also.

> And you Valerie have made me thankful that you came [in]to my family. I'm so happy that you are controlling your temper better and that you are so helpful around the home. Your unselfishness and consideration for other people is one of things I love most about you. You are a very sweet and loveable daughter. I wish you a very wonderful new year.

> And you, My Darling Wife, today I wish to offer you all my love. You have been such a dear sweet comrade all these years. I pray this Christmas you will find comfort and strength and serenity of spirit. I love you Golden Girl, more today than on any other Christmas Day. Thru next year, I'll be loving you more than in 1944. You grow into my heart each day. Your picture shows me that you are more lovely now than when we last were together. There are so few words to tell you of my love for you. I would much rather, My Queen, have my memories of you than the love of any other woman. You are truly a part of me.

Wilber's stay on New Guinea had come to an end. Training had been completed, and the division embarked yet again on ships for another objective, the invasion of Luzon, the principal island of the Republic of the Philippines. Wilber's battalion boarded the USS Fayette on December 26, carried out a final rehearsal of amphibious landings on the 27th, and departed Aitape on the 28th.

The family at home celebrated Christmas in Bangor, their first there since the somber Christmas of 1940 when Europe was in flames, and Wilber's departure was imminent. Unfortunately, I have no particular memory of the 1944 Christmas. But we surely had a decorated tree and presents, as was our custom.

USS Fayette (APA-43) at unknown location. This ship carried Wilber and about two-thirds of his battalion to the Luzon landing. The others left earlier on slower craft.
[PHOTO: NAVSOURCE ONLINE, WAYNE VANDERVOORT]

As the 43rd Division's presence at Aitape came to an end, so too did the fighting on Leyte.

On the Western front, the Allies were at Germany's borders by mid-September when their progress was slowed by stretched supply lines and German defenses. In a surprise move on December 16, the Germans carried out a major counterattack with concentrated resources in what came to be known as the Battle of the Bulge. The Allied lines in Belgium and Luxembourg were forced back with many casualties, but the defenders blocked the advance before the Germans could break out into open country. The Allied lines were restored by January 16 after many Allied and German casualties.

On the Eastern front, the Russians had reached the Vistula River outside Warsaw by August 1. They remained there, outside Warsaw, until the end of the year, cruelly refusing to come to the aid of the Polish Home Army, which took arms against the German occupiers (the Warsaw uprising, August 1 to October 2) but was destroyed by the Germans. The Russians also waited through the subsequent systematic razing of the historic city by the Germans. The Russians finally entered Warsaw on January 17, 1945. In the meantime, they had made substantial advances in the south on the Ukrainian front in Hungary and in the north toward the Baltic Sea. The major drive on to Berlin began in January 1945.

During this period, American industry was working full-tilt, providing the Pacific fleet with increasing numbers of combat vessels, aircraft, and landing craft. This output greatly exceeded Japanese production capabilities, which had peaked and were decreasing under ever-heavier stress, due to shortages of oil and raw materials. Nevertheless, the Japanese were determined to make Allied advances slow and costly.

Allied landings on the principal Philippine island of Luzon would take place on January 9, 1945. This major undertaking would be on the scale of the Normandy invasion, but launched from bases thousands of miles from the landing beaches. It was a huge undertaking, and Wilber would be an active, willing participant in that show.

UNITED STATES MARINES

Jan. 12, 1945

Dearest,

Am in the Philippines,
Am well, and having a real
time. The Bn is doing a
fine job. Don't worry about
me. Tell Mrs. Averill that
Roger is OK, also Bob Hussey.
Both are doing a magnificent
job. Love

Wilber

PART VI

FINAL BATTLES, LUZON

PHILIPPINE ISLANDS
JANUARY—SEPTEMBER, 1945

First-wave troops of the 103rd Infantry fording a stream en route to San Fabian, January 9, 1945. [PHOTO: U.S. ARMY SIGNAL CORPS, SC 200017]

26

"Some minutes are worth more than years of living"
AT SEA EN ROUTE LUZON, DECEMBER 1944–JANUARY 1945

The task forces soon to be heading to Luzon would eventually consist of hundreds of ships from many different locations in the South Pacific. Upon arrival at Luzon's Lingayen Gulf, after voyages of thousands of miles, the soldiers would be deposited directly onto the beaches. Wilber was about to begin an adventure that, as he noted, he "wouldn't miss … for anything."

Wilber and about two thirds of his unit (152nd Field Artillery Battalion) boarded the USS Fayette (APA-43) at Aitape on December 26; the remaining third had left a few days earlier on slower landing craft. The 2,500-mile voyage to Luzon would be fraught with danger because the task force had to pass through waters—Surigao Strait, Mindanao Sea, Sulu Sea, and the South China Sea—that were accessible from many Japanese-held airfields (Map 14). Suicide attacks by Japanese kamikaze aircraft had been introduced in the Battle of Leyte Gulf and continued to threaten shipping there as the Leyte fighting proceeded through November into December. The Luzon convoys would surely be attacked aggressively.

The plan was for the navy to send an advance task force, the Bombardment Group, to Lingayen Gulf to bombard the coastal defenses, clear minefields, and attack airfields. It would arrive three days before the invasion force. It too would be a target for the kamikazes.

Wilber wrote a series of letters during his 12-day voyage to Lingayen Gulf. He labeled each with a day number countdown to S Day, the invasion date. This countdown as the ship approached Luzon showed the growing tension. These letters would be mailed well after the landings in accord with censorship rules. Here are only brief excerpts from each. The first was written the day Wilber and his troops boarded the Fayette, 14 days before the invasion date (S-14 Day). The Fayette was still anchored off Aitape.

S-14 Day [Dec. 26, 1944] — This is the first of a series of letters that must be mailed after it has been announced that we are in Luzon. Yesterday was spent in a final clean up of our areas and the striking of our tents.... Today we had reveille at 0100 [1 A.M.] and at 0400 marched to the beach. I drove down and watched them come into the assembly area. At 0800 we were loaded on LCTs and taken out to the USS Fayette where we boarded by going up the nets. It was about 30 ft. high and I was worried about the possibility of men falling between the two ships or falling off the net because of their heavy packs or radios. I am quartered with Col. [Joseph] Cleland and Col. [I. M.] Oseth [of the War Dept.] in a very nice stateroom.

Colonel Cleland was commander of the 103rd Infantry Regiment and of the 103rd Regimental Combat Team of which Wilber's battalion (152nd Field Artillery Battalion) was a part. Altogether, five infantry divisions and additional supporting units would be committed to the Lingayen landing: four in the initial assault and one in reserve. They were transported from 16 different Pacific bases [Morison, v. XIII, p. 97]. The ships carrying these various forces would all arrive at Lingayen Gulf in the early hours of S day, January 9, 1945.

S-13 Day [Dec. 27 1944] — Another day has passed. We rehearsed our landing with all the assault boats going in to shore loaded with men. Of course no ammunition was fired but it was a thrill to see it. One couldn't help wondering about the boys in the boats and amphibious tractors + their future.

I go with Col. Cleland on one of the guide ships, which will stop about a mile from shore while the assault waves go on to shore. The first wave hits the beach at "H-hour" with others each four minutes.... My boys are due to go in as the seventh wave (H + 28) in LSMs so Capt. DeGlow, Sgt. Oliver and I will go in by special boat at H + 15 minutes to select their routes and positions before they arrive. We are going to try to be firing before any of the other artillery reaches the shore....

Of course my observers will be and are now with the infantry with their radios ready for us to report ready to fire. Our men are all set and morale is higher than I've ever seen. It could be we will do a real job....

This is a big affair, Norma, and I wouldn't miss it for anything. Don't forget that if I don't come thru it, some minutes are worth more than years of living and such minutes are coming to us. I love you and nothing can take me away from you. No matter what happens, I'll be caring for you.

The thrill of participating in this huge dramatic undertaking was, as Wilber noted, well worth the ultimate price he might have to pay. It offered big adventure in pursuit of a big goal. Did Wilber arrange for his artillery to make such an early landing? He had sufficient opportunity on this long voyage with the combat team commander, Col. Cleland, to explore the pros and cons of doing so. He apparently felt it most advantageous, whereas others might have considered it too risky.

The next day, Wilber wrote Norma an innocuous censor-proof letter that could be mailed before the ship departed. And on the same day, after the Fayette was underway, he continued his countdown.

S-12 Day. [Dec. 28, 1944], Hello there Good Looking and Far Away! — At 1400 today we left Aitape. It was a great sight to see all the transports move out of the anchorage, form into columns.... I hope we do well [in Luzon] and that not too many of my boys are killed.

Wilber was frank about the risks; it was a grim game they played.

S-11 Day [Dec. 29, 1944] — Today I inspected the ship for Col. Cleland, napped, played with the medicine ball for exercise, read a book ... and dreamed on deck of my home and family. I dreamed of you too last night very intimately too. Our meals on ship are outstanding....

S-10 Day [Dec. 30, 1944] — Dearest I now am on the same side of the equator with you. Really I feel actually as if I were on the way home. Of course there is still a way to go but it is good to be back in the northern hemisphere. After breakfast,... Col. Cleland and I and one of his majors then spent an hour on our plans for the landing and attack.

This show, Lover, is going to be the biggest affair out here yet.... As I go ashore, there will be firing on that 500 yards of beach to which I go, one battleship, two (?) cruisers and several destroyers.

The next day Wilber described the objectives and challenges of his unit the first day ashore.

S-9 Day [Dec. 31, 1944] — It's another day and Sunday too. I have just returned from communion service given by a fine young priest.... I think we must take a voyage some day on a ship where Episcopal services are available....

This being a large operation and we being in the initial landing waves it is of course more dangerous and a lot of people will be hurt;... my prayers this morning were that you and the children will remember [that] I'm doing the thing I feel [to be the] most worthwhile that I will ever have a chance to do and know I am content....

We land at the town of San Fabian and take it. I put my guns in position just off the beach at S.F. and support the 103[rd Infantry] in their drive inland to take San Jacinto about four miles inland…. On our left flank are some hills that overlook our zone of attack…. There is a battalion of medium [155-mm] artillery assigned to reinforce my fires, and I plan to keep them busy covering our flanks….

S-8 Day [Jan. 1, 1945] — Happy New Year Nana! Happy New Year Valerie! Happy New Year Hale! I can't think of a better plan than "Home for Christmas in '45."… Last night another convoy joined us and I found out that an unidentified ship is called a "skunk." These were skunks until they properly identified themselves.

Dear ones, I love you all and I'm so happy to have such a family. Keep your courage up this year. Take care of each other and be kind and generous to each other. No whining, no scolding, no quarrelling between brother and sister.

The countdown continued, with reassurance to Norma.

S-7 [Jan. 2, 1945] — I woke up in the middle of my dream and thought how all my life with you has been a marvelous dream, much nicer than the dreams too…. If anything happens to me on this job, I want you to remember we had more joy together than other married people have in an ordinary lifetime…. I do love you so dearly.

We have encountered four floating mines in the past 24 hours but have spotted them and had no mishaps. There have been several questionable sub contacts and they may be out ahead laying mines in our path. Most unsocial of them, isn't it?

On S-6 Day, near the Japanese-held islands of Palau, Wilber's convoy rendez-voused with the slower LSTs and LCIs of the invasion force [Morison, ibid. p. 115]. The combined flotilla would enter Philippine waters the next day.

S-6 Day [Jan. 3, 1945] — The one thing I regret the most about these voyages is the fact that you go so long without word that I am still OK. This time, Nana, I do hope you aren't being over impressed by all the Jap claims about sinking our transports. Remember I am in only one transport, not every one the Japs claim. I think I mentioned the Jap plane over us. It was a "Betty" [Japanese bomber] and was obviously a Snooper from Palau.

On the afternoon of January 4, the convoy entered Leyte Gulf (Map 14) and was joined by a Close Covering Group of four cruisers and eight destroyers. The combined convoy now extended over 40 miles and was in range of numerous Japanese airfields.

S-5 Day [Jan. 4, 1945] — Another quiet day has half passed. We can see Leyte now and all is still well. Today I checked over my equipment and refitted my straps and belts. Uncle Sam sure loads one down and the added gas mask didn't help any.

The convoy passed through Surigao Strait on the night of Jan 4–5. Thus began the most dangerous portion of the voyage westward along the northern coast of Mindanao and then up the west side of the Philippines for some 500 miles. There were an estimated 400 Japanese kamikaze aircraft on Luzon with replacements available elsewhere [Smith, ibid. p. 28]. The senior commanders were surely holding their collective breath.

> S-4 Day [Jan. 5, 1945] — Another day has passed in peace and quiet....
> After supper I went up on the bridge for an hour and watched the ships
> slide by the islands as quietly as shadows.... From the radar come reports
> of "skunks" and "bogies," then general quarters is sounded and all guns
> manned with all troops [sent] below.... I'm just down from the bridge where
> Col. Cleland + I were working up a sweat with the medicine ball....
>
> While we were there (bridge) a Jap [midget] sub fired two torpedoes at
> one of our escort ships, but missed. Then a destroyer [USS Taylor] fired a
> couple of salvos at the sub and stepped on the gas and rammed it.

The Japanese torpedoes had been fired at the cruiser USS Boise, which carried General MacArthur. The ramming destroyer was the USS Taylor; see Map 14 for the location. On the evening of January 5, fifteen Japanese planes flew over the convoy, but did not take note of it [Morison, ibid. p. 115].

On January 6, before dawn, the Bombardment Group arrived in Lingayen Gulf. The kamikaze attacks they had been experiencing en route since January 3 intensified, and on this day, 11 ships were damaged and the minesweeper USS Long was sunk. It was the worst day for the U.S. Navy since November 30, 1942, at Guadalcanal. In contrast, the transports still en route had a quiet time.

> S-3 Day [Jan 6, 1945] — Pop is still here. We are now finishing a very
> quiet day. There were only two events furnished by the Sons of Togo – one,
> some planes and two, a sub. The sub is still lurking outside in the dark, but
> I trust a lot of destroyers have an ear turned his way. The planes looked and
> went home.

Oldendorf's Bombardment Group was clearing Lingayen Gulf of mines and obstacles and would soon be firing on the landing beaches. Halsey's Third Fleet was east of Luzon providing air cover and assaulting Japanese airfields.

At daybreak January 7, the convoy was passing through Mindoro Strait, which brought it adjacent to Luzon. In the early morning, a Japanese bomb splashed near the cruiser, the USS Boise.

S-2 Day [Jan 7, 1945; 4 P.M.] — This is just a note congratulating you on the fact that you still have a husband. The Japs have showed up for a look at us but so far haven't been much trouble....

Alexander has put gas-repelling ointment on my shoes. I've packed my cottons, manuals and extra sox in my jungle pack to be brought ashore by one of my officers who comes ashore later in the day. My knife is razor sharp, my compass checked, my gas mask waterproofed.... My belt looks like this [sketch]. Around my neck are field glasses. On my arm, my knife. Over my right shoulder the gas mask. This is known as traveling light.

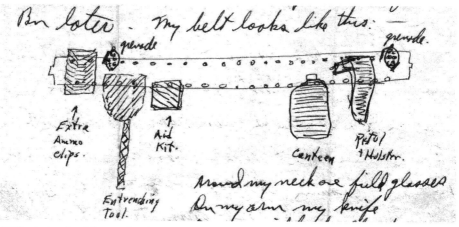

Wilber's sketch of the combat belt he would wear during the Luzon landings. The items noted were, from left: extra ammo clips, grenade, entrenching tool, aid kit, canteen, pistol & holster, grenade. [FACSIMILE: WB LETTER 1/7/45, S-2 DAY]

During the night of January 7–8, the convoy passed Manila Bay. At daybreak, the escort carriers accompanying the transports were attacked by kamikazes, one of which crashed into the USS Kadashan Bay, an escort carrier. A few moments later, another crashed into the transport USS Callaway killing 29 sailors but none of the 1,188 army troops aboard. Wilber did not mention the latter two incidents, possibly due to censorship.

On S-1 Day, the quiet apprehension aboard those transports would have been nearly palpable. A kamikaze had crash-dived into LST-912, killing four men but only slightly damaging the ship. Again Wilber did not mention the losses or damage.

S-1 Day [Jan. 8, 1945] — It is 0915 of the day before the big day and all is well. In the last 24 hours we have been alerted and placed at "General Quarters" several times....

> Last night [at 9:00 p.m.] our escort caught a large Jap destroyer or light cruiser trying to get in reach of us. Four of our ships blew him [her] out of the water in about ten minutes. It was quite a sight.

The "destroyer or light cruiser" was a small Japanese destroyer escort, the Hinoki, trying to escape from Manila Bay when it inadvertently encountered the huge convoy.

In the early hours of January 9, the ships turned south into Lingayen Gulf, and all the transports were in position by 7 a.m. Wilber wrote another innocuous censor-proof letter to be mailed aboard the ship, with no hint at all that he was then in the Northwest Pacific: "I am well and as busy as usual if not more so."

Wilber did go ashore at Lingayen Gulf as planned. He did not write a continuous narrative about the landings, but we got snippets of those moments in later letters to his sister Mary and to me.

> Feb. 21, 1945, To Mary — The naval bombardment over our heads was certainly impressive to me – probably more so to the Japs. My landing boat got lost and I practically visited all the beaches before I could convince the skipper I knew where I was to land. Of course the smoke of the shells covered things a lot so it was hard to keep oriented. Of course, it was a very pleasant surprise to find myself on the beach quite pale but otherwise OK.

> Feb. 28, 1945. To Mary — I spent your birthday [January 8 – the day before the landings] checking equipment and plans for debarking and wondering about the next morning. My battalion was the first artillery in the division to land and I was wondering if I had been wrong in recommending that we go in early. I landed at H + 15 minutes and the Bn. came in 13 minutes later. The naval fire was a stupendous sight. I wish I could name the battleships + cruisers. The Japs were trying suicide dive tactics but I didn't have much time to gawk. One strafed the beach where I was and I sure stopped working and stuck my nose in the sand for that job. After we had our howitzers ashore and so could shoot back, everyone felt much better.

> March 10, 1945. To Hale — Battery "A" [four howitzers] stopped almost at the waters edge and started firing. By the time the other two [batteries] were ashore I was able to put them a mile inland.

The landings were largely unopposed by Japanese ground forces, and the troopships were not damaged by air or artillery fire. There were a few successful attacks on navy ships, with modest damage and some loss of life, but generally the Japanese kamikaze effort had "shot its bolt" in its attacks on the Bombardment Group the previous days. Had the Japanese waited to attack the transports, the result could well have been disastrous.

27

"I'm not sure just what the Lord got"
CENTRAL PLAINS & GUIMBA, LUZON, JANUARY–MARCH, 1945

The Japanese did not defend the beaches of Lingayen Gulf but had retreated to more easily fortified positions in the mountains east and north of Lingayen Gulf and on the approaches to Manila to the south. The commander of the Japanese forces on Luzon, General Tomoyuki Yamashita, commander of the 14th Area Army had 260,000 troops at his disposal, but was short on supplies and expected no reinforcements or supplies from Japan. He could not prevent MacArthur's superior forces from taking Luzon, but was determined to husband his troops in strong defensive positions in order to delay the inevitable outcome as long as possible.

The 103rd Regimental Combat Team (RCT) landed at St. Fabian to the right of the other two RCTs of the 43rd Division. Those two had to deal with the Japanese strong points in the mountains to the left of the beachhead while the 103rd drove inland to secure towns and Japanese strong points in the hills behind the beach. This was a relatively fast-moving situation, and the artillery had to be relocated quite frequently, a big change from the earlier relatively static artillery positioning in the Solomons and New Guinea.

The 43rd Division—as a component of I Corps—engaged in four distinct phases of combat on Luzon (Map 15), three of which involved Wilber's outfit. The first, following the Lingayen landing, was the containment of the Japanese northern "Shobu Group" north and east of Lingayen Gulf, so the XIV Corps could safely drive south toward Manila.

Once ashore on Luzon the morning of January 9, the 103rd RCT drove southeast and by nightfall was just short of San Jacinto, about four miles beyond San Fabian (Map 16). By January 12, the unit had advanced, with some difficulty, another four miles to the vicinity of Manaoag and had begun the attack on heavily fortified Hill 200. (Hills were typically designated by their approximate height in feet.) Well-hidden enemy artillery proved to be a new challenge, and Wilber's artillery sought to destroy it without being destroyed in the process.

Wilber found a moment to rush off a few lines three days after the landings.

> Jan. 12, 1945, Dearest — Am in the Philippines, am well, and having a real time. The Bn. is doing a fine job. Don't worry about me. Tell Mrs. Averill that Roger is OK, also Bob Hussey. Both are doing a magnificent job.

On this date, January 12, Wilber used artillery fire to rescue a wounded Filipino guerilla near Manaoag. For this, he was awarded an oak leaf cluster for his Silver Star in lieu of a second Silver Star; the first awarded was for an event the following week. (The Silver Star is awarded for "extraordinary" personal heroism and is the third highest award for valor in the face of the enemy.) Much later in June, Wilber described the event—the rescue of a wounded Filipino guerrilla— for Norma.

> June 1, 1945 — One evening [Jan 12] ... after a mile or so we came to this scene: Somewhere in the tall grass were the Japs with two machine guns but we didn't know where. Whenever anyone tried to get to the wounded Filipino, the Japs opened up on them and had wounded several.

The two infantry colonels with Wilber organized a rescue using a machine gun, but that failed.

> So I proposed artillery. It was too close quarters to be safely used but I thought I might be able to do it.... When the first round came out I had everyone down but myself + [Col.] Wally [Devine] who never let me appear braver than him. I had to stand to see where it landed and as we heard it whistle I said to Wally, "If we read the map right, it will land across the road and if not maybe behind us on the people." Those are the hard moments in artillery.... Each time I expected to see the F. disappear because he was within dispersion limits.... Next I threw in a few volleys of smoke shell and told the soldiers to go get the F.

In an earlier letter to his sister Mary, he had written,

> February 28, 1945 — I put the fire on the machine guns and the Lord made the shells miss the boy. So we got him out and that was another high spot. They awarded me a Silver Star for that job, but I'm not sure just what the Lord got.

The prime mission of the battalion was to provide direct support for the 103rd Infantry, but counter-battery fire against enemy artillery positions was an important secondary task. This was a challenge because typically the Japanese howitzer would emerge from its camouflaged redoubt only for the brief time it took to fire. American howitzers were susceptible to Japanese artillery fire, so they had to be well placed and camouflaged. One of Wilber's jobs was to find those positions.

On January 18, Pozorrubio (Map 17) was captured and Wilber took part in some artillery spotting that he briefly described.

> Jan. 19, 1945 — Last night the Japs shelled us with a six-inch gun until we plotted his flashes and swatted him with six battalion volleys. [Each of the battalion's 12 howitzers fired six times, as fast as they could reload.] We haven't heard from him since. This A.M., I ran into six Japs. There were four of us. We had a little fire fight in which we killed one and possibly another and drove the others off. I was behind an ant hill, and the nearest one was in a hedge about 20 yards away. I flattened [?] him.

The disabling of the Japanese six-inch gun "last night" earned Wilber his first Silver Star. The citation read, in part,

> Of his own volition, Colonel Bradt went to the most forward position in order that he might determine the location of the enemy firing positions. Although under heavy artillery fire, some of which landed only feet from him, he moved to more exposed positions from which he could better locate the enemy guns. By his deliberate coolness, courage, and utter disregard for his own safety, Colonel Bradt was able to obtain data, which resulted in the destruction of the enemy positions.

Wilber's vulnerability was underscored by the two Silver-Star events together with the "little firefight" that morning.

Meanwhile, in Indiana, Wilber's mother, who had been widowed for only about six weeks, wrote to her daughter Mary and indicated that, at last, she would begin writing to her overseas son.

> Jan 19, 1945 — Wilber's letter did me a great deal of good. Now I can write him and be glad to do so.

On January 22, tragedy struck the 3rd Battalion of the 103rd Infantry. An "incautious grouping of officers and enlisted men" of the battalion attracted more than a dozen Japanese artillery rounds within just two or three minutes. Four company commanders and seven enlisted men were killed and 35 were wounded. Wilber never mentioned this tragic event in his letters, but did allude to it indirectly five days later.

> Jan. 27, '45 — It's another evening and all is still well with me and the 152. Today I went up to the 3d Bn. [103rd Inf.] front line and gave them a

little encouragement. My two officers and their parties seemed to be doing a good job. We ran into sniper and mortar and artillery fire.

This mention of the 3rd battalion getting "a little encouragement" was a deeply understated but telling reference to their tragic losses five days earlier. Wilber would often go to front-line infantry units to check on the situation and to give support to his artillery liaison and observer officers.

On January 28, the 103rd Infantry Regiment began a period of less active combat. However, this phase of the fighting was not yet over.

Feb. 5 — I was shelled twice yesterday and again just now during breakfast. However so far I have been a fast man to a fox hole. The Nips really bracketed us this A.M. [with artillery fire]. Col. Devine had filled in my hole so I joined him, which so crowded the hole, we had to tremble in unison.... Tomorrow I have a Sixth Army inspection of areas, kitchens, uniforms and equipment while we are still firing. What a war!

American troops entered Manila on February 3, but the battle for different parts of the city continued until about March 3. The 43rd Division was still busy fighting the Japanese far to the north.

Feb. 7, '45 — It is four in the afternoon and nearly time for Pistol Pete [Japanese gun] to open up on us. Our problem is to find him and silence him. The chief difficulty is that he is back in a cave somewhere in the mountains and uses a different gun each time.... Tonight after studying his shell craters and other data, we have a battery laid on each of four P.P.s most likely (we hope) to shell us. If we have guessed right, he will receive our respects promptly + with interest. If we don't have the right ones we go thru the "try + try again" routine.

X · O · Ø · O · X

At home, in mid-winter, Norma's morale was suffering; she was a de facto single mother and was far from her 15-month-old daughter.

Feb. 6, 1945 — Two letters came from you today. I can imagine the cold and discomfort of the winter is beginning … to get you pretty discouraged.... Remember Feb. is the worst month of the year in Maine. From now on the weather improves for you.

But she was researching a historical figure as a subject for her writing.

Feb. 21, 1945, [to Norma] — I don't quite catch on to this sudden interest in [John] Adams [2nd president of U.S.] but am glad the old boy is still on the job as a paternal guide. Perhaps you are a descendant of [Adams's wife] Abigail. She is probably proud of you.

Norma's interest in John Adams soon became focused on Adams's wife Abigail, whose letters to her husband are now legend. She was early to recognize Abigail's strong role as a wife responsible for home, family, and farm in wintery Massachusetts during John's long absences. Norma surely saw herself reflected in Abigail's experiences.

I was enjoying the outdoor life of Bangor in winter. A friend and I would take bicycle excursions to Pushaw Lake. The ice on the lake was so thick that trucks would drive out onto it.

X·O·Ø·O·X

On February 13, the 43rd Division completed its first mission on Luzon. Along with the rest of I Corps, it had ensured that the northern Japanese force (Shobu Group) could not plausibly attack southward and disrupt a drive on Manila by the XIV Corps. Wilber's unit, the 152nd Field Artillery, moved to an estate in Guimba (Map 15), about 40 miles southeast of Lingayen Gulf during the nights of February 14 and 15. Getting out of the combat area was not simple.

Feb. 15, 1945 — This is the end of another of those busy days.... Last night was one of those times when we had to displace under enemy shell fire. It is a very interesting experience. I could silence the Jap guns but couldn't keep them silenced. He probably pulled them back in a cave after each round so my shells couldn't destroy his guns.

That meant that I tried to outguess him and fire just as he was getting ready himself.... So my driver and I sat in a ditch beside the road for six hours (10:00 P.M. to 4:00 A.M.) playing our little game. The uncomfortable part of the business was the fact that we had to be where the shells fell. It was a good deep ditch, two feet, and it sure seemed like home whenever we heard one coming our way. Luckily we could hear them before they arrived. It sounds very risky but really wasn't unless the rare chance of a direct hit occurred. However it was very impressive to hear the fragments whiz over our heads.

Beginning tomorrow I get some rest from combat and so do the boys. It won't be a rest because the idea is to get equipment back into condition. It will however be a good change for the men to clean up, get away from the flies and out of helmets. I am fortunate in being able to find them a good bivouac in the gardens of an estate.

At Guimba, Wilber could now finally reengage with his family by responding to issues Norma had raised. Valerie and I were making our way daily to and from our school along snow-covered Garland Street.

> Feb. 18 '45 — At last I have time to start answering your letters.... You must be playing a lot lately. I'd like to see you at the piano again.... I'm glad you had a good N.Y. trip + certainly could have helped you have fun.

Norma had gotten away again, this time to New York and, we learn later (letter 3/17/44), also to Washington, D.C., to see (we surmise) little Gale.

Wilber wrote to his sister Mary with many thoughts about his mother's recent widowhood, and gave an eloquent description of his feelings about previous misunderstandings between his family and Norma.

> Feb. 18, 1945 — Since I love both Mother and Norma, I can see where trouble has started and it is probably my fault that it did start. I do know and want you to know that any mistakes of this type Norma has made were because she is so completely loyal to me. She is my wife and has been a wonderful one and I love her dearly. I expect to stand by her whether she is right or not, just as I do not expect to judge whether mother is right or wrong. In other words I have a wife and a mother and to me those words answer any questions.

Wilber faced the age-old problem of split loyalty to wife and mother.

> Feb. 24, 1945 — Our bivouac area was designated in the rice plains where trees are as scarce as in the Palouse. However after a day's search we found a large hacienda with very large grounds.... As soon as we began to repair the plumbing [and] the electric plant, the Filipinos who were former employees began to resurrect essential parts: faucets, light switches, carburetors, belts that they had hidden from the Japs.
>
> Washington's birthday is celebrated in the P.I.s and [a local attorney, José] Dacquel invited some of our men to a dance. We sent 80 and they came home most enthusiastic about the hospitality.... They also agreed the orchestra was equal to top U.S. ones.

On February 25, the 152nd Field Artillery Battalion was alerted to be prepared to move to a new position on March 1 [152nd FA Bn. Journal]. Wilber wrote Norma about friends and hospitality in the Guimba area.

Feb. 28, 1945, Lover — Things have developed into an orgy of exchange of gifts with us on the defensive.

(I still have a beautiful cane of kamagong wood Wilber was given. It is quite dense and a light brown color with dark streaks.)

On March 1, the 103rd RCT, with the 152nd Field Artillery Battalion (Wilber's unit), motored 60 miles southwest from Guimba to Mabalacat City. The 103rd RCT was to be the division reserve during the 43rd Division's containment of the Japanese Kembu Group. On March 6, the 152nd Field Artillery Battalion was relieved of its reserve status and proceeded on March 10 to a position northeast of Taytay, about ten miles southeast of Manila [152nd FA History]. The third phase of the Luzon action was about to begin.

Wilber took time to catch up on correspondence with me, and found the focused activity of combat to be "a relief"!

March 10, 1945 — My big job is really to know what the infantry is going to do and to be ready to help them. Therefore probably the most dangerous thing I do is going around alone or with one man looking for new positions [to place my howitzers]. It was while on a trip of this kind that I did run into six [Japanese]. We are back in action again and it is really a relief to be just shot at instead of trying to do all the little things we do when not fighting. The Japs shelled us last night but as usual they shelled where we weren't.

I've seen Manila and it is really a desolate sight. I also talked with several of the released U.S. and British that the Japs had held in Bilibid Prison. They hadn't been treated as badly as those in other prisons. So far I've not found O'Day or Holloway Cook.

These were Washington State friends who were in the Philippines in 1942. Cook did not survive imprisonment.

The B-29 raids on Japan were continuing with devastating fire raids on numerous cities. On the night of March 9–10, the city of Tokyo was firebombed. Sixteen square miles of city were destroyed by incendiaries dropped by more than 300 B-29 bombers. Strong winds created a "firestorm" of destruction. Over 100,000 Japanese died that night.

The Japanese island of Iwo Jima, lying roughly midway between the Marianas and the Japanese home islands, was invaded on February 19. After stubborn resistance and many casualties on both sides, the island was finally taken on March 26.

28

"Things were tight for awhile"
SHIMBU LINE & IPO DAM, MARCH–MAY, 1945

On March 14, two regiments (103rd and 172nd) of the 43rd Division began an offensive east of Manila to push the left end of Japan's southern Shimbu Group out of its strong positions and deprive it of roads and waterways. At the end of March, the 103rd Infantry was given a new task, namely to drive east across the Jala Jala peninsula into the Santa Maria Valley (Map 18). On April 1, Easter morning, the 103 RCT had assembled in the vicinity of Pililla and Tanay.

> April 1, 1945 — Happy Easter Sunday to you and the children. It is a beautiful Easter morning.... We do have so much to thank God for this Easter. All of us are well and spring is coming to you and the end of the war approaches. The news from Europe is good and we seem to be doing all right here too.

On the night of April 3–4, with great secrecy, the troops of the 103rd Infantry assembled for the southeastward drive around the large lake of Laguna de Bay; they pushed off at 3 a.m. The objective was the bridge that crossed the Pagsanjan River at Lumban, some 18 miles to the south on the eastern shore of Laguna de Bay. Its capture before the Japanese destroyed it would allow the division to link up with the 1st Cavalry Division, thus forcing the Japanese into the hills, a major strategic goal.

A battalion of the 103rd Infantry with Wilber's artillery and several tanks moved rapidly down the lakeside road, encountering occasional resistance that was pushed aside so the drive could continue—though at some risk that the Japanese would reestablish roadblocks behind them (which they did). Wilber placed artillery at four different positions as they proceeded.

Wilber begins the story of the bridge capture with a brief pencil-scribbled note written at the Japanese (southwest) end of the bridge, from a foxhole in the fading light of evening.

Apr. 5 '45 [evening; written in pencil], Dear Wife — Just a note to tell you I am OK, in the trenches for the night. It is just like old times [at Munda in the Solomon Islands]. We have been using our artillery right over our shoulders again. As usual the Nips couldn't take it. Things were tight for a while. It is getting dark so must stop. I do love you all so much.

He resumed the letter two days later, in ink.

April 7, 1945 — Everything turned out OK the other night.... Our road for the last 20 miles ran between a shore line and a young mountain range. At each critical point we dropped off a few troops and pushed ahead. The [final] critical point was a long wooden bridge [at Lumban] over an unfordable river [Pagsanjan] in a deep gorge. If the Japs were able to burn or blow up the bridge we would be stopped for days.

I moved one battery along just back of the head of the column and traveled with the point looking for positions. As soon as we reached a position in range of the bridge (5 miles) I put it [Battery B with its four howitzers] in position.... Just before we reached the bridge I lifted the artillery and we moved on the bridge. Just as Col. Cleland and myself, Maj. Colpitts (Inf.), and Capt. Averill with about ten men reached the other [side], the Japs hit the company just behind us with machine guns, anti-tank-guns and a whole lot of mortar. Obviously the company became very busy and we had a bridge to hold.

Just then Col. Cleland spotted the Japs on our side of the bridge coming back. He shot the first one with his pistol. Capt. Averill shot another and his driver Joe McCloud (Bangor, I think) still another. In fact about every one but yours truly was either hitting or missing Japs. I was flat on the ground radioing for artillery fire because there was a large group of Japs assembling about 300 yards away. Things looked pretty hot for a few minutes but the Dead Eye Dicks held out until I got the artillery in on the larger group.... After the Japs were driven off the road and a company of infantry with tanks rolled across the bridge, everyone felt much relieved.

Col Cleland went back to his C.P. then and I decided to stay until artillery plans were complete. About half an hour later the Japs attacked again ... so I stayed all night. As a result, when I returned there were some more tall stories [about me] going on around [the] division....

Did I tell you I went into a church [first] built in 1606 on Easter [April 1]. It was damaged and dirty and roof partly off, but someone had kept the light in front of the altar burning. I presume a priest was somewhere nearby. Anyway, I had a little Easter service all by myself and felt much better about it.

American tank and troops at the wooden bridge over the Pagsanjan River near Lumban,
April 5, 1945. The bridge was captured by the 103rd Infantry with Wilber's artillery
assistance on April 5. Wilber was stranded overnight on the far (Japanese) side of the river.
The Japanese built this bridge with American prisoner laborers shortly after the surrender
of Bataan in 1942. [PHOTO: U.S. ARMY SIGNAL CORPS, SC 205890]

Wilber was awarded a second oak leaf cluster for his Silver Star for this action, in
lieu of a third Silver Star.

Headquarters Battery of the 152nd Field Artillery Battalion was located in Pakil
(north of Lumban) from April 5 to 21. One of Wilber's most delightful encounters,
written several weeks later to Valerie, occurred there. It involved two little Filipino
girls who probably reminded him of his own daughter.

> June 2, 1945 — They were as clean as could be, hair combed and dresses
> as neat and clean as the girls. They were barefooted. They stood in silence
> looking me over very seriously to see if I would be cross. Then they said
> together, "Hi Joe." I answered "Hello! What is your name?" It developed one
> was Margarita and the other _____. I next gave each a stick of gum. Each
> separately and very seriously said "Thank you very much," but didn't chew it
> then. They went out and held a conference in Tagalog [the native language]
> under the nearest tree and apparently decided the social amenities had
> been observed. So they came back with a very business-like manner and
> said, "Soup please." After several repeats it finally dawned on me the poor
> little things were hungry, but I had no soup.

The girls left disappointed but returned later with a radish still with garden dirt on it and insisted Wilber eat it. He couldn't refuse, and so, risking dysentery, took a bite.

Having broken bread with them so to speak, I set the radish down and thanked them "very much" a few more times, said it was good, etc.... My heart was bleeding.... Finally I had to admit still no soup.... They were terribly disappointed, my day was ruined, War was hell, and everything was wrong in the world that couldn't even give two hungry little girls the soup they had waited so long for the Americans to bring. I nearly cried.

Just as they left I gave them the half used bar of soap I had been using. They fairly danced with joy, eyes bright, said "Yes Soup! THANK YOU VERY MUCH, We go now?" I said, "yes you go now." They raced away thru the cocoanut grove holding hands. Americans were dumb but nice. I collapsed in my chair.

On Sunday, April 15, Wilber wrote Norma.

April 15, 1945 — Your letters come almost daily now and are such a help to me. You have no idea how interesting news of your house cleanings, sewing, scout problems, and the children is to me. Besides I look in each one and find you still love me and that is the important part.

Norma had a great deal to write about when she was with Valerie and me in Bangor, unlike when she was hiding her whereabouts and activities during and after her pregnancy. On the same day, Wilber described how he used his battalion.

April 15, 1945, Dear Rex and Gerrie — My battalion has quite a reputation for crowding the front lines. On two occasions technically they were in front of the infantry but not in danger more because of it.... Time to stop and go over to the infantry C.P. for the usual check up on what the arty. can do [for them].

One colleague of Wilber's told me—with a touch of criticism—that Wilber's unit was sometimes called "Bradt's Mortars" in the Luzon action because it was often so close behind the infantry. And then there were the "special" days.

Apr. 22, '45 — Yes, we did go into a new action on the day you mentioned and went thru the Japs for three miles the first day. Since then we've had them off balance and have moved so fast they sometimes (forgot?) to fuse their tank and personnel mines which helps.... There was the ... time when my car wheels went between two percussion fuses set in 100 lb. of TNT and Fish's car stopped with his front tire one foot short of and in line with a fuse.... There are special days and just days in combat. You can see this was one of the special ones.

With its mission against the left end of the Shimbu line accomplished, the 43rd Division had played its role in rendering the Japanese southeast of Manila incapable of organized action. The 43rd Division had no time to recuperate before beginning its next and final action in Luzon.

Okinawa, in the Ryukyu Islands, a mere 400 miles southwest of mainland Japan (Kyushu), had been invaded in force on April 1 and the fighting against the strong entrenched opposition carried on throughout April, May, and June while kamikaze attacks took a heavy toll on American ships. The island was finally declared secure on July 2.

In Europe, Adolf Hitler committed suicide on April 30 in his Berlin bunker, and the German capitulation was only days away. Berlin fell on May 2, and a general unconditional surrender was signed on May 7 at Eisenhower's headquarters in Reims, France. German garrisons else-where were surrendering until May 11. May 8 was proclaimed "V-E Day" (Victory in Europe Day).

The final task for the 43rd Division in Luzon was to undertake the capture of Ipo Dam. The dam, 25 miles northeast of Manila (Map 15) in mountainous territory, provided about a third of Manila's water. A rapid capture was necessary to prevent a water shortage and to avoid combat during the forthcoming (June) rainy season.

On May 7, the attack on Ipo Dam began with the 172nd and 103rd RCTs approaching the dam from the south over about ten miles of very difficult moun-tainous terrain. The 169th RCT attacked frontally as a diversion, and Filipino guerrillas attacked from the north. Progress was slow but steady. Wilber's three batteries leapfrogged each other in order to provide continuous artillery support to the advance of the 103rd Infantry. Wilber had little time for letter writing; his first was on the fifth day of the drive toward the dam.

May 12, 1945 — Mostly I specialize in long hot hikes that are very dull and usually quite safe so far as battlefields go.... If you want to rent [the house] again, use your judgment. There is no way yet to decide what date I'll become a civilian.

Norma had apparently broached the possibility that she might not stay in Bangor for another school year and Maine winter. Springtime weather had finally arrived in Bangor and morale was rising. Valerie and I were ending our school year. Hundreds of teen bike riders crowded Garland Street at school commute times.

On this same day, Wilber wrote Valerie. He told a delightful story about the gum that Valerie had sent him.

> May 12, 1945 — I want to especially thank you for the big envelopes full of funnies. The little surprise gum or candy bar is nice too. Day before yesterday I was up in the front lines. It was a terribly hot day.... I was plugging along wishing I had water, wishing I could find a breeze, wishing the war was over, wishing we had the dam we were after, and wishing I was home, when I found a pack of charcoal gum in my pocket. I put the whole big piece in my mouth and literally "chewed" my way up to the front lines, did some survey and told the infantry commander where he was, and then "chewed" my way back to my car and water. So you see how much your thoughtfulness helped me.... The nicest part of all was the fact that I knew all that time my girl loved me. It was just like a holiday for me.

On May 13 early in the morning, the rains began, earlier than expected. Sheets of rain turned roads into quagmires; trucks, tractors, and artillery were nearly immobilized. Progress was heartbreakingly slow. Supplies were brought in by Filipino work details and dropped by air. Casualties walked to the rear if they could. In spite of this, the troops pressed on and all three thrusts gradually made headway toward Ipo Dam. Wilber described the scene to me.

> May 15, 1945 — It has rained a lot for three days now and we are [in] mud [up] to our ears. The roads we make are slippery and cars get stuck on each hill. Since it winds about thru hills, that means cars are having trouble everywhere. It is difficult for us to keep the ammunition up to the guns and then rain makes it hard to see where the enemy targets are. All in all, just now, it is a quite unpleasant war. The rainy season seems to be catching up with us.
>
> It seems good to know the war in Europe is over [on May 8] but it also seems a long way off. We didn't have any celebration because our attack here was just started. Since then we have realized it a little more. I'm certainly glad for it means a lot of boys will be home that would have died otherwise.

A month later, he wrote Norma about the drive toward Ipo Dam.

June 21, 1945 — At one time, I had 25% of my men repairing and re-laying [telephone] wire. One of my men came up to me with tears in his eyes and his voice so broken he could hardly speak. He was about to drop with fatigue. (I didn't feel too peppy either.) It was pouring rain. He said, "Col. I've repaired the lines here seven times this morning and that dozer driver tore it out seven times. I asked him and told him to stop and he just said, 'To Hell with your wire, I have to build a road.' and went ahead thru my wire again." I know he expected me to go right over and shoot the dozer driver but all I could do was explain that he too was having trouble and had an important job too. I tried to let him see I knew just how hard he was try-ing to keep his lines in and how I thought he was doing a grand job, patted him on the back and went sloshing up the next hill. One feels pretty humble about commanding the American G.I.

Ipo Dam was captured on May 17, ten days after the attack began. Mopping-up actions in the 43rd's zone continued, and it was suggested that Wilber take an infantry command.

May 18, 1945 — Two generals, Barker + Stark have suggested I take [command of] the regiment [103rd Infantry].... At present I don't care to command a regiment. I'm a bit too tired just now and besides I really like artillery....

[Note on side:] I'm so sorry about the Steinmetz boy [killed in action]. There are so many of these tragedies. Two of my friends this week here too. WB

The two friends were Wilber's 43rd Division officer colleagues, Major Hugh Ryan and Lt. Col. Stephen Nichols, both of the 192nd Field Artillery, who were badly wounded in a jeep or command car when their driver's grenade accidently exploded. This was yet another instance of "friendly fire" or "incident" that killed or injured Wilber's friends.

Then, as this phase of combat on Luzon was winding down, Wilber was given a brand new challenge.

May 20, 1945 — All the changes and promotions I mentioned in my last letter have ... changed me from artillery to infantry. Gen. Wing called me in and asked, in fact almost told me, he was making me Exec. [second in command] of the 172d Inf. The Reg[imental]. C.O. is [Col.] Geo[rge E.] Bush, whom I supported in Arundel. He requested me from all the Div. Lt. Cols., which makes it nice for me.

This appointment as executive officer of the 172nd Infantry Regiment, also of the 43rd Division, was a lateral move to another lieutenant colonel position, but it opened the way toward regimental command, a full "bird" colonel position. (The insignia of a colonel is an eagle.) The 172nd Infantry was a National Guard unit from Vermont and descendant of the Green Mountain Boys of Revolutionary War fame.

On June 8, the third and last phase of combat on Luzon was essentially over, but the war was far from over. Wilber had not yet seen the last bullet come his way, and the Japanese homeland was still untouched by Allied boots.

29

"Your old man now commands a regiment"
LUZON WRAP UP & CAMP LA CROIX, MAY–AUGUST, 1945

On May 21, Wilber was formally transferred to the 172nd Infantry Regiment as its executive officer. He soon would have the much larger responsibility of commander with the departure of Col. Bush on leave.

May 23, 1945 — This is my first day in the 172d Infantry. I've taken off the crossed cannons [of the artillery] and am again wearing the crossed rifles [of the infantry]. The new work is going to be largely administrative at least for a time. Most of the Division is quite thoroughly shocked because as they say, they have never heard of an artilleryman taking an infantry assignment.

In a letter to his sister Mary, Wilber described his immediate environment at the infantry command post.

May 25, 1945 — This would be lovely country to run about in, if the Japs weren't here. Some of the views are as beautiful as any I have seen. The people are nice and are friendly. It is interesting to watch them, especially the women carrying things on their heads. Even little three-year-old girls do it and the little boys ride carabao about and carry small machetes, most of the women smoke and are personally very modest but not at all disturbed by a bathing soldier. One of my boys lost his soap in a river and a woman who had been washing clothes downstream brought it up, soaped his back and gave it back to him. He was practically frozen by embarrassment but she gave him a nice smile and went to her washing. They are extremely clean in many ways. For example Col. Bush found one using his [Bush's] toothbrush once. Just once!

Wilber as executive officer of the 172nd Infantry, May or June 1945, probably in front of his and Col. Bush's tent, Luzon, P.I. [PHOTO: COURTESY OF GEN. GEORGE E. BUSH, 1986]

To establish priority for redeployment to the U.S., "points" were awarded to each soldier for service time, overseas time, medals (including the Purple Heart for wounds), battle stars, and dependent children under 18. Soldiers with more than 85 points could be sent home unless deemed essential. Wilber had 156 points. General Barker had his own take on the point system.

> June 1, 1945 — Barker told Waldo the same thing Wing told me about redeployment only differently. Wing told me he considered me essential. Barker's remark was "Waldo you can stick those points up your ___ for all the good they will do you." What a man!...
>
> Your old man has been leading a very quiet life recently – all desk work. The Japs are getting scarce here now, altho a few still snipe at us now + then. Ogden and I were fired at from an ambush two nights ago as we drove along a rocky narrow road. However we operate on the theory that snipers miss, and he didn't even come close.

In early June, the 172nd Infantry was moved north to the Sibul Springs-Laur region where it carried out active patrolling and established roadblocks in order to capture or destroy Japanese who had been driven from the Ipo Dam area [172nd Inf. Ipo Phase Supplement].

X·O·Ø·O·X

And Norma had her own news, repeated by Wilber.

> June 3, 1945 — Your ideas on selling the house sound reasonable to me.... I hope you don't have too much grief in your move to the Sunny South and that you find a reasonable and nice home near good schools.

Norma was selling the Bangor house, she said, to avoid another New England winter. Her prime motive surely was to be near her little girl (now 19 months old); she would move the family to Washington, D.C. This plan was understandable, but selling the Bangor house was puzzling because Wilber's position at the University of Maine still awaited him. Any negative response from Wilber was muted by his uncertainty about his own future, his ambivalence about returning to Maine, and the expense of continuing to maintain the house.

Also, by now, Wilber realized that he had to let Norma make the family decisions; by his long absence, he had essentially forfeited his right to make them. Norma had decided to follow her instincts to care for little Gale and hope that some accommodation could be worked out when Wilber returned, if he survived the war.

June 16, 1945 — The orders just came thru giving me a second cluster on my Silver Star. This was for the bridge deal that I wrote you about some time ago. Since then I've lived a relatively quiet life. That gives me 161 points....

I want to see the brown flecks in your eyes again and to walk in the snow with my arm about you. You see I do love you. Good Night Lovely Wife.

Wilber's total of 161 points was the highest in the division! But not all news was positive. Wilber had inquired about attending the army's Command and Staff School with the idea of staying in the army after the war.

June 21, 1945 — The Command + Staff School is out because of my age.... Two days ago I hiked up to one of our more distant outposts just in time to run into 24 Japs. Being a Doughboy [infantry] now, I took over, had a machine-gun set up + knocked off two before they ran. They don't fight now unless cornered.

This firefight would qualify Wilber for the Combat Infantryman's Badge, as he would learn shortly (letter 8/1/45).

On July 1, the 43rd Division was relieved of all combat responsibility on Luzon. It began its move to rainy-season camp near Cabanatuan.

June 27, 1945 — Today, Dearest, is the last day of this campaign for me. Tomorrow is the first day in the rainy season rehabilitation camp.... Maybe you can sleep a bit better for knowing it.

Dearest I love you and can hardly wait to have you in my arms again. You had better start studying your safe periods for I expect to be taking advantage of them in two or three months. Wonderful Norma. My hand is lonely for the softness of you. Happy Dreams and happy day dreams too. I am very much your husband.

Wilber was again romancing Norma at long distance. The distance, the routines and demands of war, and Norma's divided loyalties had removed much of the sexual intimacy from their relationship, but here he was reaching out for it again.

X·O·Ø·O·X

At about this time, school for Valerie and me (7th and 9th grades respectively) in Bangor came to an end. We packed up our furniture and belongings in the Bangor house, which Norma had sold. She bought a home at 4421 Alton Place NW in Washington, D.C., near Tenley Circle. We could not move into it until August 1, so we rented a summer cottage at the shore in Bethany Beach, Delaware, for the month of July.

On about July 1, Norma, Valerie, and I moved to Bethany Beach. We took along a beautiful little blond girl, Norma's baby Gale, aged one year and eight months. I vividly remember first meeting her as Norma took us into her bedroom in Monte's Washington home. Gale was described to Valerie and me as the daughter of Monte and a fictitious third wife who had since "left him," a Swedish woman named Marta Lindstrom who is listed in Monte's entry in the 1946–47 Marquis *Who's Who in America*. Mother obviously cared for this poor "motherless" child, and we were to take her to Bethany Beach for the month of July. Valerie (age 13) became the de facto live-in babysitter and felt greatly put upon by this little girl who had been raised almost solely the past year by grandmother Terkman (Monte's mother) and was, understandably, quite spoiled in our teenage eyes.

That month at Bethany Beach was memorable. Our rental was a small house one or two blocks from the beach. I spent a lot of time in the water, yearning for attention from a cute girl and for a jeep. I spent one day working in a chicken-processing plant where one worker, a German prisoner of war, was avoiding work by peacefully napping in an out-of-the-way corner, and no one was disturbing him.

The prime entertainment in town was the bowling alley. However, there was a camp for prisoners of war (POWs) on the outskirts of the village, and films were shown some evenings for the prisoners, American films with German subtitles. We kids could go and watch from the very back of the rudimentary hut in which they were shown. The German prisoners got the best seats!

We were beginning yet another phase of our lives. It would also be a new phase for Wilber as he was about to assume command of an entire regiment.

x · o · ø · o · x

The rehabilitation camp at Camp La Croix, Cabanatuan (Map 15), featured extensive recreational facilities, but it wasn't all fun and games. The training and integration of replacement troops intensified throughout the month of July. The 43rd Division was being prepared for the invasion of Japan proper. Unfortunately for the division, but not for the men, many of its experienced personnel were entitled to return to the United States based on the point system, and they did so. Wilber reflected on his own motives given the forthcoming invasion.

> July 1, 1945 — It is still in the plan for me to come home [on leave] this fall. I dream about it nights and think about it days. To be with you + the children again will be the most wonderful thing I could have given me....
>
> I probably am of little importance in the big picture. The main factor as I diagnose myself is a feeling that I cannot come home with Japs still killing and causing suffering until I can feel that I could not do so well as another

[person]. When that time comes, I'll gladly come home to stay, for then I can feel I did what I could when the opportunity was here to serve my country. Possibly the reason I feel this way is entirely selfish. I may just love the life but I don't think so. If I felt now I could face my conscience while my friends go ashore in the next landing, I would come home at once and love it.

Colonel Bush, the commander of the regiment, left for leave in America.

July 7, 1945 — Your Old Man now commands a regiment. Of course it is only while Col. Bush is away, but just the same it goes on the record. I hope I do well, and I'll sure try.... Times are sure rushing. This isn't a rest camp. It is just a preparation period and a rainy season.

On a Sunday, Wilber found himself in a blue, contemplative mood and wrote about it.

July 22, 1945 — It is late Sunday evening and I am lonely for you. Today you have been in my mind all the time. I've been remembering all the sweet dear minutes we have shared and I do so need them again. It is all right to talk about the nearing of the end of this war, but it would be heavenly to know it had been won. I know it has seemed long to you and that it has been hard for you and I shouldn't write a blue letter. I try not to feel discouraged but it has been so long away from you and home and the real people....

Don't misunderstand me. This is just a blue day.... I'm so afraid to count on my promised leave. It is so important to me that I can not really believe it could happen.... I know we will go on together after this war so why should I be so depressed? I won't be any more.

His leave was "so important" to him, most likely, because he felt he was unlikely to survive the forthcoming invasion of Japan, as he admitted in future letters. It could be his last and only chance to see his family.

Five days later, Wilber had shed his blue funk.

July 27, 1945 — Do you realize that some eighteen years ago you + I were just newly engaged and Dean Kimbrough approved? I've been thinking how wonderful it was to find you that summer.... The 172 had a decoration ceremony this week, and Gen. Wing gave me my Silver Star among many others who had done more than I.

On this date, July 28, 1945, the division received "Alert Plans" for Operation Olympic, the invasion of the Japanese homeland on the southern part of the island of Kyushu (Map 19) slated for November 1, 1945 [Barker p. 230]. Judging from the

General Leonard Wing (left) presents Wilber with the Silver Star medal, July 25, 1945.
[PHOTO: U.S. ARMY SIGNAL CORPS]

Japanese defense of islands close to the homeland—specifically Iwo Jima and Okinawa—it would be a bloodbath.

> Aug. 1, 1945 — Did I also tell you I've been awarded the "Combat Infan-
> tryman's badge"? To earn it, one must function in actual infantry combat
> while in the infantry. After I had been in a little brush with 24 Japs [June
> 19] and had taken charge of our group + done a little of what we are paid
> for, Col. Bush announced I had now earned it. I'm glad about it for artillery-
> men cannot earn it. We are in the Jap business again in a rabbit-hunting
> sort of way.

x·o·ø·o·x

On or about this date, August 1, our stay at Bethany Beach came to an end, and
we moved into the Washington, D.C., Alton Place house. I began a job as mes-
senger for the Chestnut Farms Dairy in downtown Washington on Pennsylvania

Avenue, a few blocks from the White House. I believe little Gale returned to her Q Street home under the daily care of her grandmother, in accord with the continuing fiction that Norma was not her mother.

This is only the second extant letter from Wilber to his mother after his father died in December 1944, though he had apparently been writing monthly.

> Aug. 2, 1945 — We are in a camp on Luzon training new men what we think they should know before the next scrap. At the same time as a sort of secondary effort, we still kill Japs.... It really is a pity that more of them won't surrender.

And he got one off to Norma on an auspicious day.

> Aug. 7 [6?], 1945 [evening] — Sunday I wrote you a letter but it got in the waste paper before I could finish it, so all I can say is that I did think of my family on Sunday. Tonight I am just back from a school on use of air support.

On the morning of Monday, August 6, at 8:15 a.m. (Japanese time), the U.S. dropped an atomic bomb on Hiroshima, Japan. It was 7:15 a.m. in the Philippines and was announced that evening at 11 p.m. (Philippine time) by President Harry Truman. Wilber did not mention the bombing in the above letter, which he dated the next day. Perhaps the letter was misdated and was written on Monday evening, the 6th, before the announcement. Or perhaps he did not consider it that significant an event—hard to believe, his being a chemist. The fire bombing of Japanese cities with many more casualties had not ended the fighting, and General Barker, for example, does not mention the bombing in his book.

On August 9, the Soviets entered the war against Japan by invading Manchuria. Later that day, a second atomic bomb was dropped on Nagasaki. This prompted intense debate in Japan between those wishing to fight on and those pushing for acceptance of the Allied unconditional-surrender demand in the Potsdam Declaration of July 26. The emperor was asked, early on the 10th, to choose between the two positions and came down sadly but firmly in favor of acceptance. This acceptance was passed to the Allies later that day with the proviso that the emperor would retain his "prerogatives."

The Allies responded on the 12th that the emperor and Japanese government would be subject to a supreme allied commander. How to respond to this occasioned more debate and the emperor was again consulted, with the same result. He prepared a recording of a surrender announcement for his people, and an unsuccessful military coup failed to find and destroy it. On the 14th, the Allies received word that Japan had accepted the Potsdam terms, and at noon on the 15th, Japanese time, the emperor's message was broadcast to his people [Morison, v. XIV, p. 336ff].

During my lunch hour, on those tense and anticipatory days, I would walk the few blocks down Pennsylvania Avenue from the dairy where I worked to the White House. I would stand with others silently watching the limousines arriving and departing. Would the Japanese overture lead to peace or not? I was acutely aware that I was at the geographic focus of the entire world's attention!

As he wrote this letter to Norma, Wilber knew of the initial Japanese message on the 10th, and possibly also of the Allied response on the 12th. It was a significant moment for him.

Aug. 12, 1945 — Today may be the last day of the war. I can realize how you and the children must be feeling. Here we aren't much excited because everyone feels it so strongly. We can't yet realize even that it may so soon be over. Church attendances were very high and I think we were all thinking the same things.

Now I must tell you that my leave has been cancelled. It is one of the hardest things I could be writing for I had been almost down to the day-counting stage. Now I can't begin to say how disappointed I am and how sorry I am to have raised your hopes.

The cancellation of Wilber's leave was due to the impending November 1 invasion of Kyushu, Japan, as Wilber later explained [letter 8/16/45]. It had nothing to do with the ongoing peace overtures.

So far as the plan for staying in the army is concerned, no way whereby that is possible has developed yet....

Of course, Lover, I am really too happy that I may never again have to send men into places where I expect them to die. For that I could wait a while longer to see you. The thought that the end of the fighting may be here seems unbelievable to me. I keep saying to myself that maybe there won't be any next battle, that no shells will be going by too close again. In a way I'll miss the thrill of wondering if I can wiggle out of tight places, but my intellectual self reminds me not to be regretful. All I can think is how much I love you, how now at last I can really feel that I will be home with you again.

So for Wilber, there was indeed a certain "thrill" to "wiggling out of tight places"! He went on to give his family some of the credit for his survival. It still seems a miracle that he did survive, given all those close calls.

> You, Dearest, have also won your war. Our home, thanks to you, still is complete and perfect. You have helped the children and I'll never repay you for all the letters that meant so much to me. Each hour I've known you and the children were my partners and it meant more to me than anything else in the world. We will be walking together again before too long and I hope never to be parted.... I'm glad it's over and really hope it is the last time I'll ever have to order men out to be killed.

This was Wilber's last letter before the cessation of hostilities. No longer would he face combat and possible death on Japanese shores, but rather a new and uncertain peacetime future in America.

30

"So it's over. Well! I think I'll go sit under that tree"
CAMP LA CROIX, AUGUST–SEPTEMBER, 1945

On August 14, Japan accepted the Allied Unconditional Surrender terms and on the 15th all U.S. offensive action against Japan ceased. The relief, of course, was huge, both in Luzon and for us in Washington, D.C.

At the end of the war (August 15), Yamashita's Shobu group still had about 65,000 troops of which about 52,000 comprised an organized defensive force. The original number in the Shobu group had been 150,000. At war's end, some 50,000 Japanese, including Yamashita himself, exited the mountains of northern Luzon. Yamashita had effectively carried out his planned delaying action for more than seven months.

Wilber wrote his first letter home after the cessation of combat. He deemed it to be as "historic" as the one he had written on December 7, 1941, during the attack on Pearl Harbor. It was addressed to all of us.

> Aug. 16, 1945, Dear Family, All Three of You — Congratulations to each of you for being well and fine all thru the war. You have each done your share in the winning of this war just as much as if you were fighting. Your letters to me, your care of each other and your sympathy and goodness have been the only things that made my stay here possible....
>
> I am thankful to have lived to see the end of the war. In fact I'm rather pleasantly surprised to be here considering the times I considered the odds against it. There is no question in my mind but that your prayers and the prayers of your friends [were] a great help and protection to me in the past years....
>
> As you know, my leave was cancelled, and it is OK now to tell you the reason was that the next battle was almost here. I was to be (and am now) the combat commander and was very busy with plans for the landing and action. It looked like a real job and you can be sure it is a relief to not be

facing it.... I'm very proud to have ended the war in command of a regiment? That is something I never expected.

Wilber made clear here that he would have commanded an entire regimental combat team in the Kyushu invasion, apparently even if Col. Bush had returned. Bush may have been slated for another position. Wilber re-affirmed this in his letter of 9/6/45, "In fact, for the invasion I was to command over forty-five hundred men." This would have been a huge responsibility.

The 43d didn't do any noisy celebrating. No promiscuous firing, no one hurt and no regrets. I was proud after reading the news of the hysteria elsewhere. This is really a fine division and I'll always be glad I stayed with it.

9/8/45 [to Rex] — I wrote Ruth that we didn't have a celebration nor feel like it. One soldier said, "So it's over. Well! I think I'll go sit under that tree," and he had a rather typical reaction.

Wilber dreams of his forthcoming reunion with Norma.

Aug. 21, 1945 — If you know how much I love you, you will appreciate my thoughts about our reunion. It is a dream that I can expect to be fulfilled. I do know so many sweet things we will find in that dream and can hardly wait for it.

Norma's response to this must have been mixed, a euphoria that the war was finally over and Wilber had survived it, but with no idea how her competing loyalties to little Gale and Wilber would play out.

x·o·ø·o·x

On September 2, aboard the battleship USS Missouri in Tokyo Bay, General MacArthur and Admiral Nimitz, a representative for each Allied country, and Japanese officials signed the surrender documents. The war was officially over.

The 43rd Division was ordered into Japan, near Tokyo, as early occupation troops. Entirely new plans were required and in a hurry. Wilber was rushed, but he found time to write me.

Sept. 2. 1945, My dear Son — It is a very busy time handling an infantry regiment and it seems this one has a reputation for activity. We are always getting involved in things.... I would like the following ribbons bought.... We don't earn decorations now. We wear them.

Sept. 5, 1945, Dearest Wife — A very, very short note because I have just been told censorship is lifted. If so, this will be mailed. We sail for

Tokio [sic] day after tomorrow and will be part of the occupation forces in that area. I'm combat team commander (5 ships + 4,000 men) and have been very busy these past weeks planning first the attack which was to have been next month and more recently this unopposed landing. It is a welcome change. I do love you and am on my last, I hope, job. Then HOME and you.

Wilber was developing an almost boyish enthusiasm for getting home. He too must have been having some misgivings about how his relationship with Norma would fare after the long separation. And there was, as well, his uncertainty about his future employment. Here, after boarding the ship for Japan, he describes Manila Harbor.

> Sept. 6, 1945 [Manila Harbor] — Last night I came aboard the USS Monrovia and found a long letter waiting from you.... We are sitting in the harbor and I am astounded at the change since I first saw it. That was only three days after the 37th had captured Manila [on March 3] and the harbor was full of Jap wrecks. No U.S. ships were in yet because of mines and the fact that Fort Drum was still Jap held. Now I can see hundreds of U.S. vessels. The wharves are crowded and busy.

The 43rd Division sailed for Japan on September 7. This was to be an unopposed landing under peacetime conditions. Nevertheless, the reaction of the Japanese to the forthcoming occupation was not yet known.

X·O·Ø·O·X

Accounts of the planned invasion of Kyushu (Operation Olympic) are chilling. The 43rd Division was to land on the southern end of the beaches of Shibushi Bay (Ariake Wan) on the southeast coast of Kyushu (Maps 19, 20) in order to capture nearby Japanese airfields in the vicinity of Shibushi. This was one of several landings at other locations. The Japanese were building up their forces in Kyushu, and thousands of kamikaze planes and pilots were available to attack the transports carrying Allied troops. Despite the handicaps the Japanese suffered—Allied air action hindering transportation, lack of supplies, lack of preparations and training—estimates of potential casualties in the landings reached beyond 30%, along with huge anticipated losses in the subsequent combat. Success was far from guaranteed [Drea, p. 74].

In 1983, I visited the beach where the troops of the 172nd Infantry would have landed if they had survived the kamikaze onslaught. The mountainous terrain surrounding the beaches was frightening in the context of 1945.

31

Interlude 1983, Luzon
PHILIPPINE ISLANDS, MAY 1–6, 1983

In May 1983, I visited the Philippines en route from Japan to an astronomical observing session in Australia. (I was in the midst of a six-month sabbatical in Japan.) In the Philippines, it was my intention to find the people Wilber had met and to visit the places he had been.

Wilber, ever the scientist, documented his letters with the names and addresses of the people he had met. I wrote ahead to several of them, hoping the ancient addresses would suffice. I received one response, from Emma Peralta, the wife of a protégé of Judge José Dacquel, who had befriended Wilber during his stay in Guimba. Ms. Peralta had arranged for a young relative to help me out.

TRIP AROUND LAGUNA DE BAY – SUNDAY, MAY 1

My first day in Manila, I was met by young (35-year-old) finance officer Boysie Florendo, who drove me all around Laguna de Bay, counter-clockwise, the direction opposite that of the 103rd Infantry in April 1945.

We drove first to Pagsanjan and then north a mile or two to the Lumban bridge, which Wilber had helped capture. The river there was relatively placid, 30 to 50 meters wide, with banks no more than about five meters high, hardly the deep gorge described in official histories and Wilber's letter. We found there an iron bridge built in 1949 according to the plaque mounted on it. Adjacent to it, just upstream, one could see remnants of the former bridge's wooden pilings barely protruding above the water. It was the end of the dry season and the river was very low.

I could not believe I was walking the very same grounds upon which Wilber and some 15 others had hunkered down to defend the bridge they had just crossed. To modern-day Filipinos there, it was just ordinary ground, but to me it seemed sacred.

We talked to an old man at a bus stop there and to a middle–aged man at the police station in the town of Lumban. From both, we learned of the Japanese execution, in June 1942, of ten American prisoners in front of their fellow prisoners because one of them had escaped. The prisoners were re-building the wooden bridge, which had been destroyed by the retreating Filipinos and Americans in late 1941. The story is movingly told by two of the survivors in Donald Knox's, *Death March*, pp. 181–184. These events made a deep impression on the townspeople; the capture in 1945 did not.

North of Lumban, we went by San Juan too fast for me to pick out where Battery B of the 152nd FA might have been placed. We next came to Paete and then to Pakil, where the two little girls wanted soap (though Wilber thought they meant soup) and we decided to drive into the town; a very narrow street led into the square. Some boys were playing basketball and festival (rock) music was playing at a deafening level. We thought of looking up Margarita [the little girl who wanted soap], but since the only clue I had was her age in 1945, we didn't try, and went on.

(After my return to the U.S., I made a foraging trip to the U.S. Defense Department photo archives in Washington, D.C., where I found a photo of soldiers and Filipinos celebrating the liberation of Pakil. General Wing and Colonel Cleland were prominently visible in the front row. When I received the enlarged print at home a couple of months later, I found my father in one of the back rows. He had uncharacteristically joined the group for the photograph and was looking directly at me with a grin from under a helmet. It was almost as if I had found him there in Pakil!)

We then came to Tanay. I saw a big church there and suggested that it might be the "damaged" church "built in 1606" that Wilber visited on Easter 1945—all alone—a rather touching recollection [letter 4/7/45]. The plaque on the church gave 1606 as the date of the original church, 1783 as the completion date of the current church, and 1939 as the installation date of the plaque, so the plaque was there in 1945. I concluded that this must have been the church Wilber visited; it is San Ildefonso Parish Church. I spent a quiet moment reliving Wilber's solitary Easter visit.

After dinner at a fine Philippine restaurant with Boysie, I then returned to my hotel from which I could see Manila Bay. I had known of the bay since my boyhood and here I was really seeing it! So ended my first day in the Philippines. Some day!! I looked forward to visiting the famed island of Corregidor the next day, as a simple tourist; Wilber had never set foot there.

CORREGIDOR, MONDAY, MAY 2

The trip to Corregidor (Map 21) was fascinating, a one-hour hovercraft ride from Manila. Corregidor is an island in the mouth of Manila Bay; it was an American army base and the last bastion of the American defense when the Japanese conquered the Philippines in 1942. Many of the original U.S. Army concrete buildings

Celebration of the liberation of Pakil, P.I., April 9, 1945. Wilber is at left rear in helmet (see enlargement below), General Wing (commander, 43rd Infantry Division) is front center with lei, and Colonel Cleland (commander, 103rd Infantry Regiment) is at right with hat in hand.
[PHOTO: U.S. ARMY SIGNAL CORPS, SC 266243]

were still standing but were heavily damaged and in ruins from the heavy shelling by the Japanese in 1942 and the Americans in 1945. Corregidor is a rare historic wartime memorial because its ruins have been preserved. Its isolation in Manila Bay helps make this possible.

That evening (Monday) Boysie met me and he took me to another Philippine restaurant, the Tito Rey. They had washbasins out in the open; you washed thoroughly before eating with your fingers from the seven or eight serving dishes: many types of seafood, some hot and spicy, all very good.

CUYAPO AND HACIENDA CINCO; TUESDAY, MAY 3

The next day, Tuesday, May 3, I met Emma Peralta who took me by bus—an adventurous ride in itself—up to Cuyapo where I spent the next two nights. Cuyapo is near Guimba where Wilber's unit had had two weeks of "recuperation," and it was not far from Lingayen Gulf where the landings had taken place.

I stayed with Mrs. Dacquel, the widow of the judge; she was 77 years old, chunky, and very spry. She didn't remember Wilber, but did remember entertaining American troops. I read to them—about five people—Wilber's 1945 letter about their hospitality, and they were quite touched by it. I asked them about their experiences in the occupation, and learned that Cuyapo, being rather isolated, had been left pretty much alone by the Japanese.

Later, Edgar José, a young college grad, took us to Guimba. We saw the ruins of the main home of the hacienda where the 152nd FA Bn. officers had stayed. Only the Corinthian pillars of its formerly elegant facade were still standing. About a dozen local people joined us and some told of the dancing parties on the lawn that Wilber had also described. Everyone agreed that the house and grounds were beautiful in 1945. The hacienda itself consisted of rice fields as far as the eye could see.

LINGAYEN GULF AND MANAOAG; WEDNESDAY, MAY 4

The next day, Edgar drove us to Manaoag and San Fabian—towns Wilber had gone through after landing on the beaches of Lingayen Gulf.

Our first stop on the way to San Fabian was Manaoag where Wilber had rescued the wounded Filipino guerrilla by using his artillery on Japanese machine gunners.

Portico of the main home of the Hacienda Cinco, May 1983. The 152nd Field Artillery Battalion had a two-week respite from combat here in March 1943. [PHOTO: HALE BRADT]

We talked to several officers at an army camp on "Hill 200." We ate lunch in the officers' little bamboo, straw-roofed, cool hut while we chatted and read them excerpts from Wilber's letters. I could look out over the rolling ridges that caused such trouble for the 103rd Infantry. They were quite interested in the guerrilla rescue story, but could not identify the place.

San Fabian, on Lingayen Gulf, was, in 1983, just another sleepy town with lots of motorized tricycle taxis and Jeepneys, colorful, jeep-like vehicles used as buses. The beach where the 152nd FA Bn. landed (with the 103rd Regimental Combat Team) was dotted with vacation houses, which were not there in 1945. People were swimming, but regretfully I had not brought my bathing suit. Contemplating the scene, I imagined the very different atmosphere of January 9, 1945.

MANILA AND AMERICAN MILITARY CEMETERY; MAY 5–6

The next day, May 5, I took the bus with Emma Peralta back to Manila. There, various relatives of Wilber's Cuyapo acquaintances began to get word of my presence, and I became even busier! I found that the Filipinos enjoy their food and their families, and they know how to entertain their guests.

They took me to the Manila American (military) Cemetery. The grave markers there are white marble crosses except for some with a Star of David, rather than the simple headstones at Arlington National Cemetery. The crosses in their neat rows,

Grave of Lt. Norbert Heidelberger and me at the Manila American Cemetery, May 1983. The text on the cross reads: "NORBERT J HEIDELBERGER; 1 LT 169 FA BN 43 DIV; NEW YORK AUG 15 1943." I also located the graves of Wilber's two other forward observers who were killed in the Munda action, Lieutenants Earl Payne and Arthur Malone.
[PHOTO: HALE BRADT]

with their sharp shadows in the hot Philippine sun, were a striking sight. After the war, the Pacific military dead were moved here from the combat-area gravesites unless their families requested they be returned to the U.S. Here, I found the graves of the officers Wilber had lost in the Solomon Islands: Lts. Malone, Payne, and Heidelberg. Sadly, their families probably never saw their final resting places.

So ended my stay on Luzon. That evening (Friday, May 6), with several small gifts in hand from my Filipino friends, I was on a plane bound for Australia and the astronomical work I was being paid to do. My visit had been rich in impressions of places and people and long-ago events. I will never forget the hospitality the Filipinos showed me; it was as warm and welcoming as it had been for Wilber in 1945.

After my Australian astronomical observing run and a week in the Solomon Islands, my Pacific tour was coming to an end. I had relived my father's 1100-day Pacific odyssey during my own 30-day mini-odyssey. As I was winging my way back to Japan, so too had Wilber been heading there in 1945, but much more slowly on the USS Monrovia.

Oct. 5, 1945
U.S.S. Gen. Pope
in North Pacific.

My Dearest Lovely Wife,
There is little point to writing this letter for I hope to tell you all the thoughts of it with your hand in mine. Darling my duties are nearly over in the army. Anytime that I have had brought trouble it has meant so much to me to know you were waiting with confidence in me. You have helped me to show patience with those whose performance was poor. You have been beside me in lonely spots and have shown me faith and love to shorten long days and hours.

PART VII

JAPAN AND HOME

SEPTEMBER—DECEMBER, 1945

Soldiers returning to San Francisco on the USS General John Pope after lengthy war service in the Pacific Theater, October 8, 1945. [PHOTO: BRK00012314_24A; *SAN FRANCISCO NEWS-CALL BULLETIN* NEWSPAPER ARCHIVES, COURTESY BANCROFT LIBRARY, UNIV. OF CALIFORNIA, BERKELEY]

32

"Tokyo and Yokohama are ruins"
KUMAGAYA, JAPAN, SEPTEMBER, 1945

With the war officially ended, Wilber faced a new challenge: the occupation of Japan. His September 7, 1945, departure for Japan coincided with the beginning of the school year for Valerie and me. Valerie was in eighth grade at Alice Deal Jr. High School and I in tenth grade at Woodrow Wilson High School, both public schools in Washington, D.C., and both within walking distance of our Alton Place home. I took up a paper route delivering the *Washington Post*. Rising before dawn, I would deliver 40 papers in the neighborhood by bicycle.

The USS Monrovia (APA-31) carrying Wilber and part of the 172nd Regimental Combat was destined for the port of Yokohama in Tokyo Bay. Wilber wrote Norma and his brother Rex.

> Sept. 8, 1945, Dearest Wife — We are just leaving the shelter of Luzon and starting thru the Luzon Straits between that island and Formosa. So far the weather is good and the sea smooth, but it is reported we will see rougher water beyond the Straits....
>
> Tonight for the first time overseas we sail with the lights on and the portholes open. There is nothing so hot as the hold of a ship with all ports closed. This is the first convincing indication to us that the war is over. I hope for more evidence soon....
>
> Sept. 8, 1945, Dear Rex — I'm sitting on the deck of the USS Monrovia on the way to Tokyo. It is good to have a little less on my mind than I expected to have on my trip to Japan. Incidentally plans were well completed on that job. I knew which hills I was to take and what some of the difficulties were. All in all it is a relief to hope the next landing will be unopposed. We were to be a "spearhead" division again, and I never did care for the term....
>
> The attack plans were changed to occupation plans, and we have been rushing on them until yesterday. Yesterday we sailed, and I've slept since

[then] more than in three days before.... I'm very tired but find myself in good physical and mental condition except for a bad case of homesickness.

The 172nd Infantry arrived in Yokohama on September 13 and debarked dockside early the next day [WEB Journal]; there was no longer the need to climb down nets into small landing craft. The unit moved immediately to the Kumagaya airbase, 45 miles northwest of Tokyo. Their occupation duties were to keep order and to collect weapons.

> Sept. 15, 1945, Hello Darling — Am just outside Tokyo and as busy as can be now. No trouble. Am OK. Will write as soon as possible. Tokyo + Yokohama are ruins. WB

> Sept. 17, 1945, Dear Son Hale — There are some Jap soldiers all around me now. They are sweeping out the Hq. bldg. We use them to do all kinds of work such as digging ditches, latrines, cleaning up areas, handling heavy equipment. They work well but one can't tell what they are thinking. I suspect they aren't at all except what the Emperor tells them.

> Day before yesterday I was driving thru some country where no Americans had been yet. It was interesting to see the Jap reactions. Many women would dash inside their houses, others would hold their hands over their children's eyes, some boys were very formally turning their backs, others saluted, still others just gawked. Many men would fold their arms and bow very formally or salute, or take off their hats. They were very helpful as to directions whenever my Nisei (U.S. Jap) asked them questions.

The 43rd Division next received VERY big news.

> Sept. 19, 1945 — Today is the big day. We have just received orders for the 43d to return to U.S. as a division and soon. I have real hope of being with you, not for X-mas, but for Thanksgiving. Dearest I'm so happy. The sun would be shining for me even if it were pouring.

It was probably on this day that I was in a high-school study hall listening to the student-read daily news over the school public-address system, when I heard, "The 43rd Division will be returning home from Japan." I let out a little yelp of pleasure, which attracted only a brief questioning glance from the presiding teacher. No further note was made of the announcement, and the classroom reverted to its atmosphere of quiet industry. I was probably the only person in that whole school who was affected by the news, but I was not inclined to make more of a fuss.

Here again, Wilber shared with his brother Rex some of his darker thoughts about the planned invasion.

The beach at Shibushi Bay, looking south, May 1983. The mountains behind me reach up to almost 3000 feet. The 172nd Infantry, Wilber's unit, would have landed at this southern end of the beach on November 1, 1945. They had been given "the point considered most critical." [PHOTO: HALE BRADT]

Sept. 20, 1945 — We had already made plans for the landing on Japan and there would have been many casualties. In fact I didn't expect to come thru that one alive.... The 43rd was one of the assault divisions in the landing and my regiment was given the point considered most critical to the success of the division action. That meant we couldn't take our time but would have to drive thru anything we met the costly way.

All was now "orderly confusion" as the regiment prepared for departure.

[ca. Sept. 23, 1945] — We "progress." Everything is all orderly (?) confusion while we transfer all the low point personnel to divisions remaining here and receive those with high points. We count and recount everything from shirts to trucks, rush supplies here and yon and build tent camps for the regiment that is to relieve us. But it is fun. Our date for boarding ship now is the 27th.... The [campaign] ribbons came yesterday and were fine. Hale surely acted promptly on that matter.

Just now it is pouring rain and I'm glad to be under a roof. It is hard to realize my tenting days are practically over. Every hour or so, I feel good realizing we didn't have to fight our way ashore and to Tokyo. We earthquaked last night – no thrill!

I can't think of anything to mention or write about because I'm coming home, I'm coming home. I'm really coming home. I love all of you so much and have dreamed of this so long that I really am almost delirious.

After hectic preparations, the move to Tokyo and their ship home was at hand. Here is Wilber's last overseas letter, except for two (one lost) written en route home.

Sept. 26, 1945, Hello Star of My Life — Tomorrow we go aboard ship! These past days have been as hectic as combat. It is times like this that I am thankful for a good staff. They really are a fine lot and I am saved a great many details and much work....

The return won't be a rest for I'll have about five thousand men and officers and that means a lot of organization because they come from three divisions. However being the senior commander on ship, I'll have the only stateroom for one person that is intended for generals....

My present intentions include at least a month's rest, which may be on a "Leave" status or after release and a session in the hospital to clarify my physical condition. My shoulder and back have improved steadily since I had a special seat put in my Jeep and my dysentery has disappeared but I want to be sure I'm cleaned of any of the tropical bugs I may have accumulated.

On the 27th, the regiment moved to Tokyo and boarded the USS General John Pope (AP-110), a large transport ship named after a Civil War (Union) general. Loading the 172nd Infantry and the 2nd and 3rd Battalions of the 169th Infantry was completed by 5 p.m.

33

"My heart rests in your dear hands"
OCTOBER–DECEMBER, 1945

The USS General Pope left Tokyo at 9 a.m. on September 29, 1945 [WEB Journal]. Wilber was the senior officer aboard. He apparently wrote only one letter to Norma during the voyage and another to his mother. The former was an outpouring of gratitude for her support and love during the long war.

> USS Gen. Pope in North Pacific, Oct. 5, 1945, My Dearest Lovely Wife — There is little point to writing this letter for I hope to tell you all the thoughts of it with your hand in mine. Darling my duties are nearly over in the army. Anytime that I have had trouble, it has meant so much to me to know you were waiting with confidence in me. You have helped me to show patience with those whose performance was poor. You have been beside me in lonely spots and have shown me faith and love to shorten long days and hours....
>
> It has been memory of you and your sweetness and beauty that has held my love and desires. I have been true to you and have touched no other woman. This has been hard thru the long months but I knew you too were needing caresses and denying yourself....
>
> There have been times when I lacked the courage to continue the pace I had set for myself, when it was a temptation [to] not go into dangerous places that day. On those days you have reassured me and led me thru the hard places....
>
> Neither do I forget the two fine children you bore me.... I shall love you and cherish you thru eternity. My life will be yours to use. My heart rests in your dear hands. Never try to leave me, Beloved, for I can never let you free.

He had such an idealistic, wonderful view of Norma. Sadly, he could not see the complexities of her feelings and her life, in part because Norma could not bring herself to share them with him. In retrospect, that ending is chillingly ominous.

The General Pope arrived in San Francisco on October 8, 1945, three years and one week after Wilber had departed San Francisco. This may have been San Francisco's first view of returning troops after the war's end. In June 2010, I located a photo (see Prologue) of Wilber taken by a newspaper reporter who met the ship on the day of its arrival in San Francisco harbor. It is a precious memento; it is the only extant photo of Wilber after his return. Another photo shows the happy soldiers exhibiting a souvenir Japanese flag.

The 43rd Division was deactivated from federal service at Camp Stoneman, Pittsburg, California, and Wilber's unit, the 172nd Infantry, was formally released on October 13, 1945. From Stoneman, each man was sent to an army separation center near his home. For Wilber, this was Fort Meade, Maryland. He departed California on October 17, after sending a telegram home. He crossed the country on a government transport plane. He later told of his difficulty sleeping during the long flight given the noise, hard floor, and cold of the cargo bay; his head wound bothered him a great deal, he said. Upon arrival in the Washington, D.C., area, he checked into Fort Meade, and arrived at our home on the evening of Friday, October 19.

We heard a knock on the door, I opened it, and there he was in full dress uniform. I immediately received a one-armed hug; his valpack (a military folding suitcase) was in the other. Mother screamed happily from the kitchen and there were hugs and smiles all around. I do not remember more of that evening, except that he advised us, with a grin, not to be alarmed if we saw him wandering around in the back yard at night; he was not accustomed to indoor bathrooms. For Valerie, age 13, she remembers her father's return as "one of ineffable joy. I loved the way he smelled like he did before he went away to war."

Two days after his arrival, on Sunday, October 21, he and I went to see the famous concert violinist, Fritz Kreisler, in a recital at Constitution Hall [*Washington Post*, October 21, 1945]. Mother must already have had the tickets for herself and me, so we decided that Wilber and I would go instead. I was studying violin, so it was considered important that I attend, and he was a lover of classical music. This was one of the two father-son outings we had after his return.

Norma, Valerie, and I had been in Washington for only about 11 weeks when Wilber arrived home and thus our acquaintances were few. Wilber was a complete stranger to the area. There was no influx of visitors and friends to see him, which probably would have been his preference anyway. His one close contact in Washington was his brother Paul, who lived four miles away. He and his family were away during the weekend Wilber arrived, but they came to see him Monday evening. Josephine, Paul's wife, told of the visit in a letter to Elizabeth, her mother-in-law.

October 25, 1945 — Wilber looked very tired when we got there so we thought we'd only stay awhile, but he got more and more animated and interested the more he talked, and pretty soon it was 10:30 and we couldn't believe it.

Norma is well but also has a case of "battle fatigue," I think. The kids [Hale and Valerie] looked fine and are doing well at school....

P.S. Norma just called to say that Wilber, who is now stationed at Ft. George Meade, near here, has entered the hospital there for a general checkup before he is discharged.... When he sees you will depend on how long they will take to clean up these small things wrong with him.

You must be proud of Wilber, mother. He is a fine man! I meant to tell you that Hale [your grandson] is serving a morning paper and is studying violin under the concertmaster of the symphony orchestra here in Washington.

I remember that evening well. Wilber told the entire Baanga story in detail, the story he had never written up because it was "a depressing and unfortunate affair in several ways" [letter 10/22/43]. How I wish I had a recording of that evening.

Wilber entered the Fort Meade hospital as an outpatient on October 24. The shrapnel in his eyebrow, I was told, entailed risks whether removed or left in place. He was still on malarial medication and was seeing a psychiatrist. He would come home weekends and sometimes more often. I do not remember his being or acting depressed; he appeared fully communicative to me, though as a 14-year-old, I might not have been sufficiently attentive. My memories of those six weeks include the following:

– Wilber suggested I drop my *Washington Post* paper route because it could interfere with my studies. If I did, he and Mother would provide enough allowance for my necessary expenses, to which I acquiesced.

– I went to Fort Meade with Wilber one weekend day. We took the trolley to the bus station near Lafayette Park opposite the White House. He was dressed in his uniform, with its three rows of ribbons, the crossed rifles of the Infantry, the Combat Infantryman's Badge, six gold hash marks signifying three years overseas, and the Lt. Col. silver oak-leaf insignia; it made quite an impression on me and, I noticed, on others.

– In our conversation in Lafayette Park, he told me that Mother wanted to separate from him. He told me this in a matter-of-fact way without any particular emotion. I got the sense that it was a problem to be solved, not a family disaster. Years later, when I asked Norma about her desire to separate from Wilber, she said that she had planned it to be only temporary and that she would have moved to a room in a nearby home and would have still kept house for our family.

– I failed to turn off the gas burner for the hot water when I left the house although I had said I would. The overheated tank with no pressure release valve could have exploded, but it was caught in time. Wilber's comment to me later was simple: "You said you would turn it off." In the Pacific, he had written that he had had to give his junior officers the opportunity to learn from their mistakes. I had learned first hand just how he did that.

What did I learn from Norma about this period in later years? She told me that she had needed "courting" before being taken sexually, and that Wilber had not sufficiently appreciated that need, though his romancing in his letters had been very compelling. She said that things had been tense between them, and that he had slept with his pistol (loaded I presume) under his pillow. This was not far-fetched according to his military colleagues; they had always done this in combat areas. She also said that once, when she was leaving the bedroom after a tense discussion, he had said, chillingly, "One more step and you will be sorry," which truly frightened her.

In the last years of her life, when Norma had finally been able to share the story of Gale's birth with us (see the Epilog below), I asked her if she and Wilber had ever talked frankly about their intimacy issues or about Gale, and she answered me by saying, "One day when he was sitting at the dining room table, I came up behind him and put my hands on his shoulders, whereupon he said, 'Why do you do that if you don't love me?'" Perhaps neither of them could bear to bring up the unspeakable truth of Gale's birth.

Gale's existence had not been a secret since we had met her in Washington the previous summer and had taken her with us to Bethany Beach. Wilber would have known through our letters that she was with us and that she was Monte's daughter by the (fictional) departed wife. Had Wilber by now deduced Gale's true parentage? The dates of Gale's birth and infanthood matched perfectly the period in which Norma had been on her own and was so uncommunicative about her activities and whereabouts. It is inconceivable to me that Wilber would have failed to make the obvious connection.

On November 20, Wilber wrote to his sister Mary, who had suggested he relocate to Michigan, but did not mail the letter; it was found on his desk after he died and forwarded to Mary.

> [Tuesday], Dear Little Sister [Mary] — I don't know just what I will be doing yet, but am pretty sure I won't spend the first winter in the north part of the country. Michigan U. sounds fine, but I nearly freeze here, so I regret-fully decline your hospitable offer. Thanks anyway. Paul and Jo were over the other day, and it was surely good to see them…. All in all, I've no complaints about my luck when I think how many friends are still [buried] out there.

Paul and Josephine had apparently visited our home the previous weekend, November 17–18. This was most likely only their second visit since Wilber's return.

On Thanksgiving Day, Thursday November 22, the Bourjailys joined the Bradts for dinner at 4421 Alton Place. There were four Bradts, with Wilber in his uniform, complete with ribbons, insignia, and overseas hash marks. The Bourjailys included Monte, little Gale, Monte's mother Terkman, and his sister Alice, an army nurse. Alice and Terkman helped Norma in the kitchen. Even today Gale remembers Wilber's dress uniform and sitting on his lap; his uniform greatly impressed her. She was one month past her second birthday.

It may have been while she was on his lap that Wilber—according to a story Norma told us much later—put his hand on Gale's head, pulling her hair clear of her high rounded forehead and commented that it "sure looks like a Sparlin forehead." There was hardly space for the proverbial elephant in that small crowded living room.

On the evening of Thanksgiving, Elizabeth wrote to Wilber, her son, but decided not to send the letter. Instead she sent it to Mary with notes in the margins. Elizabeth was 70 years old.

Nov. 22, 1945, "Dear Son — There seems to be some secrecy as to why you are in the hospital. It makes me wonder if there isn't something serious the matter. The last paragraph of your last letter was dated October first and you [said] that you were nearing the Aleutians. Yet the letter was not mailed until 8 p.m., Oct. 29th. Were you unable to mail your letter when you reached this country? I've had letters from others mentioning your "back," a "bug you've picked up," a "fragment of a shell," and "resting." No explanation of any of them. I am not frail nor am I unable to take things as they come. I'd rather [hear the truth] than be kept in the dark."

I find it remarkable and almost unbelievable that Wilber had not written or called his mother in the five weeks that he had been back in the U.S. He had apparently written his scheduled monthly letter during the Pacific crossing, October 1, but did not mail it until Oct 29th when the next was due. Perhaps he was simply tired of being the peacemaker between Norma and his mother, and, with no definite plan for his future, he might not have been inclined to face his mother, or perhaps in a depressed state of mind, he wasn't thinking clearly.

The following letter from Wilber to his brother Rex was located in Fort Meade Hospital after Wilber died and was forwarded to Rex by Norma. Wilber's openness about his state of mind and body was about as frank as one could get.

27 Nov. 1945 [Tuesday], Dear Rex — You have no idea how much I appreciated your thoughtfulness in presenting my name for the job you

wrote Paul about. Also your confidence in my ability was indeed encouraging particularly since it came just at the time I was and am wondering if I have any ability as a chemist. It was necessary to explain just why I couldn't be interested at the time. In the first place I had no idea how long I would be kept in the hospital and in the second place I was too tired to even talk with anyone about a job.

The situation with me is pretty well clarified now. I've been quite thoroughly examined and several things of a minor nature cleared up and others treated. I'm free of an intestinal parasitic infection, have malaria but have successfully gotten off malaria [medications], teeth OK, a fragment of steel in my right forehead has been located and will probably be left alone, a back injury is apparently going to entitle me to a good cane for they can't find anything by X-ray. However it doesn't bother me enough to matter.

The "fragment of steel in my right forehead" is the only concrete evidence I have that a piece of shrapnel was actually there, in his eyebrow. His autopsy report does not mention it.

The reason I'm still being held here is simply combat fatigue. I'm just plain tired, so tired that at first writing was difficult and enunciation poor and I tended to be hysterical [teary]. It seems that when I relinquished my command and was told officially I was tired, I just all at once realized and admitted it to myself and then was tired. I am much improved after a month here mainly due to a lot of sleep and freedom from responsibility so will likely be released soon.... The children are well and make good records at school. They have certainly proven that the presence of a father is of little consequence....

We had a good Thanksgiving [Nov. 22] together at home and I hope you all had the same.

The calm mention of Thanksgiving seems to signify that it had not been a defining event for him. The presence of a father might have seemed of "little consequence" as Valerie and I continued our daily schooling and activities with only nominal attention to our parents, like most teen-agers. In fact, Valerie and I strongly felt his presence during his long absence through his letters and our prewar memories.

The day before he died, Wilber drafted a letter to Paul Cloke, dean of the School of Science and Engineering at the University of Maine; he had been Wilber's immediate superior at the university. Wilber still held, but was on leave from, his faculty position and head of department there. Here again he is unusually candid about his state of mind.

Nov. 30 [1945], Dear Paul — The general findings indicate a rather complete condition of fatigue, which has already shown considerable improvement. However, it is rather definite now that I should not try to go back to work in February. Consequently in view of your statement that a July return would be acceptable to the University, I would appreciate that privilege.

He then went on to discuss why he might not choose to return to the university at all: schools, weather, salary, and an interest in industrial work. Wilber was giving Cloke fair notice that he might not come back to Maine. He was "too tired" to consider "any job."

X·O·Ø·O·X

On Friday evening, November 30, 1945, the entire family went to my high school, Woodrow Wilson, to see the fall musical put on by the students, Gilbert and Sullivan's *Trial by Jury*. (An archived news announcement in the *Washington Post* confirmed the date for me.) We walked to the school, perhaps a 15-minute trip, as we had no car at the time. This day was Norma's 40th birthday. I remember no celebration but we probably took note of it with a candle-lit cake at supper before going up to the high school.

It may have been on this occasion, after the musical, that—as I recall—Norma desperately wanted to go to Monte's house to take care of Gale who was sick, but Wilber insisted she stick with the family. I don't remember the details, but for Norma, this stood out as a painful memory of those days. She was torn between two obligations and possibly could still not discuss with Wilber what he most likely had already deduced.

The following morning, Saturday, December 1, 1945, Wilber did not return to Fort Meade as planned because he was suffering from a recurrence of malarial symptoms—chills and a fever. He had recently been taken off malarial medicines. Valerie and I left the house early for our respective dance and violin lessons. Norma called to us as we headed out, "Don't forget to say goodbye to your father," which we dutifully and off-handedly did. After we left, Wilber went down to the basement to sort out souvenirs for Christmas presents.

According to Norma, the door to the basement was open and she and Wilber had spoken back and forth to each other a couple of times about the Christmas presents. At about 9:15 a.m., Norma heard a loud bang from the basement, whereupon she ran out the front door into the street, screaming for help.

271

UNITED STATES POSTAGE 3 CENTS

Dr. Roy C. Kirk
1601 Sayre St

Dear Roy and Irene,
— or Irene and Roy —

You may have
heard our terrible
news — but if not
it is my painful duty
to tell you that
our dear Doc

left this world
on Dec. 1st
He had been home
for six weeks at
Ft. Geo. Meade
Regional Hospital.
Don't worry about
us and please
forgive this brevity
as I have far too much to do.

Love, Norma B.

PART VIII

EPILOG

1945–2016

Little Gale at about 20 months. [PHOTO: BRADT-BOURJAILY FAMILY]

34

"I have never known such deep despair and ill health"
DECEMBER 1945–JUNE 1947

On the Saturday (December 1) he died, Wilber was 45 years old, exactly two months shy of his 46th birthday. Valerie was 13, I was six days away from my 15th birthday, and Norma had turned 40 the day before. Norma told me not long afterward that when she heard the gunshot, her first impulse had been to run to the basement door but was stopped by a vision of Valerie and me blocking her way. She remembered, and I also recall, that Wilber had either written or said that he felt he had the will power to live long enough to shoot any enemy soldier who had just shot him. So she ran out to the street instead.

Wilber had suffered a gunshot wound to his chest from his personal .45 caliber Colt pistol, the one given him in 1936 as a departure gift by his Washington State military colleagues when we moved to Maine. An autopsy performed at the army's Walter Reed General Hospital on Sunday, December 2, showed that the bullet had perforated his heart and passed completely through his chest. His death was ruled a suicide, based in part on powder burns on his chest.

Valerie and I returned home separately and reacted very differently to the news of the "accident" as described in the Prologue to this work. I remember that I did not suffer painful grief, but rather was shocked into a complete absence of feeling; I simply went numb. Thirteen-year-old Valerie responded with a quiet anger; she collected her necessities in a paper bag and fled to a neighbor's home. I remained at home.

On Sunday, the newspapers carried the story. *The Washington Post* heading (without photo) at the bottom of the front page, read, "Professor Turned Hero Found Dead of Gunshot Wound Here." The *Washington Star* heading on page A-6 (with photo) was, "Fatal Shooting of Colonel, Pacific Hero, Probed by Army."

That morning, a young navy medical corpsman—Stonewall Sparlin—from Minnesota saw the story; he was attending the navy's deep-sea diving school at the Washington Navy Yard. He realized that the story involved his half-sister Norma

Neither knew the other was in Washington. He immediately got in touch with us, and he made our home his home for the next several months while he was stationed in Washington. "Stoney" was a levelheaded, good-natured, handsome fellow who was like a big brother to Valerie and me.

On Monday, I went to school and had a pretty typical day. I did not volunteer the fact of Wilber's death to my friends, though some may have been aware of it from the newspapers. At most I might have received a quiet acknowledgement from a sensitive teacher. At the end of the day, I told my friend Archie Beard that I would not be at school the following day, Tuesday. He asked me why, and I, flushed with embarrassment and with a self-conscious grin (!), delivered the blockbuster news, that I was going to my dad's funeral. That awkward painful moment is permanently burned into my brain.

That evening (Monday) we went by car to the funeral home. There were no visitation hours or wake. Mother went into the funeral home accompanied by either Stoney or Monte, or one of Monte's sons. I remained in the car. She returned saying she had kissed Wilber's lips. Even today, I can hardly bear to imagine the anguish and guilt she must have felt.

On Tuesday, Wilber was buried at Arlington National Cemetery. It was cold and cloudy with a light rain. Our funeral party was small: Norma, Wilber's brother Paul and his wife Jo, Wilber's other brother Rex, Stoney, and General Cleland, Wilber's associate in Luzon, who escorted Mother. Monte was there with his army-nurse sister Alice and probably his mother Terkman. I was there, but Valerie had refused to go. There was a brief service in the cemetery chapel. The burial immediately followed under a small tent over the gravesite. There were the customary prayers, the playing of taps, the rifle salute, the removal of the U.S. flag from the coffin, its ritual folding, and its presentation to the widow.

The burial plot is Section 10, number 10599 RH. The standard simple tombstone erected shortly thereafter carried the wrong birthdate, February 2, 1900; the correct date is February 1. The light-hearted joke Wilber had endured his entire life about his birthday being (almost) on Groundhog Day (February 2) persisted even after his death. He would have appreciated the humor in that. Some years later, the tombstone was replaced by one inscribed with the correct date.

On Wednesday, I was back in school and so was Valerie. Norma was intent on keeping our lives on as even a keel as possible; resuming our normal routines seemed the best way to do that.

In the wake of Wilber's death, Norma found comfort in the Catholic priests at the neighboring St. Ann's Church. The priests assured her, charitably, that God would decide Wilber's spiritual fate with compassion even though suicide is a grave sin in Catholic theology. By contrast, the local Episcopalian minister was very noncommittal on this matter and this offended her. Thus began her lifelong devotion to the Catholic Church.

All who knew Wilber were, of course, stunned by his sudden and unexpected death after his survival through so much combat. There are some extant letters that revealed some of these feelings. A few weeks after Wilber's death, Norma wrote to Wilber's brother Rex and his wife Gerry.

> Dec. 22, 1945 — Your goodness and kindness have remained with us comfortingly. I could not properly express my appreciation of your having come to us, and of all your attentions to Hale and Valerie, to our home and to Wilber and myself.... Last Saturday [Dec. 15] night, I collapsed, miscarried (6 wks. pr.) here at home, hemorrhaged, and was taken to the hospital close to a nervous breakdown. I was kept under sedatives until Monday, when they operated, and also quite asleep all week.... My brother Stoney is now here on 5-day leave and helping us....
>
> Don't worry about my not crying. I did a lot of both before + after you left. I am getting better, though Gerry will understand how my back feels (like crumpled paper).

The same day, December 22, Josephine, Paul's wife, wrote to her mother-in-law, Elizabeth, in which she expressed a deep anger toward Norma.

> Dec. 22, 1945 — I wrote you a letter about Norma the other day in the heat of anger (it was really heat too; I was burned up.), but I'm not going to send it.... However, I'm going to give you a slight warning. If Norma writes you a lot of stuff, take it all with a great deal of salt before you believe it. A word to the wise is sufficient. Tell Mary this too, if you wish because Norma's getting all the sympathy and more than she needs.

The "lot of stuff" may well have been Norma presenting Gale as Monte's baby by a third wife, a story that Jo probably could see through quite easily.

However, another letter that Paul and Josephine—the nicest and gentlest of all the Bradts—wrote to Mary a month later was equally condemning and "told all," but did not mention Gale's parentage. The faults they itemized hardly explain their rage. First, they faulted Norma for changing her story after her first tearful confessions to Josephine in which she said (if we take the letter at face value) that she and Wilber had been having an argument when she heard the gunshot and that she did not go to the basement to help Wilber upon hearing the shot because she was afraid he would shoot her too. Later she changed her story, namely that it was Hale and Valerie quarrelling and that she was afraid that in going to Wilber's side she would faint and not be able to get help. They also criticized her as too controlling of her children. Perhaps the out-of-wedlock birth was so shocking they dared not mention it in this letter. Their rage could also reflect their own painful guilt for not having visited Wilber more than twice in those few weeks he was home.

Wilber and Norma may well have continued the argument of the night before about little Gale's illness and Norma may well have been afraid of being shot by Wilber. She probably came to realize that those statements would not play well to critical ears and adjusted her story to be more benign, an understandable reaction in those circumstances. As for overly controlling her children, Paul and Jo misinterpreted two instances—Norma wanting us to get to bed on a school night and wanting me to return home across town by bicycle before dark—as evidence of excessive control. In fact, Norma left me very much to my own devices during those years.

x·o·ø·o·x

Shortly after the New Year, Norma was still notifying friends of Wilber's death.

January 12, 1946, Dear Roy and Irene, or Irene and Roy — You may have heard our terrible news – but if not it is my painful duty to tell you that our dear Doc left this world on Dec. 1st. He had been home for six weeks at Ft. Geo. Meade Regional Hospital. Don't worry about us and please forgive this brevity as I have far too much to do. — Love Norma B.

At some time during the few months after Wilber's death, Monte and Gale moved into our home. Monte's mother Terkman was also with us for a time. Monte had left government service by then and was attempting to start a new business, the Globe (newspaper) Syndicate, featuring political columnists and comic strips. Norma's secretarial and editing skills filled an important need in the business. She surely received a monthly survivor's pension from the Veteran's Administration. This and syndicate income may have saved her from having to seek a nightclub job as a pianist or paid clerical work. I do not remember the sleeping arrangements in our little Alton Place house, but I am sure they were quite circumspect.

Norma took the $10,000 insurance payment (about $130,000 today) she received from the U.S. government and placed it in irrevocable trusts for Valerie's and my college educations at $5000 each. She did this quite early when her prospects for income were nebulous at best. Putting this beyond her own reach for our benefit was admirable and, for her, the beginning of a long self-imposed penance.

How did I fare after my father's death? I had not had a father at home the preceding five years, so I soldiered on much as before. I was new to the school and neighborhood, but soon became active in the school chorus and later the orchestra.

Monte Bourjaily and Gale, early 1946 in Washington DC. She was two and he 52. Monte was the only father she knew. [PHOTO: BRADT-BOURJAILY FAMILY]

I also came to know the contingent of students I encountered in the more challenging classes. Outside of school, I found time for biking and photography, often with one or two friends. Guns in the house were forbidden, of course, so my shooting career was over.

On Sundays, I would often go rock climbing with the group my Uncle Paul had helped found (Rock Climbing Branch of the Appalachian Trail Club of Washington, D.C.). In the summers of 1946 and 1947, I returned to Grace Boys Camp in New York

State, which I had attended in 1943, first as a senior camper and then at age 16 as a junior counselor. I specialized in taking the campers out on hiking-camping trips.

Valerie had a hard time with the new family arrangement, and the tensions would sometimes run high. She was not a happy 13-year old. Monte's authoritarianism would have been anathema to any 13-year-old and was especially so to strong-willed Valerie as she coped with the loss of her father. In September, she returned to her New Jersey boarding school, St. John Baptist, for ninth grade and eventually graduated from high school there. The school provided both the order and the freedom she needed.

A year after Wilber's death, Norma wrote our cousin Connie Lou and her parents (Rex and Gerry) about the past year.

> [Postmark Jan. 5, 1947] — It has been a terrible year. I have never known such deep despair and ill health.

Like all of us, Norma carried on with her daily tasks, supporting the family along with Monte's syndicate business. She continued with most of the routine household duties, though I remember doing lots of dishes. Monte was very old-school in such matters and helped little, but he was a determined, hard worker; after supper he would invariably return to his syndicate work.

Five months later, Norma wrote again to Rex, a year and a half after Wilber's death.

> June 4, 1947 — We went to Arlington [Cemetery] on Memorial Day (we are there often of course) and covered the grave with a blanket of crimson roses from our yard. It looked so beautiful....
>
> The city of Bangor recently dedicated a Book of Honor of all their [Bangor's] war dead. We were invited but could not go, and they sent us a duplicate of Wilber's page. The book will be in the Bangor library in an illuminated case, and a page will be turned each day forever, God willing....
>
> St. John's Episcopal Church in Bangor has recently dedicated a large stained glass window to the four boys [from the church] who lost their lives in service, and Wilber's name is incorporated there. Some day you may want to go and see this window.

The library in Bangor still displays that book under glass and still turns it to a new page nearly daily, and the church window is still at St. John's.

35

"I think we might grow to love each other. Don't you?"
1947–2016

Norma and Monte Bourjaily were married September 6, 1947, by Bishop Basie of the Antiochian Orthodox Christian Church in Brooklyn, New York. Monte's two divorces precluded marriage in the Roman Catholic Church. He was 53 and she 41. Monte meshed well into the family, although his temper, when provoked, could be a problem. With time he mellowed. He took his new family seriously and treated Valerie and me as his own children.

Was the Norma-Monte marriage a love match or a way to do the "right thing"? Monte and Norma grew accustomed to each other as they joined forces to raise the combined family after Wilber's death. Their marriage two years later ensured that Gale would have her father's presence as she grew up, and it gave Monte another chance at fatherhood. As the years passed, Monte and Norma became true companions in the deepest sense. And there was intimacy: on March 21, 1950, Norma, at age 44, gave birth to another daughter, Dale Anne.

Monte continued to pursue his newspaper syndication business at which he was so very talented. Over the years, it evolved into primarily an editorial service. In the 1950s, he ran newspapers in Grafton, West Virginia, and in Bangor, Maine, and established a home in Spring Lake, New Jersey. He continued writing his daily editorials until very late in his life.

Elizabeth, Wilber's mother and our grandmother, lived on the Versailles farm through the 1950s. Norma did not intrude on Wilber's family, but ensured that Valerie and I stayed in contact with her, our only living grandparent, and also with our Bradt aunts and uncles.

The half-true story that Gale was Monte's daughter by a (non-existent) third wife soon became awkward because Gale had always believed that Norma was her mother. The "true" story presented to Valerie and me in 1950 was yet another half-truth: Gale was the daughter of Norma and Wilber, in accord with her birth

Studio photo of the six Bradt-Bourjailys in Grafton, West Virginia, early January 1952. Valerie (right rear) and I (left rear) were home from college for the holidays. Monte, Dale Anne, Norma, and Gale are in front. [PHOTOGRAPHER: UNKNOWN]

certificate. Norma told us that Wilber had returned briefly to the West Coast in early 1943 to make arrangements for his division related to the sinking of the SS Coolidge, and she had met him there.

It may have been a year later (1951) when a family friend suggested to Valerie and me—we were in our late teens—that half of each story was true and that Gale's biological parents were, in fact, Monte and Norma. This placed the scarlet letter on my own family! I was taken aback by this idea and recall telling this shocking possibility to a few friends upon my return to college. My reaction was to not probe further. Norma's story was not implausible, so for the next 30 years, I chose to live with the ambiguity that Gale's father could be either Monte or Wilber. I simply did not know.

In 1953 when Gale was ten years old and the family was living in West Virginia, Monte formally adopted Gale. A new birth certificate was issued—as was the practice in those days—with Monte listed as the father, Norma as the mother, and the child's name as Abigail Therese Bourjaily. This caused some angst on Norma's part because the birth date preceded their marriage date by four years. After the adoption, we all began to call Gale by her new name, Abigail or Abby, as was her preference. Abigail grew into adulthood believing the family dogma that Norma was her mother and that Wilber, the deceased war hero, was her biological father. As an adult she became aware of her ambiguous paternity, but never forced the issue.

I began my immersion into Wilber's letters late in 1980 on my 50th birthday; Abby was 37. My research finally made it abundantly clear that Wilber had not returned to the United States during his three years of overseas duty. Before I could call her with this epochal information, she had gone, unbeknownst to me, to Florida and interviewed Norma about her long life. When she got to the war years, she begged Norma to tell the story of her birth, which she did by telling a story that made it seem clear. My news then, a few weeks later, was no surprise to Abby.

I had heard Norma tell the story in other contexts that did not, however, carry the import of this telling. Here is Norma's story as Abby told it to me.

> In Washington State, Wilber and I occasionally ate in a Chinese restaurant with friends [probably Charlie's Place in Pullman; letter 2/22/43]. Charlie, the owner, had a wife who still resided in China. On several occasions over the years, he greeted his customers with cigars and the happy announcement that he was the father of a new baby boy or girl, born to his wife in China. When asked how this could possibly be since he never went to China, he answered, "I have a very good friend in China."

Thus Norma was aware in her last years that we all knew who fathered Abby. I think she had long believed that if we had learned of her infidelity, we would have blamed her for Wilber's death and despised her for it. It must have been a great relief to her to learn that her children could absorb the true story without hating her. We knew that Wilber's suicide had had many causal components. Most of all, we couldn't hate Norma because she was, after all, our mother.

Wilber's mother eventually accepted Abby as a family member. When Abby was 15, she initiated a correspondence with her "grandmother Bradt." Elizabeth was 83. It probably took Elizabeth aback to receive Abby's letter, and she might well have thought ill of Norma for allowing or encouraging Abby to write. To her credit, Elizabeth rose above such considerations and responded warmly.

> February 5, 1959 — Your Christmas card should have been acknowledged weeks ago but I find a first letter so hard to start. Once I'm started, I'll not know when to stop. I thank you for your Christmas card. It was a surprise. I was pleased with your grades. Hope you keep them among the top ranks.... I hope there will be a "next time" [another letter] for I think we might grow to love each other. Don't you?

Me, my grandmother Elizabeth, my 1930 Ford Model A Roadster, the old Bradt log house (background), and the barn (behind and to right of the house) on the Bradt Versailles farm in 1952. I had just graduated from college in New Jersey and was on my way to navy duty in California. I was 21 and she was 77. She lived nine more years, until 1961. [PHOTO: HALE BRADT]

Two years later, Elizabeth noted that Abigail was graduating from high school and I from graduate school.

> June 12 [1961] — Yesterday was your [graduation] day and I thought of you often. Hale and Dottie [Hale's wife] were sure to say you were the prettiest girl graduate, and it doesn't take any stretch of the imagination to believe they were right. Now, the thing to do is to prepare for school again on a much larger scale.... When is Hale's commencement? A graduate from M.I.T. is something for which to be proud, but a Ph.D. is a lot more.

It pleases me still that my grandmother felt this way. Elizabeth died on July 20, 1961, at age 86 in her bed in the house my grandfather Hale had built on their farm. I regret to this day that I had not taken my 18-month-old daughter—Elizabeth's namesake—to Indiana to see her before then, as Wilber had taken me to see my great-grandmother in 1931.

Elizabeth left the Versailles farm to her children or their heirs, giving her daughter Mary Higgins a life interest so she could live there during the balance of her life. Mary did so almost to the end, 26 years later, and became a much-admired local legend in her own right. She was the Versailles "grandmother" of my two girls.

Paul Bradt, Wilber's brother, was living with Mary in the Versailles farmhouse when he died on April 5, 1978; Josephine had died in 1975. This letter from Mary, a month later, to Abby and her husband Tom, told of my visit and offered Abby an important reassurance.

> 9 May 1978, Dear Abby and Tommy — Rex mentioned that you were worried about whether or not you were blood kin of ours. Do not worry about that; you want to be a Bradt and we Bradts want you to be one of us. Is not that enough? How much better to be wanted and one of us than to be a member of [a] family who was never mentioned nor admitted to the family circle. In fact, if you want us, it is mutual, and so it is settled; you are one of us. Both Rex and Ruth in her letter to me spoke of how charming you both were.

Two years later, Wilber's youngest sister Ruth Wilson wrote to Norma. Norma was 74 and Ruth 64. Here again was some reconciliation, understanding, and reassurance.

> Aug. 25th, 1980, Dear Norma — One of the reasons I am so glad to hear from you – I was glad to know I was no longer bitter about Wilber's death. I'm ashamed to say I was at the time. I realize it was much harder on you than me. Such things are so hard to understand – I guess no one really can. You and Monte certainly did a good job raising your family to be so nice and deserve a lot of credit.

And another two years later, Ruth wrote to Abby, who was then 38. Ruth was able to look inward at her own feelings.

> May 15, 1982, Dear Abby — I want to thank you and Norma for letting me get acquainted with you. I will admit I was bitter after my brother's death. I suppose I felt Norma had betrayed my trust in her. Because Wilber had loved her so much, I did also. I believe it was the last letter I received from him in which he said how very tired he felt – that when he went to war

285

he had tried to leave things as if he would never return and that he could hardly believe he was really coming home. I've thought of that many times and it helped me understand things I believe. Maybe it will help you also.

Norma could have kept you, Hale, and Valerie away from us. It probably would have been easier for her to have done that. However, knowing you three has made the pain much less. I am no longer bitter but appreciate her patience with me....

I hope you will always consider me your Aunt.

That Wilber's sisters could express their acceptance of both Norma and Abby late in life is very heartwarming for me. I never heard such sentiments from the brothers, but their warm engagement with me over the years said as much.

Life continued on for all of us. I finished high school in 1948 and went on to Princeton University where I majored in music and then served two years in the U.S. Navy during and after the Korean conflict. I returned to Princeton for a year of physics courses and then earned my PhD in physics at MIT. I was fortunate in being able to stay on as a faculty member for a long career there. I have been married since 1958 to Dorothy, a special education teacher and mother of our two daughters. One daughter has two children.

My sister Abigail attended Manhattanville College in Purchase, New York, married a dentist, managed his dental practice, and became a superb home designer and leading expert in classic cars; she often serves as a judge at Rolls Royce rallies. They are the parents of three children and now live in Maryland. Our youngest sister Dale Anne lives in Europe. She has worked in government and private agencies dealing with sustainable farming and other environmental issues on an international scale. She has four children.

Valerie, after graduating from St. John Baptist School in 1950, went on to college at Barnard and Columbia University, married, had three boys and became a prominent journalist in Maryland. She covered Maryland for WTOP and Washington, D.C., for Group W and CNN television. She reported on the Vice President Agnew scandal in 1973, and her live reporting of the 1972 shooting of the presidential candidate, Alabama Governor George Wallace, in Laurel, Maryland, was broadcast around the world. She is now deeply committed to supporting the prison ministry of the Episcopal diocese of Maryland.

Toward the ends of their lives, Monte and Norma enjoyed visits to St. Petersburg, Florida. In 1978, they sold their large New Jersey home and moved to Florida where they purchased a condominium. Monte had already had one or more strokes, but was still quite mobile. He died in St. Petersburg on May 6, 1979, and was buried there.

Norma and Valerie at Norma's 80th birthday, November 30, 1985, at Abigail's home in
Allenwood, New Jersey. Norma died 11 weeks later on February 17, 1986.
[PHOTO: HALE BRADT]

Norma died of heart failure at age 80 in 1986 and was buried in St. Catharine's
Cemetery in Spring Lake, New Jersey. Monte's body was moved from Florida to be
beside her there, at Norma's request. Possibly in response to my mother's death, I
grew quite close to my Aunt Mary, Wilber's sister, and found myself quite interested
in the Indiana farm where Wilber had grown up and where she then lived. In 1987,
I purchased my relatives' interests in the farm, and after Mary died late that year,
managed it from afar (Massachusetts) as best I could. In 2001, it was deeded to the
State of Indiana as an adjunct to the adjoining Versailles State Park.

x·o·ø·o·x

We are left wondering why Wilber chose such a self-destructive act.

It is, of course, impossible to know; the act itself is illogical. In his depression,
he must not have been able to imagine a credible path forward for his life. He
may also have thought—impulsively and tragically in error—that he could solve
a complex family problem simply by removing himself from the scene. Sadly, he

didn't realize that life was not as cheap as he had been forced to think in order to tolerate the combat losses of friends, unknown Japanese soldiers, and even himself in the planned invasion of the Japanese homeland. It wasn't so simple. And the ultimate cost was greater than he, or any of us, could possibly have imagined.

How do we assess Norma's role in the story? She was a victim of her own will and aspirations. Choosing to leave the tight society of Bangor, Maine, in 1941, in an attempt to advance her artistic skills in New York City, she became vulnerable to her own need for attention and affection. This led to years of anguish, guilt, cover-ups, and lies. Her anxieties and actions may well have been rooted in an insecure and possibly abusive childhood. Nevertheless, her strength and convictions were clear, shining through in her continuing creativity, her devotion and attention to Wilber and her children—including her wartime baby—and especially in her commitment to her postwar family. She was a survivor when Wilber was not. He was a hero, but so was she a heroine.

Regrettably, Wilber did not live to know the fine people Valerie and I married, nor our children, his grandchildren; but his spirit lives on through them, and through the descendants of his university students and the men he led through a dramatic Pacific odyssey.

THE END

For more on the Wilber's War story or as a memorable gift:

WILBER'S WAR TRILOGY

Wilber's War:
An American Family's Journey through World War II

Citizen Soldier (Book 1)
Combat and New Life (Book 2)
Victory and Homecoming (Book 3)

ISBN 978-0-9908544-0-1
(Boxed set, hardcover, 39 maps, 269 photos/facsimiles)
www.wilberswar.com

Acknowledgments

I have been pursuing the story of my father Wilber and mother Norma for more than 35 years and have been aided by so many individuals and organizations that it is not possible to properly acknowledge them all, but I will do my best.

First and foremost, my sisters Abigail and Valerie deserve my utmost gratitude for letting me tell our family's story and for moral support throughout. Abigail's husband Tom has been an enthusiastic supporter, and Donald, Valerie's husband, has provided sage editorial advice.

This work could not exist but for those who husbanded my father's letters for the 35 years it took me to wake up to their existence and intrinsic value, namely my mother, my Bradt grandmother, and my cousin Alan, my Uncles Rex and Paul, and Prof. Irwin Doublass of the University of Maine, all of whom are now deceased. My aunt, Wilber's sister Mary Higgins, chose to give me a collection of letters between Wilber's mother and father written in the 1910s and 1920s, and between Mary and her mother in later decades. These shed important light on the familial relationships that were so influential in my father's life.

In the early 1980s, I hired students and secretaries—Trish Dobson, Pam Gibbs, Brenda Parsons, and Nancy Ferreira—to type Wilber's letters into a primitive stand-alone word processor. They were persevering, patient souls who took a serious personal interest in the story. I used those files to create the volume *World War Two Letters of Wilber E. Bradt* (by Hale Bradt, 1986), a complete compilation of Wilber's letters of which I created only 40 copies, mostly for relatives. The trilogy, *Wilber's War: An American Family's Journey through World War II* (2016), was a distillation of the complete letters with much more supportive material. This volume is a further distillation.

General Harold R. Barker, Wilber's immediate superior in the 43rd Division, wrote his *History of the 43rd Division Artillery*, which is rich in technical detail—operation orders, maps, and rosters of officers, medal winners, wounded, and killed. It pertains directly to the units Wilber commanded. This, along with other published histories and documentation in Wilber's papers, provides context for the events Wilber described. At my request in 1981, when she was 75 and still quite alert, my mother typed an eight-page summary of her life that was a valuable view of her life as she then, perhaps somewhat wishfully, remembered it.

Conversations and correspondence with Wilber's military and civilian associates and his siblings in the 1980s materially enriched this story. Especially helpful were Howard Brown, Waldo Fish, and others of the Rhode Island National Guard; Donald Downen of the Washington State National Guard; Irwin Douglass of the University of Maine; and Robert Patenge, formerly of the 169th Field Artillery Battalion. My 1983 conversation with Japanese Colonel Seishu Kinoshita, who fought opposite Wilber on Arundel, was an emotional highlight for both of us. Howard Brown died in 2014; the others long before. My Aunt Mary Bradt Higgins was especially helpful with her wonderful memory and facility with the typewriter. Her sister Ruth and brother Rex were also generous with their recollections and so were my mother's relatives, especially her sister Evelyn and Evelyn's daughters, Jane and Julie. My Bourjaily stepbrother, Paul Webb, and the former wife of his brother Vance, Tina Bourjaily, were helpfully responsive to my queries.

My visits in 1983 and 1984 to the Pacific sites of Wilber's odyssey (Solomon Islands, Philippine Islands, New Zealand, and Japan), and my meetings with the people he encountered, added important dimensions and perspective. In New Zealand, Olive Madsen, Minnie and Sidney Smith, and Dawn Jones Penney were most helpful. In the Solomons, my guide Alfred Basili got me around efficiently in his motorized canoe, Liz and Ian Warne provided hospitality on Kolombangara, and Claude Colomer took photos for me after I had immersed my camera in seawater, and so did the Warnes. In the Philippines, Mrs. José Dacquel, whom Wilber had known, Emma Peralto, Boysie Florendo, and the deLeon family made my visit most fruitful. Boysie spent a day driving me to sites on the Laguna de Bay, and young Edgar José drove us to Lingayen Gulf in his 1969 Ford Mustang, with the music playing loudly as we cruised down roads reminiscent of the U.S. in the 1930s. These Pacific visits were facilitated by my residence in Japan while on sabbatical leave in 1983 at the Japanese Institute of Space and Astronautical Science. I remain grateful for its generous support of my scientific endeavors.

I was fortunate to have started this project when many of my informants were still living. In recent years, I have been in contact with families of soldiers and in one case a sailor who served with Wilber, namely the families of Charles D'Avanzo, Robert Patenge, Donald Mushik, Lawrence Palmer, Saul Shocket, and Marshall Dann. Their recollections and generous sharing of memories and photographs further added to the story.

Faculty, archivists, and librarians at the universities Wilber and Norma attended or taught at (Washington State University, Indiana University, University of Cincinnati, University of Maine) helped flesh out those aspects of their lives. Staff at the National Archives in Suitland, Maryland, Washington, D.C., and College Park, Maryland, on my half dozen visits over the years, were expert at finding needed documents. Also helpful were librarians and archivists in New Zealand (Auckland, Christchurch, and Wellington), and at the City of Nouméa, New Caledonia; Bancroft Library of the University of California, Berkeley; Bangor Public Library, Maine; Columbia University; Tacoma Public Library, Washington; Seattle Museum of History and Industry; U.S. Army Center for Military History; Japanese Center for Military History of the National Institute of Defense Studies (IDS); and elsewhere. It was Dr. Hishashi Takahashi of IDS who put me in touch with Col. Kinoshita.

I am most grateful to Robin Bourjaily, Maura Henry, and Richard Feyl for readings and editorial comments on near-final drafts of the trilogy. Frances King did heroic service as editor and manager of the final phases of that work and this one also, and Lisa Carta's attention to detail and superb design sense made both works special. Marketing advice and publicity has been provided by Suzanne Fox, Mallory Campoli of Smith Publicity, Inc., Michael Sperling, and others.

The many Bradts, Sparlins, and Bourjailys I have queried and visited over the years have helped create this story. In many respects, it is their story too. Many friends and colleagues have suffered my recounting parts of the story to them over these past decades. My daughters, Elizabeth and Dorothy, and my wife, Dorothy, have borne the burden more than most, and they did so with grace.

I, of course, take sole responsibility for errors and misrepresentations herein.

Bibliography

The following references have been particularly helpful to me. They do not by any means comprise a comprehensive list of World War II Pacific Theater sources. Many of these volumes and documents are now available on the Internet.

Official military journals, histories, and operations reports of the following units during World War II, U.S. National Archives and Records Administration (NARA)

172nd, 103rd, and 169th Infantry Regiments of the 43rd Infantry Division.

152nd, 169th, 103rd, and 192nd Field Artillery Battalions of the 43rd Infantry Division.

27th, 145th, 148th, and 161st Infantry Regiments; see also Karolevitz reference below.

43rd Infantry Division Historical Report, Luzon Campaign, 1945.

History of the 103rd Infantry Regiment, 43rd Division, January 1, 1945–May 31, 1945. [Detailed narrative history of the entire Luzon campaign for the regimental combat team that included Wilber's artillery battalion]

Logs of naval units

LCI-65

LCI (L) Group 14

Histories sponsored by the U.S. military

United States Army in World War II, The War in the Pacific Series. Sponsored by the U.S. Army Chief of Military History, U.S. Government Printing Office, 1949–1962:

Morton, Louis. *Strategy and Command: The First Two Years.*

Morton, Louis. *The Fall of the Philippines.* [1941–42]

Miller, John, Jr. Guadalcanal, *The First Offensive.* [Guadalcanal campaign, 1942–43]

Miller, John, Jr. *Cartwheel, the Reduction of Rabaul.* [New Georgia campaign, 1943]

Miller, Samuel. *Victory in Papua.* [Eastern New Guinea campaign, 1942]

Smith, Robert Ross. *Approach to the Philippines.* [Northern New Guinea campaign, 1944]

Cannon, M. Hamlin. Leyte: *The Return to the Philippines.* [Leyte campaign, 1944]

Smith, Robert Ross. *Triumph in the Philippines.* [Luzon campaign, 1945]

Williams, Mary. *Chronology 1941–1945.* [World War II events]

MacArthur, Gen. Douglas, *The Campaigns of MacArthur in the Pacific, Reports of General MacArthur, Volume 1*, U.S. Army Center for Military History, CMH Pub 13-3, 1994.

Morison, Samuel Eliot. *History of the U.S. Naval Operations in World War II*. New York: Atlantic, Little, Brown, 1948–60:

Vol. III, *The Rising Sun in the Pacific*.

Vol. V, *The Struggle for Guadalcanal*.

Vol. VI, *Breaking the Bismarck Barrier*.

Vol. VIII, *New Guinea and the Marianas*.

Vol. XII, *Leyte*.

Vol. XIII, *The Liberation of the Philippines*.

Memoirs and histories by participants

Barker, Harold R. *History of the 43rd Division Artillery*. Providence RI: John F. Greene Printer, 1961.

Eichelberger, Robert L. *Our Jungle Road to Tokyo*. Rockville, MD: Zenger, 1949.

Halsey, William F. and J. Bryan III. *Admiral Halsey's Story*. Rockville, MD: Zenger, 1947.

Krueger, Walter. From *Down Under to Nippon*. Rockville, MD: Zenger, 1953.

Ockenden, Edward. *The Ghosts of Company G*. Infinity, 2011. [The TED Force in New Guinea]

Sledge, E. B. *With the Old Breed*. New York: Ballantine Books, 1981.

Zimmer, Joseph E. *History of the 43rd Infantry Division 1941–1945*. Baton Rouge, LA: Army and Navy Publ. Co., undated, ca. late 1940s.

Other histories and memoirs

Bauer, K. Jack and Alan C. Coox. "Olympic vs. Ketsu-go," *Marine Corps Gazette*, August 1965, v. 49, No. 8.

Bourjaily, Vance. "My Father's Life," *Esquire Magazine*, March 1984, p. 98.

Bradt, Hale. *Wilber's War: An American Family's Journey through World War II*. Salem, MA: Van Dorn Books, 2016.

Day, Ronnie. *New Georgia: The Second Battle for the Solomons*. Bloomington: Indiana University Press, 2016.

Donovan, Robert. *PT 109*. New York: McGraw-Hill, 1961.

Drea, Edward J. "Previews of Hell." *Quarterly Journal of Military History*, vol. 7, no. 3, p. 74. Aston, PA: Weider History, 1995. [Planned invasion of Kyushu]

Drea, Edward J. *Defending the Driniumor: Covering Force Operations in New Guinea, 1944*. Leavenworth Papers No. 9, Combat Studies Institute, 1984.

Estes, Kenneth W. *Marines Under Armor*. Annapolis, MD: Naval Institute Press, 2000.

Goodwin, Doris Kearns. *No Ordinary Time*. New York: Touchstone, Simon & Schuster, 1994.

Hammel, Eric. *Munda Trail*. London: Orion Press, 1989.

Hasegawa, Tsuyoshi, ed. *The End of the Pacific War, Reappraisals*. Stanford, CA: Stanford University Press, 2007.

Keegan, John. *The Second World War*. New York: Viking Press, 1989.

Knox, Donald. *Death March*. New York: Harcourt, Brace, Jovanovich, 1981, pp. 181–184, 227, 1981. [The Lumban bridge story]

Karolevitz, R. F., ed. *History of the 25th Infantry Division in World War II*. Nashville, TN: Battery Press, 1946, 1995. [Actions of the 27th and 161st Infantry Regiments]

Larrabee, Eric. *Commander in Chief*. New York: Simon & Schuster, 1987.

Paull, Raymond. *Retreat from Kokoda*. Australia: Wm. Heinemann Press, 1958.

Potter, E. B. *Nimitz*. Annapolis, MD: Naval Institute Press, 1976.

Skates, John R. *The Invasion of Japan*. University of California Press, 1994.

The Official History of the Washington National Guard, Vol. 6, Washington National Guard in World War II. State of Washington: Office of the Adjutant General. [Also contains WW I and the 1935 strike duty]

Unpublished or self-published documents

Antill, Peter. *Operation Downfall: The Planned Assault on Japan, Parts 1–4*. http://www.historyofwar.org/articles/wars_downfall1.html (1996).

Bourjaily, Monte F. "Re: Monte Ferris Bourjaily," 1936. [Résumé with references]

Bradt, Hale V.D. *Story of the Bradt Fund, the F. Hale Bradt Family, and their Versailles, Indiana Farm (1906–2001)*. Self-published, 2004. [Early years of Wilber Bradt's life]

Bradt, Hale. *The World War II Letters of Wilber E. Bradt*. Self-published 1986. [The nearly complete letters, transcribed and privately bound and distributed]

Bradt, Norma S. *Memoir, 1981*. [Eight page self-typed document]

Bradt, Wilber E. *Personal Journal (1941–45)*. [Five handwritten notebook pages of dates, places, incidents]

Fushak, K. Graham. *The 43rd Infantry Division, Unit Cohesion and Neuropsychiatric Casualties*. Thesis, U.S. Command and General Staff College, 1999.

Higgins, John J. *A History of the First Connecticut Regiment, 169th Infantry 1672–1963*. Unpublished, 1963.

Patenge, Robert. *Memories of Wilber E. Bradt, 1997*. Booklet prepared for Hale Bradt. [Patenge was a survey officer in the 169th Field Artillery Battalion under Wilber Bradt in the Munda campaign.]

Saillant, Richard. *Journal of Richard L. Saillant*. Transcribed by Joseph Carey. [Saillant was an officer in the 118th Engineers of the 43rd Division until April 1944. The Munda campaign is vividly described.]

Zimmer, Joseph E. *Letters from Col. Joseph E. Zimmer to his wife, Maude Files Zimmer, 1942–1945.* Transcribed by Maude Zimmer. [Zimmer was an infantry officer in the 43rd Division who served in the 169th Infantry, 103rd Infantry, and other elements of the 43rd Division from 1941 until May 1945.]

Newspaper archives, 1941–45

Bangor (Maine) *Daily News*

The New York Times

Wellington (New Zealand) *Evening Post*

Washington (D.C.) *Post*

Washington (D.C.) *Star*

Notable conversations with 43rd Division participants and one Japanese officer:

Howard Brown (1981 through 2012)

Warren Covill (1981)

Seishu Kinoshita, Kyushu, Japan (1983)

Albert Merck (1984, 2009)

William Naylor (1984)

Robert Patenge (1997)

Index

A **bold face** number indicates a chapter or, if a page range is given, a larger part.
An *italic* page number indicates an illustration or a map.
WB = Wilber Bradt; "Hale" is Wilber's son; "F. Hale" is Wilber's father.

Proof

Made in the USA
Charleston, SC
06 August 2016